teach yourself

politics
peter joyce

For over sixty years, more than
40 million people have learnt over
750 subjects the **teach yourself**
way, with impressive results.

be where you want to be
with **teach yourself**

For UK order enquiries: please contact Bookpoint Ltd, 130 Milton Park, Abingdon, Oxon OX14 4SB. Telephone: +44 (0) 1235 827720. Fax: +44 (0) 1235 400454. Lines are open 09.00–18.00, Monday to Saturday, with a 24-hour message answering service. Details about our titles and how to order are available at www.teachyourself.co.uk

For USA order enquiries: please contact McGraw-Hill Customer Services, PO Box 545, Blacklick, OH 43004-0545, USA. Telephone: 1-800-722-4726. Fax: 1-614-755-5645.

For Canada order enquiries: please contact McGraw-Hill Ryerson Ltd, 300 Water St, Whitby, Ontario L1N 9B6, Canada. Telephone: 905 430 5000. Fax: 905 430 5020.

Long renowned as the authoritative source for self-guided learning – with more than 40 million copies sold worldwide – the **teach yourself** series includes over 300 titles in the fields of languages, crafts, hobbies, business, computing and education.

British Library Cataloguing in Publication Data: a catalogue record for this title is available from the British Library.

Library of Congress Catalog Card Number: on file.

First published in UK 2001 by Hodder Arnold, 338 Euston Road, London, NW1 3BH.

First published in US 2001 by Contemporary Books, a Division of the McGraw-Hill Companies, 1 Prudential Plaza, 130 East Randolph Street, Chicago, IL 60601 USA.

This edition published 2003.

The **teach yourself** name is a registered trade mark of Hodder Headline Ltd.

Typeset by Transet Limited, Coventry, England.
Printed in Great Britain for Hodder Arnold, a division of Hodder Headline, 338 Euston Road, London NW1 3BH, by Cox & Wyman Ltd, Reading, Berkshire.

Hodder Headline's policy is to use papers that are natural, renewable and recyclable products and made from wood grown in sustainable forests. The logging and manufacturing processes are expected to conform to the environmental regulations of the country of origin.

Impression number 10 9 8 7 6 5 4 3 2
Year   2010 2009 2008 2007 2006 2005 2004

iii

contents

preface

This book is designed as an introduction to the study of politics. It is aimed at both the general reader and those commencing an academic study of this subject. It is especially relevant for 'A' level politics students and those studying politics on first-year undergraduate courses who have no prior knowledge of the subject area.

As an introduction, the material presented in this work is selective. It concentrates on the institutions of government and the political systems operating in first world (or post-industrial) liberal democratic states. It seeks to provide the reader with an understanding of the operations of liberal democratic political systems and the differences that exist between them. The key issues which are discussed are supplemented by a range of examples drawn from a variety of relevant countries.

Each chapter contains questions related to the issues discussed. The aim of these questions is to encourage readers to further their studies especially by relating general concerns to specific countries with which they are familiar. This may be done, for example, by reading newspapers and journals in conjunction with this work.

It is hoped that this introduction to the study of politics will encourage readers to pursue their investigations further. A brief list of more specialized texts is suggested at the end of the book as a guide to further study.

Peter Joyce
February 2001

01

key issues in
the study of
politics

In this chapter you will learn:
- what is meant by the term
  'politics'
- key terms associated with
  the study of politics
- why similar systems of
  government operate
  differently

Definition

What is politics?

We are all familiar with the term 'politics'. It is encountered in the workplace, perhaps in the form of 'office politics'. We talk of the 'political environment' which fashions the content of public policy. But what exactly is involved in the study of politics?

Human relationships are crucial to the study of politics. Human beings do not live in isolation. We live in communities. These may be small (such as a family) or large (such as a country). Politics embraces the study of the behaviour of individuals within a group context. The focus of its study is broad and includes issues such as inter-group relationships, the management of groups, the operations of their collective decision-making processes (especially the activities and operations of the state) and the implementation and enforcement of decisions. The regulation of conflict between individuals and groups is a particular focus of political analysis to which the study of the concept of power and the manner in which it is exercised is central. The study of politics thus involves a wide range of complementary subject areas which include political theory, political history, government and public administration, policy analysis and international relations.

In the following sections we discuss a number of key issues that relate to the study of politics. These are usually referred to as 'concepts' and they provide us with an underpinning on which a more detailed examination of the political process in liberal democracies can be built.

Political Culture

What is political culture and why is it of relevance to the study of politics?

We expect to see a number of common features in a liberal democratic political system. These include institutions such as a chief executive, legislatures and courts, organizations such as political parties and pressure groups, processes such as elections and the possession by individual citizens of a range of personal freedoms. However, their composition, conduct, powers,

Alternative views concerning the formulation of political culture

Liberal theorists suggest that a country's political culture is fashioned by its unique historical development and is transmitted across the generations by a process termed 'political socialization'. Agencies such as the family, schools, the media and political parties are responsible for instructing citizens in such beliefs and values.

Marxists, however, tend to view political culture as an artificial creation rather than the product of history. They view political culture as an ideological weapon through which society is indoctrinated to accept views which are in the interests of its dominant classes.

relationships and operations differ from one country to another. Within a common framework, the workings of the political system in each liberal democracy are subject to wide variation. In France, for example, there is a wide degree of tolerance for conflict as a means of settling political disputes. In Sweden, however, the spirit of compromise tends to guide the actions of key participants to the political process. In the United Kingdom there is a tradition of evolutionary rather than revolutionary change.

These variations arise from what we term 'political culture'. This refers to an underlying set of values held by most people living in a particular country concerning political behaviour, one important aspect of which is the degree of trust which citizens have in their political leaders. These attitudes influence the conduct of political activity by both politicians and the general public. When we refer to a country's political culture we are emphasizing the similarity of views held within any particular country. We are suggesting that within any one country there is a tendency for the majority of people to think, feel and act in a similar manner concerning the conduct of political affairs. But these sentiments may be quite different from the core values espoused by citizens in other liberal democracies.

The extent of a common political culture can, however, be overstated. Within any country differences are likely to exist concerning fundamental values related to political behaviour. The term 'homogeneity' denotes a wide level of similarity in these attitudes but universal agreement is not accorded to them.

Factors such as de-industrialization (which has resulted in the emergence of an 'underclass' in many liberal democracies) or immigration (which has led to the development of multi-ethnic societies) have fundamental significance for the existence of universally agreed sentiments underpinning political behaviour. These may give rise to a heterogeneous society (in which dominant attitudes are challenged by sub-cultural values) or result in a looser attachment to mainstream values by some sections of society.

States and governments

What is the difference between a 'political system', a 'state' and a 'government'?

A political system is the constitutional framework through which demands are put forward and decisions are made. It has no physical dimension or formal existence but consists of the institutions, processes and relationships which are involved in the processes of agenda setting, policy formulation and decision making.

Political systems can be distinguished from each other in a number of ways. This process of differentiation is termed classification. There are three broad types of political systems – liberal democratic, communist and totalitarian. The extent of civil rights in liberal democratic political systems facilitates a wider degree of public participation in political affairs than is permitted in the other two systems.

A state consists of a wide range of permanent official institutions (such as the bureaucracy, police, courts, military, parliament and local government) which are responsible for the organization of communal life within specific geographic boundaries. These are usually referred to as a 'country' or 'nation' and the state enjoys sovereignty within them. Decisions that are taken in the name of the state are binding on all members of that society and may, if necessary, be enforced by the legitimate use of power to prevent, restrain or punish breaches of the law.

There are a wide range of views concerning the operations of the state. Liberal analysis suggests that the state is neutral and independent of any class interests. It arises out of the voluntary agreement of its members and serves impartially to mediate the conflicts which arise within society, seeking to promote the national interest above sectional concerns. Elite theorists, however, suggest political power is wielded by a ruling elite whose interests are maintained and advanced by the state. Marxism identifies this ruling elite as the economically powerful, the bourgeoisie, and views the state as a mechanism that will mediate between the conflict between capital and labour (which they assert to be inevitable) in order to sustain class exploitation and profit accumulation.

The term 'state' is often used synonomously with the term 'government'. This latter term refers to the institutions concerned with making, implementing and enforcing laws. In a narrower sense, however, government is often associated with those who wield executive power within a state, who give direction to its activities. In liberal democracies, political parties compete for control of the state and in this sense governments have a limited and temporary existence whereas states are permanent.

The role of the state

What is the legitimate scope of state activity?

There are widely differing views concerning the desirable scope of state activity. Differences exist both within states over historical periods of time, as well as between them concerning the appropriate functions which should be performed. Historically, the role of the state was confined to a few key areas, which usually included defence and foreign affairs. However, many states with liberal democratic political systems were subject to pressures during and following the Second World War, which drastically increased the role of state activity. In Britain, for example, this period witnessed the development of the Welfare State, an acceptance that the maintenance of full employment was a proper state responsibility and the placing of several key industries under state control and direction.

During the 1980s, however, government influenced by new right ideology, especially that of Margaret Thatcher in the United Kingdom and Ronald Reagan in America, succeeded in reversing the trend towards increased state activity by 'rolling back' the frontiers of the state in both economic and social areas of activity. In the economic sphere, the free market and private enterprise were seen as superior to state control or involvement, which was depicted as both wasteful and inefficient. It was further alleged that the role played by the state in people's lives was detrimental. Those who received state aid (for example, in the form of welfare payments) were depicted as being dependent on the state who thus relinquished their ability to take decisions affecting the conduct of their everyday lives. The thinking, active citizen had thus been transformed into a passive recipient of handouts while those in employment were adversely affected by the high level of taxation needed to finance the existing activities performed by the state.

Power, authority and legitimacy

Why do we obey our rulers?

A major concern of a government is to secure the obedience of its citizens to its decisions. There are two broad explanations concerning why a government is able to secure popular compliance to its objectives or policies. These centre on an understanding of the concepts of power and authority.

Political obligation

Political obligation is the theory which seeks to explain why, and under what circumstances, citizens are required to obey their governments. There are various explanations for this, although an important one is the idea that the existence of government and the powers which it exercises are based on the consent of the governed. This is a central belief put forward in social contract political philosophies, which further assert that should a government undermine the rights and liberties of the citizen, which it was established to protect, it is morally acceptable to disobey the state's laws and, in extreme circumstances, to institute a new government which does possess the consent of its people.

Power

Power consists of a relationship between two parties in which one has the ability to compel the other to undertake a course of action which would not have been voluntarily carried out. The preferences of one party become binding on the other because the former has the ability to compel compliance by the threat or the use of sanctions. The desire to avoid the sanction thus ensures the obedience of one party to another. Governments may exercise power over their citizens but other political organizations (such as pressure groups and social movements) may wield power by their ability to use force or violence to further their aims.

The nature of power is a fundamental issue related to the study of politics. In his book, *Power: A Radical View,* written in 1974, Stephen Lukes identified three dimensions to power – the one-dimensional view (which focused on whose views prevailed in decision making), the two-dimensional view (which involved examining both decision making but also non-decision making) and the three-dimensional view (which focused on the ability to control the political agenda by manipulating people's needs and preferences).

Power is different from influence which entails the ability of those who are not participants to a policy-making process to be able to affect the content and nature of its decisions. Their ability to do so may include the intellectual weight of arguments which they are able to put forward.

Power entails the ability to compel obedience. A body exercising power has the ability to invoke sanctions in order to secure compliance to its decisions. The fear of the sanction thus ensures that the body which may invoke it is able to achieve its goals. A government which possesses power is thus obeyed as its citizens are afraid of the consequences of disobedience. Dictatorships may often govern in such a fashion, executing those who dare disagree with its policies. In liberal democratic political structures coercion is often coupled to resources at the government's disposal, enabling it to offer rewards as well as threats to secure obedience.

Who holds political power?

There is considerable disagreement concerning the distribution of power within a society.

Pluralists argue that power is widely distributed throughout society and that the role of the state is to adjudicate in the constant competition which exists between competing groups and interests. Decisions thus reflect the process of bargaining between such diverse bodies.

Elitist theories, however, contend that power is concentrated in the hands of a relatively small, organized group of people and that this minority is able to force its will on the majority of citizens. Marxists identify the ruling elite as those who possess economic power and are able to use the political system to further their own interests.

Authority

The second explanation to account for governments being able to exert control over their citizens is the authority possessed by such institutions. Authority is based on moral force. An individual or institution which possesses authority secures compliance to its suggestions primarily if there is general agreement that those who put forward such ideas have the right to propose and implement them. Citizens thus obey governments because there is a general consensus that it has the right to take decisions even if the content of them is not generally popular.

The sociologist Max Weber suggested that authority could be derived from one or other of three sources. The first of these was traditional authority, where acceptance of the right to rule is based on custom. Popular consent is accorded to decisions made by those from a background which traditionally exercises the functions of government within a state. Hereditary monarchs (who rule by virtue of birth) enjoy this form of authority. Second was charismatic authority, which is derived from characteristics, that are personal to a political leader. The main criterion for obedience is that the public stand in awe of the person taking decisions. Charisma is particularly associated with dictators, including Adolf Hitler in Germany and Juan Péron who served as President of Argentina between 1946–55 and 1973–74. The final source was legal-bureaucratic or legal-rational authority. In this case, compliance to decisions made by rulers is based on the office which an individual holds within a state and not his or her personal characteristics. It is thus the prestige accorded by the public to an office which influences the ability of an official to secure acceptance to his or her wishes.

In liberal democratic political systems the political office occupied by those who give orders forms the main basis of their authority. We accept that presidents or prime ministers have the right to give orders by virtue of the public positions which they occupy. However, political leaders frequently derive their authority from more than one source: in Britain the association of the prime minister with government carried out in the name of the monarch gives this office holder authority derived from both traditional and legal-bureaucratic sources.

In liberal democracies governments possess both power and authority. They are obeyed partly because there is general consent that they have the right to govern, but also because the police, courts and penal system may be used as a sanction to force compliance to their laws. Power that is divorced from authority is likely to produce an unstable political structure in which violence, disorder and revolution threaten the existence of the government.

Legitimacy

Legitimacy entails popular acceptance of the exercise of power within a political system. It is closely linked to the concept of authority, being commonly applied to political systems whereas authority is generally applied to specific public officials. Legitimacy is a quality that confers acceptance of the actions undertaken by the government from those who are subject to them. Those who are subject to such rules may not necessarily approve of them, but legitimacy involves an acceptance that the government has the right to make decisions and that the public has a duty to obey them.

In liberal democratic political systems, legitimacy is founded on the notion of popular consent. Governments derive their position from elections. This is a process in which all citizens are entitled to participate and in countries are required to if voting is compulsory. The support obtained at an election is the basis of a government's claim on the obedience of its citizens to the actions which they subsequently undertake provided that they act in accordance within the established rules of political conduct. Marxists, however, emphasize that legitimacy entails public acceptance of the distribution of power within society. This is not derived from genuine popular approval but, rather, is the product of ideological control exerted in the interests of the ruling class over the masses, which is designed to secure their acceptance of political, social and economic inequality.

Legitimacy, whether it derives from manipulation or genuine popular approval, is important in establishing stable government able to draw upon the obedience of its citizens. This may, however, be undermined by political, social or economic factors such as repeated failures by governments to act in accordance with the wishes of their citizens or by perceptions that those who occupy political office seek to use their position to bring them personal benefits. Factors such as these may result in what is termed a 'legitimation crisis' in which citizens question the right of the government to act.

The rule of law

What is the 'rule of law' and why is this principle of importance to liberal democracies?

The rule of law is a fundamental constitutional principle in liberal democracies. It asserts the supremacy of the law as an instrument that governs both the actions of individual citizens in their relationships with each other and also controls the conduct of the state towards them.

The rule of law suggests that citizens can only be punished by the state using formalized procedures when they have transgressed the law and that all citizens will be treated in the same way when they commit wrongdoings. Nobody is 'above the law', and the punishments meted out for similar crimes should be the same regardless of who has committed them. This suggests that the law is applied dispassionately and is not subject to the biases and prejudices of those who enforce it. Additionally, all citizens should be aware of the contents of the law. The rule of law, therefore, provides a powerful safeguard to the citizen against arbitrary actions committed by the state and its officials, and is best guaranteed by a judiciary which is independent of the other branches of government.

This principle may be grounded in common law (which was historically the situation in Britain) or it may be incorporated into a codified constitution, as is the case in America.

Although many of the requirements embodied in the principle of the rule of law constitute practices which are widely adhered to in liberal democracies, most liberal democratic states deviate from the strict application of the rule of law. Factors, which include social background, financial means, class, race or gender, may play an influential part in determining whether a citizen who transgresses the law is proceeded against by the state and may also have a major bearing on the outcome of any trial. Additionally, governments may deviate from strict application of the rule of law when emergencies occur. Marxists equate the rule of law with the protection of private property rights which they view as underpinning the social inequalities and class exploitation found in capitalist societies.

The Rule of Law in America

The freedom of citizens from arbitrary actions undertaken by government is incorporated into the Constitution. The procedure and practices which must be followed when citizens are accused of criminal actions are laid down in this document, most notably in the Fifth and Fourteenth amendments. The requirement that no citizen shall be deprived of 'life, liberty or property' without 'due process of law' is imposed as a condition affecting the operations of both federal and state governments. The Fifth amendment also provides the citizen with further protection in their dealings with government. No person may be tried twice for the same offence or be compelled to give self-incriminatory evidence in a criminal trial.

Equality

What is equality and how can it be achieved?

Equality refers to the ideal of citizens being equal. There are several forms this can take.

Initially, equality sought to remove the privileges enjoyed by certain groups within society so that all of its members were able to lead their lives without impediments being placed upon them derived from factors such as birth, race, gender or religion. This is termed formal equality and is based on views such as the assertion in the American Declaration of Independence (1776) that 'all men are created equal'. This perception of a shared common humanity underpinned the extension of civic rights to all members of society. These included the rule of law (which emphasized equality of all citizens before the law) and reforms such as the abolition of slavery and the removal of restrictions to voting thus providing for universal male and female enfranchisement.

Although formal equality removed the unfair disadvantages operating against some citizens, it did not tackle the underlying social or economic factors which might enable some members of society to achieve more than others. Other forms of equality have addressed this issue. Social equality is especially concerned with improving the status and self-esteem of traditionally disadvantaged groups in society. Equality of opportunity has underpinned reforms to aid materially the poorer and weaker members of society. This can be achieved by some measure of redistribution of wealth which in the United Kingdom gave rise to the welfare state or to measures (including equal opportunities and affirmative action programmes) designed to help disadvantaged groups (including women, racial minorities and persons with physical handicaps) who have experienced discrimination in areas such as employment opportunities, pay and housing allocation.

Some socialists favour equality of outcome, which seeks a common level of attainment regardless of an individual's background, personal circumstances or the position in society which they occupy. This may entail a levelling-out process whereby some members of society are penalized in order to ensure social equality. The abolition of wage differentials (so that all persons were paid the same wage regardless of the job they performed) would be one way to secure equality of outcome.

Affirmative action

Affirmative action (or 'positive discrimination') refers to a programme of measures designed to give preferential treatment to certain groups which have historically been disadvantaged as the result of discrimination encountered within a society. Such groups may include racial minorities who suffer from problems which include social and economic deprivation and political marginalization, but may also embrace other minorities such as persons with physical handicaps, homosexuals who have been the victims of popular prejudice, which may have affected issues such as employment opportunities.

Affirmative action is a more radical approach than equal opportunity programmes. The latter seek to ensure that members of disadvantaged groups do not experience discrimination in areas such as job applications or interviews and will be treated on a par with applicants not drawn from minority groups. Affirmative action, however, seeks to ensure that positive steps are taken to guarantee that members of disadvantaged groups can gain access to facilities such as jobs, housing and education. One means of securing this is through the use of quotas: this would ensure, for example, that in an area in which 25 per cent of the population were from an African-Caribbean background, employment opportunities in the public and private sectors would reflect this.

Affirmative action programmes were initiated in America by the 1964 Civil Rights Act. Title VI of that Act prohibited discrimination under any programme which received any form of federal financial assistance and Title VII made it illegal to discriminate in employment matters.

To be effective, affirmative action needs to be underpinned by strong sanctions which may be applied against those who continue to discriminate against disadvantaged groups. In America, for example, the courts are empowered to hear class actions (that is, an application on behalf of an entire group which alleges discrimination which, if successful, will result in all members being compensated). However, critics of this approach believe that failing to treat all members of society equally can result in injustices. In America, for example, unhappiness with the application of affirmative action to university admissions (which could mean that qualified candidates were overlooked in favour of less qualified ones for whom a set number of places had been set aside) resulted in the Supreme Court case of *Regents of the University of California* v. *Bakke* (1978) which prohibited the use of rigid racial quotas for medical school admissions (although it did not prevent race being considered a factor when determining admissions, a situation which was latterly confirmed by the Supreme Court in 2003 in a decision affecting the admissions policy of Michigan State University's law school). New right politicians were sceptical of affirmative action, believing that the position of disadvantaged minorities would be enhanced through the expanding economy rather than as the result of affirmative action programmes.

Questions

1 What do you understand by the term political culture? Outline the main features of the political culture of any country you are familiar with.
2 Distinguish between the terms 'power', 'authority' and 'legitimacy'.
3 Conduct a study of the application of the rule of law in any one country, indicating the extent to which this principle applies and does not apply there.
4 Distinguish between the terms 'formal equality' and 'social equality'. What measures are associated with achieving these ideals?

Taking it further

This chapter has provided an introduction to the study of politics and has referred to some key issues which underpin this subject. A key requirement for those of us who study politics is the need to keep abreast of current affairs. This is most easily done by reading a 'quality' newspaper which in the United Kingdom include the *Independent*, the *Guardian*, the *Daily Telegraph*, the *Times* and (on Sundays) the *Observer*. Contemporary events are also catered for in magazines such as the *Economist*.

There are a number of good text books which address the issues referred to in this book in greater detail. These include, Bill Coxall and Lynton Robins, *Contemporary British Politics* (Basingstoke: Macmillan/Palgrave, 2001), Rod Hague and Martin Harris, *Contemporary Government and Politics* (Basingstoke: Macmillan/Palgrave, 2001), Andrew Heywood, *Politics* (Basingstoke: Macmillan/Palgrave, 2002) and Barrie Axford *et al.*, *Politics – An Introduction* (London: Routledge, 1997).

In addition there are also specialist journals which deal with contemporary political issues. In the United Kingdom the most useful introductory journal is *Talking Politics*. More specialized knowledge can be obtained from *Parliamentary Affairs*, *Political Studies* and *The British Journal of Political Science*.

The internet is a crucial tool which enables us to keep abreast of contemporary issues. Iain Dale, *Directory of Political Websites* (London: Politicos Publishing, 2001) provides a list of around 1,500 websites which students of politics will find useful. In addition the *Guardian* newspaper's website at www.guardian.co.uk/politics provides an up-to-date summary of contemporary political issues.

02

liberal democracy

In this chapter you will learn:
- the key features of a liberal democratic system of government
- the importance of elections in liberal democratic states
- how the public can influence decision making in liberal democracies

Definition

What do we understand by the terms 'democracy' and 'liberal democracy'?

A democratic society is one in which political power resides with the people who live there: it is they who are sovereign.

Democratic government was initiated in the Greek city state of Athens in the fifth century BC. The word 'democracy' is derived from two Greek words, *demos* (meaning 'people') and *kratos* (meaning 'power'). The term literally means 'government by the people'. Initially, major decisions were taken by meetings at which all free males attended. It was possible for government to function in this way when the population was small and when the activity of the state was limited. Today, however, ancient city states have been replaced by bigger units of government with a greater range of responsibilities delivered to larger numbers of people. It is necessary, therefore, to invent a political system through which the notion of popular sovereignty can be reconciled with an effective decision-making process. We term such a political system 'liberal democracy'. It has two fundamental characteristics. Government is 'liberal' in terms of the core values which underpin it and 'democratic' concerning the political arrangements that exist within it.

Political systems

We have previously stated that a political system is the constitutional framework through which demands are put forward and decisions are made. It has no physical dimension or formal existence but consists of the institutions, processes and relationships which are involved in the processes of agenda setting, policy formulation and decision making.

In liberal democratic political systems, demands by the public can be made through a number of channels which include political parties, pressure groups, the media, elections and extra-parliamentary political action. The suggestions which are put forward in this manner are key aspects of the agenda for the consideration of the formal institutions of government (the legislature, judiciary, executive and bureaucracy) who may also put forward policy proposals of their own. These institutions determine whether to act on demands which are presented to them and if so through what means. Their actions may involve repealing contentious legislation, enacting new laws or taking policy or budgetary decisions.

The term 'system' implies that the component parts which shape decision making form part of an integrated structure, in which stability is secured by the actions undertaken by governments broadly matching the demands placed upon it by public opinion, however this is articulated. If this fails to be the case, disequilibrium may occur in which demands outstrip a government's willingness or ability to match them. This may result in revolution.

The core values associated with liberal democratic political systems accord to the traditional liberal belief in limited government and are designed to ensure that a broad measure of civil and human rights exist. These may be guaranteed by devices which include a constitution, a bill of rights, the separation of powers, a system of checks and balances and, crucially, the rule of law.

A democratic political system is one whose actions reflect the will of the people (or at least the majority of them). Popular consent in liberal democratic political systems is secured through representation: liberal (or, as it is sometimes referred to, representative) democracy entails a small group of people taking political decisions on behalf of all the citizens who live in a particular country. Those who exercise this responsibility do so with the consent of the citizens and govern in their name. However, their right to take decisions depends on popular approval and may be withdrawn should they lose the support of the population to whom they are accountable for their actions. In these cases, citizens reclaim the political power they have ceded and reallocate the responsibility for government elsewhere. Elections, which provide a genuine opportunity to exert popular choice over the actions and personnel of government, are thus an essential aspect of liberal democracies. This requires that all adults having the right to vote, the regular holding of elections and political parties being able to compete openly for power.

Liberal democratic political systems are associated with the capitalist economies of first world countries. Marxists allege that an incompatibility exists between the political equality and social inequality found in such countries. They dismiss liberal democracy as 'bourgeois democracy' whose values and operations are underpinned by the defence of private property ownership and whose legitimacy is secured through the ideological control exercised by the ruling class.

There are wide variations in the political structures which exist within liberal democratic political systems. A major distinction is between those (such as America) which have presidential systems of government and those (such as the United Kingdom) which have parliamentary systems. In some, the executive branch of government tends to be derived from one political party but in others is drawn from a coalition of parties, perhaps making for a more consensual style of government. These issues are discussed more fully in later chapters of the book.

Accountability

Accountability (which is often referred to as responsibility) denotes that an individual or organization to whom power has been delegated is required to submit to the scrutiny of another body or bodies to answer for the actions which have been undertaken. Additionally, the body or bodies to whom the organization or individual is answerable possesses sanctions which can be used in the event of actions being undertaken which are deemed to be unacceptable.

There are two forms of accountability. The individual or organization may have to seek prior permission before taking actions. Alternatively, accountability may entail an individual or organization being free to take actions but required to report what has been done to another body. This is termed *ex post facto* accountability.

In liberal democratic political systems governments are accountable to the electorate. While in office they may take decisions but the electorate has the ultimate ability to remove them from power at a national election if they disapprove of what has been performed. Elections are thus an essential aspect of liberal democracy which enable the public to exert influence over the legislative and executive branches of government and hold them accountable for their actions. Effective accountability also requires that citizens are in possession of information by which to judge the activities undertaken by public officials. Many liberal democracies provide for this through freedom of information legislation enabling public access to official documents.

Additionally, governments in liberal democratic political systems are accountable to legislatures. They may be required to submit their policies to the scrutiny of legislative bodies and in parliamentary forms of government, such as that in the United Kingdom, legislatures possess the ability to remove the government by passing a vote of 'no confidence' in it.

Communist and totalitarian political systems

What other political systems are there in addition to liberal democratic ones and what are their main characteristics?

Political systems can be distinguished from one another in a process of differentiation which is termed classification. Two other systems exist in addition to liberal democratic ones – communist and totalitarian.

Communist political systems (sometimes referred to as socialist democracies) are political systems based on the ideas of Karl Marx. The most notable feature of communist states is the paramount position of an official socialist ideology and the domination or total monopolization of political affairs by the official Communist Party whose leading members exerted control over institutions such as trade unions, the media and the military and over key state-provided services such as education. Considerable differences existed between them although, in general, these countries were characterized by the existence of little or no private property ownership, a planned economy (which was viewed as essential to achieving equality and classlessness) and a comprehensive welfare state. Communist states include the former Soviet Union and its East European satellite neighbours but following the 'collapse of communism' in Eastern Europe between 1989–91, is now confined to a smaller number of countries which include the People's Republic of China, Vietnam, Cuba and North Korea.

Totalitarian political systems are those in which the state controls every aspect of the political, social, cultural and economic life of its citizens. It is governed by a ruling elite whose power is based upon ideological control which is exerted over the masses underpinned by the use of coercive methods. Civil liberties, human rights and the ability of citizens to participate in decision making are very limited if not totally absent in such societies. The term 'authoritarian' applies to societies which are also governed by an elite with considerable power, although this is not always exerted over every aspect of civil life as is the case with totalitarianism.

The ideology which is found in totalitarian societies is subject to wide variation. Communist political systems exhibit totalitarian characteristics as they are totally under the control of the Communist Party. Other totalitarian regimes may be dominated by the ideology of fascism, in which only one political party is permitted to exist and representative institutions such as directly elected legislatures are typically absent. Totalitarian regimes may also be based upon a religious ideology. In areas where Sharia law is enforced, Islamic religious leaders occupy prominent political positions and political parties function in accordance with the Koran and Sharia. A main feature of theocratic government is its intolerance of viewpoints other than those of the dominant religious sect.

Totalitarian regimes differ from oligarchic ones. An oligarchy is a political system in which power is held by a small group of persons who govern in their own interests rather than seeking to advance a political ideology. These interests may be economic or may consist of the desire to wield power. As with totalitarian regimes, few political freedoms exist in oligarchic regimes since the general public is not allowed to play any part in politics and are frequently characterized by brutality and coercion meted out by the police or military who exercise a prominent role in civil affairs. Oligarchies embrace a wide variety of political arrangements including military dictatorships and one-party states, and are typically found in less-developed countries.

Political freedoms and liberal democracies

What political freedoms are required to exist in liberal democractic political systems?

Liberal democracies require mechanisms whereby the general public can exercise choice over who will represent them and also to dismiss such persons if they feel that policies lacking popular support are being pursued. This suggests that elections are essential to the operations of liberal democratic political systems. These enable the public to exert influence over the composition of the legislative and executive branches of government and subsequent actions which they undertake. They also serve as the means whereby a country's citizens can make a retrospective judgement on the record of those who exercise functions of government.

However, elections are not confined to liberal democracies. Countries with alternative political systems may also utilize them. An essential characteristic, therefore, of elections in liberal democracies is that these contests should provide a genuine opportunity to exert popular choice over the personnel and policies of government. Liberal democracy thus requires a range of political freedoms to serve as the environment within which elections occur. Let us consider some of these essential freedoms.

Freedom of political expression

Elections will only provide the public with meaningful political choice if a diverse range of opinions can be articulated. Measures which impose censorship on the media or which place restrictions or bans on political parties, trade unions or other forms of political activity must be pursued extremely cautiously by liberal democratic governments. The freedom of speech, thought and action are essential features of liberal democracies, distinguishing them from more totalitarian systems in which the ability to dissent is circumscribed. An impartial judicial system and freedom from arbitrary arrest are also necessary aspects of such political systems.

The timing of elections

Elections facilitate popular control over the activities of government only if they are held regularly and if their timing is not totally determined by the incumbent office holders. In some countries, legislators or executives hold office for a fixed period of time at the end of which fresh elections must be held. In America, for example, the president is elected for a four-year term while members of the House of Representatives and the Senate serve for two and six years respectively. Other countries do not hold elections at predetermined intervals. In the United Kingdom, for example, the executive has the ability to determine when general elections are held subject to the proviso that fresh elections to the House of Commons take place at least every five years.

Nonetheless, a line needs to be drawn between what is acceptable political behaviour and what the state is justified in wishing to prohibit. This affects issues such as what political parties are allowed to say and the means they use to put their case across to the electorate. We refer to this as political toleration.

One justification for imposing restrictions on political toleration is where parties fail to support the basic principles underlying liberal democracy: thus it might achieve power through the ballot box but once installed in power will transform a country's political system into a totalitarian one. The 1947 Italian Constitution banned the re-formation of the Fascist Party on these grounds while the 1958 French Constitution stipulated that political parties must respect the principles of national sovereignty and democracy. A similar provision applies in the 1949 German Constitution.

The doctrines put forward by a political party may, further, be viewed as threatening not merely to a country's political system but to the very existence of the state itself and justify limits on political activity. Fear of the Soviet Union and communism (which was believed to be embarked upon a quest for world domination) was prominent in America during the 1950s. The American Communist Party was banned by the 1954 Communist Control Act and perceived sympathy for communism led to discriminatory actions against individuals such as dismissal from employment.

The methods used by political organizations may also justify curbs being placed on political toleration. Organizations whose views, opinions or statements offend other citizens (and may possibly provoke violence against them) may be subject to restrictions in order to maintain public order. Groups which actually carry out acts of violence to further their political objectives are also likely to be the subject of state constraints. In the United Kingdom, for example, groups which utilize violence to further their political ends banned (or 'proscribed') by the 2000 Terrorism Act.

To ban or not to ban?

Decisions by a government to place restraints on political activities might influence the structure and operations of the party which is subject to them. An organization which becomes subject to what it regards as restrictive intervention may respond by going 'underground' and adopting a cell structure, the essence of which is a covert, secret and conspiratorial organization for which membership is highly selective. This may also affect the tactics which the organization uses. A group which is driven underground may adopt violent means to further its aims. It may become labelled a 'terrorist' group.

The size of the electorate

The exercise of popular control over government necessitates a broad electorate in which the vast majority of the population possess the right to vote. We refer to this as the franchise. In the nineteenth century the franchise in many countries was based on property ownership: those who owned little or no property were not regarded as citizens and thus were unable to play any part in conventional political activities. The enfranchisement of adults, regardless of wealth, gender or race is necessary to ensure that government accurately reflects the wishes of their populations and progress towards universal adult suffrage is a major measurement by which progress towards establishing liberal democracy can be judged.

The conduct of elections

Public involvement in political activities occurs only when elections are conducted fairly. Factors which include the secret ballot and freedom from intimidation are required to ensure that the outcome of election contests reflects genuine public sentiments. Liberal democracy also requires incumbent office holders to accept the verdict delivered by the electorate and not to oppose it by methods which have sometimes been utilized by non-democratic systems of government. These include setting election results aside by declaring them null and void or supporting a military take-over to preserve the political status quo when an election has demonstrated popular support for fundamental change.

Eligibility to be a candidate for national office

There are a wide variety of regulations in liberal democracies governing eligibility to stand as a candidate for national office. In the United Kingdom these rules are very broad. Any citizen over the age of 21 (subject to disqualifications laid down in legislation enacted in 1975) may seek election to parliament. A candidate merely requires endorsement from ten registered voters in the constituency he or she wishes to contest and a deposit of £500 (which is returned if the candidate secures over 5% of the votes cast in the election). In other countries the rules are more complex. Candidates may be required to be nominees of political parties which in turn may be subject to controls governing their ability to contest elections. These may require a party to demonstrate a stipulated level of support in order to be entered on the ballot paper. In the 1995 elections to the Russian parliament, for example, each party had to submit 200,000 signatures gathered in at least 15 of the regions in order to enter the contest.

Representation

To what extent are the opinions of the population effectively represented in liberal democratic political systems?

We have argued that liberal democracy involves a small group of people taking political decisions on behalf of the entire population. This typically takes the form of what we term 'territorial representation' whereby legislators represents a specific geographic area and those who live there. There is, however, an alternative form of representation termed 'functional representation'. This entails legislators representing specific sectional or vocational interests rather than being directly elected by the general public. The Irish *Seanad* is partly constituted on this basis.

In the sections that follow we consider whether those entrusted with the responsibility of representation adequately reflect public opinion. There are a number of factors which are relevant to this objective being effectively accomplished.

The development of the party system

Parties may enhance public involvement in policy making, although the extent to which they achieve this is dependent on factors such as the size of their membership. Further, the development of party systems may distort the relationship between an elected official and his or her electorate. Voters may support candidates for public office on the basis of their party label rather than their perceived ability to put forward the needs of local electors. While in office, party discipline may force elected officials to sacrifice locality to party if these interests do not coincide. The extent to which this happens depends on the strength of party discipline which is stronger in some liberal democracies such as the United Kingdom, Australia and New Zealand than in others such as America where local influences (termed 'parochialism') play a significant part in determining a voter's choice of candidate for public office.

The electoral system

Electoral systems vary in the extent to which those who are elected accurately reflect the voting preferences of members of the general public. A fundamental division exists between the first-past-the-post electoral system and proportional representation. In the United Kingdom, for example, the former has been charged with distorting the wishes of the electorate and producing a legislative body which does not accord with popular opinion as expressed at a general election.

The status of elected officials

Those who are elected to public office may fulfil the role of either a delegate or a representative. A delegate is an elected official who follows the instructions of the electorate as and when these are given. A delegate has little freedom of action and is effectively mandated by voters to act in a particular manner. A representative claims the right to exercise his or her judgement on matters which arise. Once elected to office a representative's actions are determined by that person's conscience and not by instructions delivered by voters. A representative can, however, be held accountable by the public for actions undertaken while occupying public office.

The status of UK members of parliament

The eighteenth-century statesman, Edmund Burke, argued that an MP should apply his judgement to serve the interests of the nation as a whole rather than having to obey the wishes of a local electorate.

A member of parliament is subject to no formal restraints on his or her actions once elected. The system of recall which is practised in some American states has never applied in the United Kingdom. A member of parliament cannot be forced to resign by local electors: their only power is their ultimate ability to select an alternative representative when the next election occurs.

There are informal pressures which may influence the behaviour of United Kingdom members of parliament, for example the discipline exerted by the party system. But even this may prove an ineffective restraint on their behaviour.

The social composition of public office holders

The term 'characteristic representation' suggests that the institutions of representative government can only validly represent public opinion when they constitute a microcosm of society, containing members from diverse social groups in proportion to their strength. However, in many liberal democracies key divisions in society (such as its occupational make-up or its class, ethnic or religious divisions) are not reflected in this manner. Many liberal democracies were slow in according women the right to vote. New Zealand granted this in 1893 and the United Kingdom (on a restricted basis) in 1918. However, white, male, middle-class persons of above average education continue to dominate the composition of such bodies which are thus socially unrepresentative although possibly reflective of the characteristics required to achieve success in all aspects of social activity.

The lack of social representativeness may result in the institutions of government becoming out of tune with public opinion and being seen as an anachronistic defender of the status quo when the national mood demands reform and innovation. This problem may be accentuated by the procedures adopted by legislative bodies: the seniority system used by the American Congress tended to entrench the conservative influence over post-war American domestic affairs and persisted until changes to these procedures were introduced during the 1960s and 1970s. Groups who perceive that their needs are being inadequately catered for by the institutions of government (such as women, youth or racial minorities) may resort to alternative means of political expression which may have long-term consequences for the authority of such bodies.

The composition of the UK House of Commons

At the 2001 general election 659 members of parliament were elected. Of these, 118 (17.9 %) were women and 12 (1.8 %) were from ethnic minority communities. The remaining 529 (80.3%) were white males. Most European parliaments contain more women members.

Public involvement in policy making

What mechanisms other than elections might be used to enable the general public to be involved in policy making?

We have seen that elections play a major role in liberal democratic political systems. They enable the population to select a small group of people who perform the tasks of government. However, the ability to elect representatives and (at a subsequent election) to deliver a verdict on their performance in public office does not give the general public a significant role in political affairs. In many liberal democracies, therefore, other mechanisms exist which seek to provide citizens with a more constant role in policy making. In this section we consider some of the ways in which this objective can be achieved.

Pressure groups

Pressure groups provide the public with opportunities to influence the policy-making process. The existence of pressure groups and the competition which occurs between them is viewed as an indispensable aspect of a pluralist society in which power is dispersed and policy emerges as the result of a process of bargaining and conciliation conducted between groups.

Extra-parliamentary political action

What we term 'conventional political activity' entails viewing a country's legislative assembly as the main arena in which political decisions are formally made. Alternatively, extra-parliamentary political activity involves actions undertaken by groups of citizens who seek to influence a state's decision-making process through ways other than this. To do this they may utilize a wide range of methods which include demonstrations, industrial disputes, civil disobedience, direct action, riots and terrorism. Extra-parliamentary methods (which may be associated with organizations such as pressure groups and social movements) offer an alternative means of political action to that provided by conventional political activity.

The ability to engage in extra-parliamentary political activity is an important feature of all liberal democratic political systems and it possesses a number of advantages to aid their operations. These include enabling citizens to involve themselves in the government of their country beyond periodic voting in elections and permitting them to exert influence over specific items of policy which are of concern to them. Extra-parliamentary politics may succeed in raising minority interests: the emergence of women's issues and environmental concerns onto the political agenda owed much to the activities of groups willing to utilize extra-parliamentary methods. Extra-parliamentary politics also guard against political apathy resulting from a tendency to defer all political decisions to a country's leaders which could result in a totalitarian system of government.

Sleaze

The level of public support given to conventional political activity is influenced by factors which include perceptions as to whether those elected to public office are motivated by serving the public or furthering their own interests. Accusations of 'sleaze' have exerted a considerable influence on the political affairs of a number of liberal democracies in recent years and may help to explain the use by the public of extra-parliamentary methods to attain their political objectives.

Sleaze describes the abuse of power by elected public officials who improperly exploit their office for personal gain, party advantage (which may especially benefit party leaders to secure or retain their hold on power) or for sexual motives. The term also embraces attempts to cover up such inappropriate behaviour either by those guilty of misconduct or by their political colleagues.

In the United Kingdom, the government's emphasis on the need for a return to conservative traditional values of self-discipline and the importance of the family in its 'back to basics' policy of 1993 was undone by revelations that a number of members of the government were engaging in extra-marital affairs. The prime minister initially refused to intervene, arguing it was a personal matter. A further problem was the 'cash for questions' accusation in 1994 that a small number of Conservative members of parliament had accepted money to table parliamentary questions. This resulted in the appointment of a Committee on Standards in Public Life whose recommendations included establishing an independent parliamentary commissioner.

In America, sleaze took the form of allegations that President Clinton had a sexual relationship with Monica Lewinsky. Initially, both Clinton and Lewinsky swore on oath that they had not had an affair. However, doubt was subsequently cast on the truthfulness of these denials and Clinton admitted to having had an 'inappropiate' physical relationship with her. The report of a special counsel, Kenneth Starr, to the House of Representative's Judiciary Committee accused the president of perjury, abuse of power, obstruction of justice and witness tampering. In December 1998 the House of Representatives' judicial commitee approved four articles of impeachment, two of which were subsequently endorsed by the House of Representatives. This decision resulted in a trial before the Senate at which he was acquitted in February 1999.

In Ireland a special enquiry, the Moriarty Tribunal, was established in 1998 to examine the financial affairs of the former *Taoiseach,* Charles Haughey, and in 1999 the former Chancellor of Germany, Helmut Kohl, was accused of channelling donations to his party, the Christian Democratic Union, into a secret fund. In 2000 allegations of underhand financial dealings in Paris when Jacques Chirac was mayor were put forward and in 2001 a number of people, including the former French foreign minister and president of the Constitutional Council, Roland Dumas, were placed on trial in connection with complicity in the misuse of the funds of the Elf oil company.

There are, however, problems associated with extra-parliamentary politics. Violence and public disorder may arise, perhaps based on a desire by a group to achieve political aims through intimidation or coercion rather than through education. In these cases a government may be required to intervene in order to prevent citizens or their property being subject to the threat or actuality of violence. Conventional politics conducted through the ballot box may be viewed as an irrelevant form of activity if other means are widely practised and are seen to be successful, and such actions may also undermine a government's capacity for governing if it is forced to follow a course of action advocated by groups using extra-parliamentary methods. A government in this situation may appear weak which may create a desire for the imposition of 'strong' government.

Opinion polls

Opinion polls seek to determine the views of the public by putting questions to a small group of people. There are several ways in which this group might be selected. The two main ways are through the use of a random or a quota sample. The first addresses questions to a segment of the public who are chosen by a method which lacks scientific construction. In Britain, for example, a random sample might consist of every thousandth name on the register of electors in a particular parliamentary constituency. A quota sample, however, seeks to address questions to a group of people whose composition is determined in advance. By this method, questions are directed at a group who are perceived to be a cross-section of the public whose views are being sought. It will attempt, for example, to reflect the overall balance between old and young people, men and women and working- and middle-class people.

Opinion polls may be utilized to ascertain public feelings on particular issues. The findings of polls can then be incorporated into the policy proposals put forward by political parties. They are especially prominent in election campaigns. They are used to assess the views of voters on particular issues which may encourage parties to adjust the emphasis of their campaigns (or the content of their policy) to match the popular mood. They are also employed to investigate the outcome of elections by asking voters who they intend to support. The belief that this activity does not merely indicate public feelings but may actually influence voting behaviour (for example, by creating a bandwagon effect for the party judged by the polls to be in the lead) has prompted countries such as France to ban the publication of poll results close to the actual contest.

How accurate are opinion polls?

Although opinion polls are widely used they are not consistently accurate especially when seeking to predict the outcome of an election contest. In 1995 the polls wrongly predicted a major victory for Silvio Berlusconi in the Italian regional elections (which his party lost) and a clear victory for Jacques Chirac in the first round of the French presidential election (in which he was defeated by the socialist, Lionel Jospin).

There are several reasons that might explain the shortcoming of opinion polls. Some people may refuse to answer the pollsters' questions. This may distort the result if the refusal to answer is disproportionately associated with one segment of electoral opinion. Polls rely on those who are questioned telling the truth and subsequently adhering to the opinions which they express to the pollsters. The 'last-minute swing' phenomenon suggests that members of the general public may change their minds and depart from a previously expressed opinion. Polls may also find accuracy difficult when the public is evenly divided on the matter under investigation.

Consultation and participation

Members of the general public may also secure involvement in policy making through mechanisms which allow them to express their views to policy makers on particular issues. Consultation implies the right to be heard. Citizens may be invited to express their opinions on particular matters to which the policy makers listen but are not required to act on. Participation, however, involves a shift in the power relationship between policy makers and the public. Policy making is transformed into a joint exercise involving governors and the governed.

Consultation and participation might be regarded as beneficial to liberal democracies as they permit the policy preferences of the public to be considered or acted on by public officials. However, the lack of information in the hands of the general public might make meaningful discussion impossible and may result in the public being manipulated into giving their backing to contentious proposals put forward by the policy makers.

Exit polls

Exit polls are a form of opinion poll. They are conducted after an election has taken place and ask citizens as they leave the polling station whom they have voted for.

Exit polls are a particular aid to the media who frequently sponsor them in order to be in a position to predict the winner of a contest soon after voting has ended but before the official results are declared. Exit polls are usually accurate, although in the 2000 American presidential election the closeness of the contest between George W. Bush and Al Gore resulted in difficulties. In some states (including Florida) the media predicted one or other of these two candidates as the victor on the evidence of exit polls only to be forced to retract this assertion as the ballots were counted.

Referendum

What is a referendum and does this provide a desirable way to increase the role of the general public in policy making?

Referenda give the general public the opportunity to vote on specific policy issues. They are utilized widely in some liberal democracies such as Switzerland and the Scandinavian countries but more sparingly in others such as the United Kingdom.

Advantages

The main advantages associated with referenda are discussed in the following sections.

Direct democracy

Referenda permit mass public involvement in public policy making. We term this 'direct democracy'. There are various forms of referendum. They may entail the public being given the opportunity to approve a proposed course of action before it is implemented or to express their views on actions previously undertaken by a government. In America referendum are frequently used in state government. A widely used version is the petition referendum which enables a predetermined number of signatories to suspend the operation of a law passed by the state legislature which is then placed before the public at a future state election.

Referenda avoid the dangers of public office holders not accurately reflecting public opinion by enabling the citizens themselves to express their approval or disapproval of issues which affect their everyday lives. The power exercised by policy makers over the content of public policy is reduced and they are required to pursue actions which are truly reflective of the views of the public.

It is important, however, that the initiative to hold a referendum should not solely rest with those who discharge the functions of government. Referenda will only provide a mechanism to secure public involvement in policy making if the public themselves have the right both to call one and to exercise some control over its content. In New Zealand, for example, the 1993 Citizens' Initiated Referenda Act gave 10 per cent of registered electors the opportunity to initiate a non-binding referendum on any subject. This must be held within one year of the initial call for a referendum unless 75 per cent of members of parliament vote to defer it. A related measure is the initiative petition which is used in approximately half of the American states. This enables a set number of a state's voters to put a proposed law on a ballot paper which becomes law if approved by a majority of voters regardless of whether the state legislature chooses to enact it.

Determination of constitutional issues

It is not feasible to suggest that referenda should be held to ascertain the views of the public on every item of public policy. However, they do provide a means whereby major issues (perhaps of considerable constitutional importance) can be resolved. In many European countries referenda were held on membership of the European Union or treaties (such as Maastricht) which were associated with it because of their implications for fundamental matters such as national sovereignty. In the United Kingdom referenda were held in 1997 to enable people living in Scotland and Wales to give their views on the government's devolution proposals for these two countries. In 1998 referenda were held in Northern Ireland to assess the public mood on the Good Friday peace agreement and in the Irish Republic to approve the amendment of its Constitution which laid claim to the six counties of Northern Ireland.

Disadvantages

There are, however, a number of problems associated with referenda. These are considered now.

Devalue the role of the legislature

Referenda may devalue the role performed by legislative bodies. In some countries (such as France) they were deliberately introduced to weaken the power of parliament. Although they can be reconciled with the concept of parliamentary sovereignty when they are consultative and do not require the legislature to undertake a particular course of action, it is difficult to ignore the outcome of a popular vote even when it does not theoretically tie the hands of public policy makers. Thus the Norwegian Parliament announced in advance of the 1972 consultative referenda on entry into the European Economic Community that its outcome would determine the country's stance on this issue.

Unequal competition

Competing groups in a referenda do not necessarily possess equality in the resources which they have at their disposal and this may give one side an unfair advantage over the other in putting its case across to the electorate. This problem is accentuated if the government contributes to the financing of one side's campaign, as occurred in the early stages of the 1995 Irish referendum on divorce.

Complexity of issues

The general public may be unable to understand the complexities of the issues which are the subject of a referendum. This may mean that the level of public participation is low or that the result is swayed by factors other than the issue which is placed before the voters for their consideration. For example, the September 2000 referendum in Denmark to reject entry into the single European currency, the Euro, was determined more by arguments about the erosion of national identity and independence rather than the economic arguments related to joining the Euro.

Underlying motives may not be progressive

We should also observe that a referendum is not always a progressive measure designed to enhance the ability of the public to play a meaningful role in policy making. Dictators may use them instead of representative institutions such as a parliament, asserting that these bodies are unnecessary since the public are directly consulted on government policy. The use of referendum by Germany's Nazi government (1933–45) resulted in the 1949 West German Constitution prohibiting their future use.

Referenda may also be proposed by governments to preserve party unity on an issue which is extremely divisive. The British referendum in 1975 on the Labour government's renegotiated terms for membership of the European Economic Community was primarily put forward for such partisan reasons. This avoided the government having to take a decision which might have split the party.

'Mob rule'
A referendum may facilitate the tyranny of the majority with minority interests being sacrificed at the behest of mob rule. This may mean that political issues are resolved by orchestrated hysteria rather than through a calm reflection of the issues which are involved.

Examples of the use of referenda

Referenda are widely used by liberal democracies as the following examples demonstrate.

Ireland   Proposals to amend the constitution, following enactment by the *Oireachtas* (parliament), must be submitted to a referendum. In 1995 a proposal to amend the constitution and legalize divorce was narrowly approved, having been decisively rejected in 1986.

France   Referenda have been initiated by some presidents to appeal directly to the public over the heads of either the National Assembly or the government. De Gaulle's 1962 referendum secured popular approval for the direct election of the president and demonstrated how a referendum can be used to enhance presidential power.

Low turnout

Public interest in referenda is not always high and is affected by factors which include the extent to which established political parties are able to agree on a stance to be adopted and campaign for this. Some countries which utilize referendum have a requirement that turnout should reach a stipulated figure in order for reforms to be initiated. This seeks to prevent minorities securing control of the political agenda. In Portugal, for example, a turnout of 50 per cent of the electorate is required for a referendum to have binding authority.

'Teledemocracy'

Referenda are one mechanism of direct democracy. But there are others. What is termed 'teledemocracy' can also be used to achieve the objective of enhanced popular involvement in public policy making. This involves a television audience being supplied with the technology to make an instant response to matters which appear on their screens. Experiments have taken place in countries which include America and New Zealand. Although these have often been concerned with marketing commercial products and entertainment, they could be further developed to facilitate members of the general public being regularly involved in the formulation of policy, perhaps through their participation in spontaneous polls concerning options which are debated before them.

The role of the military in civilian affairs

What constraints govern the involvement of the military in civilian affairs in a liberal democracy?

In some areas of the world, governments are controlled by members of the military. Government is conducted by soldiers rather than politicians. Nigeria, for example, has been ruled by military governments for most of the period since independence in 1960 and military intervention is a frequent occurrence in the politics of Pakistan.

In liberal democratic political systems we are likely to view the military as an institution concerned with defending the interests of our country at home or abroad. But we sometimes see soldiers performing duties in our own country too. Such tasks are of a civilian rather than a military nature. Thus we need to consider how the involvement of the military in civilian affairs in liberal democracies differs from that which it performs in totalitarian political structures.

In a liberal democracy the military is subject to civilian control. This means that it does not intervene in civil affairs at its own discretion but awaits a request to do so from what is termed a civil authority. This control extends to implementing objectives which are determined by politicians who may subsequently be called upon to account for the actions of the military. In America the president is the commander in chief of the armed forces. In the United Kingdom historically the authority which requested military intervention in civilian affairs was a magistrate. Today government ministers and chief constables play key roles in decisions of this kind. There are three circumstances in which military intervention in civil affairs may be justified in contemporary Britain. These are military aid to the civilian communities (which covers events such as providing help to the public in the wake of natural disasters, for example, floods), military aid to the civilian ministries (in which military aid is sought to provide a service required by the public when such has been withdrawn, for example in a strike) and military aid to the civil power (when military support is needed to ensure public order). Troops were deployed in Northern Ireland after 1969 under this latter contingency.

Questions

1 Outline the main features of a liberal democratic political system with which you are familiar. How do these features contrast with the key characteristics of communist and totalitarian political systems?
2 With reference to any national legislature or local government body with which you are familiar, indicate the level of representation secured by women and ethnic minority communities. In your view should elected bodies of this nature seek to mirror the social composition of society?
3 With the use of examples, consider whether referenda are a help or hindrance to the operations of liberal democracy.

Taking it further

This chapter has referred to a number of common features affecting liberal democratic states. These general issues can be supplemented by more detailed reading which includes Barry Holden, *Understanding Liberal Democracy* (London: Harvester Wheatsheaf, 1993).

In addition to specialized books which discuss the politics of one specific liberal democracy, there are many which offer a comparative account of some of the issues which are discussed in this chapter. One good example of this is Jurg Steiner, *European Democracies*, (Harlow: Longman, 1998).

It is also important to appreciate that the political arrangements in liberal democratic states are not set in stone and that changes are frequently made. You can keep abreast of current developments by using the internet: in the United Kingdom information on contemporary issues can be obtained from the Government Information Service whose website is www.open.gov.uk.

03

political ideologies

In this chapter you will learn:
- what is meant by the term 'political ideology'
- the distinction between 'left' and 'right' political ideologies
- outlines of key left- and right-wing political ideologies

Definition

What do we mean by the term 'political ideology' and why is it important for the study of politics?

Ideology is commonly defined as the principles which motivate political parties, in particular providing a vision of the society which they wish to create. Ideology thus serves as a unifying force between party leaders and supporters: all are spiritually united in the promotion of a common cause.

Ideology is not, however, always the guiding force in party politics. American political parties appear far less ideological than their western European counterparts. Even in these countries, parties (especially when in power) are often forced to respond to events rather than to fashion them. Parties on the left of the political spectrum have sometimes been accused of abandoning ideology in favour of pragmatism (that is, responding to events as they occur without referring to any preconceived ideology) or of redefining their ideology to make them more electable.

There is a danger that politicians are perceived as seeking office for the power which it gives them as individuals where political ideology is not prominent as a driving force motivating a political party. This may influence the level of popular involvement in political affairs. The absence of pronounced ideology may also result in a situation in which electors find it difficult to differentiate between the political parties. The term 'consensus' is used to describe a situation in which similar goals and policies are put forward by competing political parties.

Marxists adopt a more precise definition of ideology. Here it refers to a coherent set of ideas, beliefs and values through which an individual can make sense of the social world they inhabit. This ought to derive from a person's social class. However, Marxists contend that liberal democracies are dominated by the ideology of the ruling class (or bourgeoisie) which secures the acquiescence of the working class (proletariat) to exploitation and social inequality. The dominance accorded to bourgeois ideas in such societies (arising from the control they exert over agencies such as the education system and the media) results in the proletariat suffering from what Friedrich Engels referred to as a 'false consciousness' whereby they fail to appreciate the fact that they are exploited and thus consent to the operations of the existing social system which is thus accorded legitimacy by this intellectual form of control.

Political spectrum

The term political spectrum is used to place different political ideologies in relationship to one another thereby enabling the similarities and differences that exist between them to be identified.

The various political ideologies are grouped under the broad headings of 'left', 'right' and 'centre'. The right consists of fascism and conservatism, the centre consists of liberalism and social democracy and the left comprises socialism, communism and anarchism. Anarchism is located on the far left of the political spectrum and fascism is on the far right. This terminology was derived from the French Revolution in the late eighteenth century: the left was associated with revolution while the right was identified with reaction.

The terms 'right', 'left' and 'centre' lack precise definition but are used broadly to indicate the stances which the different ideologies adopt towards political, economic and social change. Historically, the right opposed this, preferring tradition and the established order of the past. The left endorsed change as a necessary development which was designed to improve the human condition. The centre was also associated with change, but wished to introduce this gradually within the existing economic and political framework which the left sought to abolish as a prerequisite to establishing an improved society.

The political spectrum is concerned with ideologies, not with the political systems or practices with which they may be associated. Communism and fascism (which are on the opposite ends of the political spectrum) are both associated with totalitarian political systems in which citizens are deprived of a wide range of civil and political liberties and in which personal freedom is sacrificed to the common interests which are defined by the state. However, the nature of the society with which these two ideologies is associated is entirely different.

Individualism and collectivism

Individualism and collectivism constitute one important way of distinguishing between political ideologies.

Individualism places the interests of individual citizens at the forefront of its concerns and is viewed as the opposite of collectivism. As a political doctrine it suggests that the sphere of government should be limited so as not unduly to encroach on the ability of individuals to pursue their own interests and thereby achieve self-fulfilment. As an economic principle, individualism opposes government intervention in the workings of the economy in preference to support for the free market and laissez-faire capitalism (which sees no place for government imposing restrictions affecting matters such as wages and conditions of work).

Individualism is historically linked to liberalism, where the classical notion of limited government (derived from natural rights) held that individuals should be as free as possible from state interference since this would deprive them of their ability to exercise responsibility for the conduct of their lives. It could, however, be justified in order to prevent actions by some which would impede the ability of others to advance their interests. This belief would, for example, justify legislation against monopolists since these prejudiced the position of individual entrepreneurs. By the same token, state involvement in social policy (especially to protect the poorer and weaker members of society) was rejected by liberals for much of the nineteenth century on the grounds that individuals should be responsible for their own welfare.

Individualism was thus historically viewed as the opposite of collectivism. However, some strands of liberal thought have suggested their compatibility by arguing that individual enterprise is hindered by circumstances such as the operations of the economy which are not of the individual's own making. State action directed at those who are placed in such circumstances can thus be justified in the belief that it would remove impediments preventing people from being able to assert control over their own destinies.

The 'new right' enthusiastically adopted many of the ideas associated with classical liberalism in the 1980s, in particular support for the free market and opposition to social welfare policies. In America individualism underpins the opposition voiced by militia movements against government involvement in people's lives.

Collectivism entails the sacrifice of self-interest to commonly agreed goals. These are often asserted by a central political authority which results in the state taking an active role directing the resources at its command to achieve these objectives.

Collectivism is usually depicted as the opposite of individualism since group needs are placed above the pursuit of individual interests. However, some aspects of liberal thought argue that these ideas are not incompatible since the sense of co-operation and fraternity which is developed through collective endeavour enables individuals to develop their personalities to a greater extent than would be possible if they existed in isolation.

Collectivism emerged in the United Kingdom towards the end of the nineteenth century when various socialist organizations advocated a more vigorous response by the state to social problems, especially poverty, which would entail an enhanced level of government intervention in the economy and some redistribution of resources from the more affluent members of society. Some within the Liberal Party (the 'new Liberals') also moved towards advocating activity by both central and local government to improve social conditions. This resulted in legislation in the early twentieth century to benefit the poorer and weaker members of society which ultimately developed into the welfare state.

Collectivism is traditionally closely identified with socialism, especially those who view state ownership of the means of production (achieved through policies such as nationalization) as the way to achieve a more just society. However, collective action can be organized through social units other than the state (such as communities that possess a wide degree of political autonomy) and may underpin economic ventures such as co-operatives in which people can work together and pursue common aims within a capitalist economic system.

Left-wing political ideologies

What are the main features of political ideologies located on the left of the political spectrum?

A number of political ideologies are identified with the left of the political spectrum. This section identifies them and outlines their main features.

Anarchism

Anarchism literally means 'no rule' and is a form of socialism which rejects conventional forms of government on the basis that it imposes restraints on individuals without their express consent having been given. Accordingly anarchists urge the abolition of the state and all forms of political authority, especially the machinery of law and order (which they view as the basis of oppression providing for the exercise of power by some members of society over others). Most anarchists deem violence as the necessary means to tear down the state.

Anarchists assert that government is an unnecessary evil since social order will develop naturally. Co-operation will be founded upon the self-interest of individuals and regulated by their common sense and willingness to resolve problems rationally. They assert that traditional forms of government, far from promoting harmony, are the root cause of social conflict. Private ownership of property, which is a key aspect of capitalist society, is regarded as a major source of this friction.

Some aspects of Marxism (especially the view that under communism the state would 'wither away') are compatible with anarchist views. Anarchist thought has been concerned with developing social structures outside conventional forms of government in the belief that the elimination of the state would eradicate exploitation and that co-operation, fraternity and a fair division of goods and labour would be facilitated in smaller forms of social organization. These have included syndicalism (which sought worker control of industry to be achieved by strike action), communes and a wide range of co-operative endeavours (which were characterized by relatively small groups of individuals owning and operating a productive enterprise which is managed for their mutual economic benefit).

Communism

Communism (sometimes referred to as socialist democracy) is a political system based on the ideas of Karl Marx. According to Marxist theory, communism occurs following the overthrow of capitalism and after an intermediary phase (referred to as socialism) in which the Communist Party functions as the vanguard of the proletariat, ruling on their behalf and paving the way for the eventual establishment of communism. This is characterized by the abolition of private property and class divisions and the creation of equality in which citizens live in co-operation and harmony. In this situation the state becomes unnecessary and will 'wither away'.

States which have called themselves 'communist' have not achieved the ideal situation referred to by Marx. Considerable differences existed between them (especially the former USSR and China whose approach to issues such as social equality was dissimilar) although in general, these countries were characterized by the existence of little or no private property ownership, a planned economy (which was viewed as essential to achieving equality and classlessness) and a comprehensive welfare state.

The most notable feature of communist states is the paramount position of an official socialist ideology and the domination or total monopolization of political affairs by the official Communist Party. As the massacre of opponents to the communist regime in China at Tiananmen Square in 1989 evidenced, dissent is not encouraged in communist states. The control which the Communist Party exerts over government means that the judiciary is less able to defend civil and political liberties as is the case in liberal democratic political systems.

Communist states included the former Soviet Union and its East European satellite neighbours but, following the 'collapse of communism' in Eastern Europe between 1989–91, is confined to a smaller number of countries which include the People's Republic of China, Vietnam, Cuba and North Korea. The communist heritage of the former states has resulted in weak party systems and limited levels of public participation in political affairs. Civil liberties are relatively poorly protected. A considerable degree of state ownership remains, although vigorous attempts are being made to move towards a capitalist economy.

Marxism–Leninism

Marxism–Leninism combines the ideas of Karl Marx and Vladimir Ilych Lenin. Marx asserted that actions and human institutions were economically determined and that the class struggle was the key instrument of historical change. Lenin was especially concerned with the organization of a post-capitalist society. Marxism–Leninism formed the basis of the political system which was established in Russia following the 1917 Revolution.

Marxist theory, like elitism, questioned the pluralist nature of society. It held that in industrialized societies the elite consisted of the economically dominant class, the bourgeoisie. Their wealth was the underpinning for their political power in which the state was used as an instrument to dominate and exploit the working class (or proletariat). Although those who owned and controlled capital were not necessarily the same as those who exercised political power, the economic interests and cultural values of the former determined the actions undertaken by the latter. Popular consent to such decisions is especially reliant on the ideological control exerted over the population by this economically powerful elite.

Marx stressed that social classes were in an inevitable state of competition with one another and that the exploitive nature of capitalism made a proletarian or working-class revolution inevitable. Exploitation would result in increased class consciousness. This would develop into class conflict, resulting in a revolution involving the overthrow of the ruling class and the emergence of a new society based on what he termed 'the dictatorship of the proletariat'. The new socialist society would be characterized by the abolition of private property ownership which was viewed as the basis of the inequalities of the class system.

Marx said little concerning how a socialist society should be organized. This was a major concern of Lenin's. He argued that it was the role of the Communist Party to act as the vanguard (that is, leader) of the proletariat which would direct the revolution and control society while true socialism was being constructed. A key objective of this period would be to rescue the masses from the false consciousness which had been cultivated by the previous regime. This meant that a one-party state operated in countries controlled by Marxist–Leninist ideology.

Most Eastern European communist parties subscribed to Marxist–Leninist doctrines. These were, however, challenged elsewhere. Maoism, named after the Chinese leader Mao Tse-Tung, viewed the peasantry rather than the industrial proletariat as the revolutionary class and, in common with Leon Trotsky, he also rejected the centralized power exerted by the Communist Party in favour of the popular involvement of the masses in the revolutionary transformation of society.

Socialism

Socialism arose in reaction to the exploitive nature of capitalism. It rejects a society in which inequalities in the distribution of wealth and political power result in social injustice and is committed to the ideal of equality. Socialists seek a society in which co-operation and fraternity replace the divisions based on class lines which characterize capitalist societies. There is, however, considerable disagreement concerning both the nature of an egalitarian society and how it would be created. These stem from the diverse traditions embraced by socialism.

The roots of socialism include the economic theories of David Ricardo (who suggested that the interests of capital and labour were opposed), the reforming activites of Robert Owen (who advocated the ownership of the means of production by small groups of producers organized into societies based upon the spirit of co-operation), the Christian impulse (which was relevant to socialism through its concern for the poor and the early experiences of Christians living in a society in which property was held in common) and the writings of Karl Marx and Friedrich Engels who asserted that inequality was rooted in private property ownership and the class system which derived from this.

The varied impulses which influenced socialism explain the differences within it. A key division is between fundamentalist and reformist socialism (or social democracy). Fundamentalist socialists believe that state control of all means of production is indispensable to the creation of an egalitarian society and is thus viewed as their main political objective. They reject the free market and instead have historically endorsed the centralized planning of the economy and the nationalization (or 'socialization' as it is termed in America) of key industries to achieve this goal. Reformist (or revisionist) socialists, however, believe that an egalitarian society can be created by reforming the capitalist system rather than abolishing it. This version of socialism is commonly referred to as social democracy. This has resulted in nationalization being applied to selected industries on a piecemeal basis and an acceptance of the coexistence of state-owned and privately owned industry within what is termed a mixed economy. Central economic planning has typically been used to supplement the workings of the free market rather than seeking to replace it.

Feminism

Feminism is not a coherent political ideology. However, its desire to change the power relationships in society make it compatible with ideologies on the left of the political spectrum.

Feminism refers to a wide range of theories which assert that the power relationship between the sexes is unequal and which views this problem as a social construction rather than a natural situation arising from biological differences between male and females. Feminist ideas inspired campaigns waged from the late nineteenth century onwards seeking equal legal and political rights for women, but the modern feminist movement derived from North America in the 1960s.

There are a number of strands to feminist thought. Liberal feminism seeks to combat discrimination experienced by women in the public sphere and seeks equality of treatment. Measures to secure formal equality embodied in equal rights legislation (such as the United Kingdom's 1970 Equal Pay Act and 1975 Sex Discrimination Act) derive from this perspective.

Radical feminism seeks the liberation of women. They focus not on inequality but, rather, on the system of sexual oppression which was termed 'patriarchy' (or 'rule by men'). Radical feminists believe that patriarchy is the key power relationship in society and is reproduced in each generation by the family. They believe that sexual equality requires a revolution in cultural and social values and cannot be attained by providing additional legal rights for women within the existing social structure. Marxist feminism attributes the oppression of women to the operations of capitalism which gives rise to economic dependency which is viewed as the basis of women's oppression. They assert that only in a communist society would this situation be remedied. Socialist feminism concentrates on the way in which the twin forces of patriarchy and class oppression interact in a capitalist society and place women in a socially subordinate position. Unlike radical feminists, however, they do not view the interests of men and women as being permanently opposed. Post-modernist feminism rejects the certainty and objectivity which underlay the Marxist view of class interests. They do not see all women as being subject to the same processes and believed that different groups encounter different experiences.

Feminist politics are especially associated with extra-parliamentary political action, although in some countries they are advanced by women's political parties. One example of this is Iceland's Women's Alliance which was formed in 1983 to promote women's and children's issues

The centre and centre-left of the political spectrum

What are the main features of social democracy and liberalism?

This section outlines the key aspects of liberalism and social democracy which are identified with the centre-left and centre of the political spectrum.

Social democracy

Social democracy rests within the reformist (or revisionist) tradition of socialism. It suggests that social inequalities can be addressed by an enhanced level of state intervention within the existing structure of the capitalist economic system. The influence of social democracy was increased after 1945 when capitalism was seen to be bringing many benefits to working-class people (such as a rising standard of living and social mobility) in a number of countries which in turn tended to reduce the hostility between the social classes.

Lord John Maynard Keynes was especially influential in the development of social democratic politics. He argued that a market economy subject to an enhanced degree of state intervention to manage demand could provide an effective solution to the problem of unemployment. His policy of demand management was adopted by a number of socialist parties as an alternative to state control of the economy.

Social democracy also sought to remove social problems affecting the poorer members of society through the establishment of a welfare state. This was a mechanism to provide for the redistribution of wealth within society since the welfare state would be financed by public money obtained through the taxation of income so that the rich would contribute towards addressing the health and welfare needs of the poor. Social democracy was also associated with other policies designed to improve the access of poorer members of society to a range of services such as housing and education.

There are a number of key differences between fundamentalists and social democrats. The latter have a negative view towards nationalization, viewing it as one means among many which may be used to secure state influence over the workings of the economy. This view is to some extent flavoured by a perception that state ownership of industry (where this occurred in countries such as the United Kingdom) resulted in bureaucracy and inefficiency without substantially improving the position of the working class. Fundamentalists assert that social democratic policies such as the welfare state serve not to create a socialist society but, rather, to hinder the development of class consciousness thereby perpetuating capitalism and its essentially exploitive nature.

The third way

The 'third way' embraces the goals of opportunity and social inclusion based on support for capitalism. Many social democratic parties in Europe (such as the United Kingdom Labour Party and the German Social Democratic Party) shifted towards the 'third way' during the late 1990s.

The first way was the approach of new right governments of the 1980s. The emphasis which they placed on the free market intensified social divisions. Much of the wealth that had been created had not been invested which meant that it had failed to percolate throughout society and instead had created an 'underclass' who felt themselves to be permanently excluded from society, deprived of work, power and prospects.

The second way consisted of social democracy which placed considerable importance on nationalization of key industries and public utilities. The third way sought to retain private ownership but to reshape the way it worked by seeking to combine a company's responsibilities to its shareholders with responsibility to the wider community which included their customers, the workers they employed and the localities where they operated.

The third way was underpinned by stakeholding which was directed towards the pursuit of social justice and the provision of wider opportunities for all within a market economy. It sought to equip individuals with the skills and capacities necessary to succeed in the highly flexible and constantly changing labour markets of modern capitalism but could also be depicted as a reform which was essential to the smooth operations of a market economy. A dynamic market required flexibility which was hindered by a permanently excluded underclass. The stakeholder economy was thus an approach which would provide for economic efficiency at the same time as dispensing a measure of social justice. In addition to these individual principles, stakeholding can be governed by collective ideals. The collective model of stakeholding has a wider agenda, covering issues which include the ownership and control of companies and constitutional change.

Liberalism

Modern liberalism emerged from the fight for religious freedom waged in late sixteenth- and seventeenth-century western Europe. The close link which existed between Church and state ensured that the objective of religious freedom was associated with political dissent. Liberal theorists argued that the social order was a compact (or contract) voluntarily entered into by those who were party to it rather than being a structure handed down by God. Social contract theory was developed by liberal theorists such as Thomas Hobbes and John Locke. The belief that government emerged as the result of rational choice made by those who subsequently accorded their consent to its operations ensured that the rights of the individual were prominent concerns of liberal philosophers. The people were viewed as the ultimate source of political power and government was legitimate only while it operated with their consent.

As a political doctrine, liberalism emphasized individualism and asserted that human beings should exercise the maximum possible freedom consistent with others being able to enjoy similar liberty. They sought to advance this belief through their support for limited government and their opposition to the intervention of the state in the everyday lives of its citizens, arguing that this would dehumanize individuals since they were not required to take responsibility for their own welfare but instead became reliant on others whom they could blame if personal misfortunes befell them. As an economic doctrine, liberalism was traditionally associated with the free market, laissez-faire capitalism and free trade.

The perception that social problems such as unemployment and poverty were not the fault of the individual but, rather, were dependent on factors such as the workings of the economy over which the individual had no control resulted in significant changes to liberal ideology. In many countries liberals advocated state intervention in welfare provision and economic management. In the United Kingdom, this approach was especially associated with Lord William Beveridge and Lord

John Maynard Keynes, and in America with the 'New Deal Liberalism' pursued by President Franklin Delano Roosevelt. Traditional liberal principles, however, subsequently influenced the new right in the 1980s.

Freedom

Freedom suggests that individuals are able to live their lives as they see fit with no impediments being placed on their actions. However, this assertion would find little support outside anarchist thought: other ideologies suggest that some form of regulation needs to be applied since unrestrained freedom would enable some members of society to harm others. A key issue affecting freedom, therefore, is the relationship between the individual and the state and under what circumstances it is acceptable for the state to undertake interventions which intrude on some or all of its members.

Liberal thought saw a close distinction between freedom and rights. Freedom was especially associated with civil liberties and was defined in a negative sense whereby individuals were deemed free to undertake actions unless the interests of others required that constraints should be placed upon them. Freedom was equated with privacy and minimal state activity since this would limit an individual's freedom of action.

The concept of freedom was later developed in liberal thought into that of positive freedom which viewed a more vigorous form of state activity as essential to enable individuals to exercise freedom which was defined in terms of self-fulfilment. Industrial capitalism had created conditions whereby large numbers of individuals lived in poverty and distress and were thus not able to exercise freedom. Socially and economically deprived individuals thus needed state action (typically in the form of a welfare state and intervention in the management of the economy) to create conditions in which they regained autonomy over the conduct of their lives.

A reaction against state intervention occurred in a number of liberal democratic countries in the later decades of the twentieth century. Neo-liberals focused on an economic definition of freedom which was equated with the advocacy of free market capitalism and the reduction of state interference in social and economic affairs. It was asserted that state intervention had eroded freedom by constraining consumer choice, by transforming recipients of state aid into a position of dependency whereby they lost the freedom to exercise control over their everyday lives and by sacrificing individual autonomy to the power wielded by large-scale bureaucracies.

Progressivism

Progressivism is generally identified with the centre-left of the political spectrum and seeks social and political reform which is deemed to be beneficial to the majority of the population. These reforms are put forward within the existing framework of capitalist society and thus exclude those groups that seek revolutionary change or upheaval. Constitutional reform is a particular concern of progressive movements, whose objective is to bring government closer to the people.

In America, the progressive movement initiated a number of political reforms between 1890–1920, many of which affected state government. These included the use of referendum, which typically took the form of the petition referendum enabling a predetermined number of signatories to suspend the operation of a law passed by the state legislature which would be placed before the public at a future state election. A further reform was the initiative petition, which enabled a set number of a state's voters to put a proposed law on a ballot paper which became law if approved by a majority of voters regardless of whether the state legislature chose to enact it. Most states have adopted some form of referendum and around half utilize the initiative petition.

Other reforms associated with American progressivism included enabling a set number of electors to re-call an elected representative at either state or federal level (which has the effect of 'de-electing' this person) and the introduction of direct election of senators, civil service examinations, a method to enable popular choice to determine the selection of candidates put forward by political parties (termed 'primary elections') and the long ballot. In Congress progressive pressure succeeded in drastically reducing the power of the Speaker of the House of Representatives to control its actions. Progressive parties have also stood in presidential elections in 1912, 1924 and 1948, the most successful of which was the 'Bull Moose Party', led by former President Theodore Roosevelt. This was a splinter from the Republican Party and obtained 88 electoral college votes in 1912.

In the United Kingdom progressive opinion is not located in one political movement but has historically been spread across the major parties. It is currently identified with the Liberal Democrats and Labour Party and left-wing Conservatives.

Right-wing political ideologies

What are the main characteristics of conservatism and fascism?

This section discusses the main aspects of ideologies on the right of the political spectrum.

Conservatism

The essence of conservative ideology is scepticism towards change. The desire to 'retain things as they are' is especially concerned with what are deemed to be the key institutions and values on which society is based. These include support for private property ownership. This results in opposition to any form of social (including moral) upheaval, support for firm (but not despotic) government and a belief that political institutions should evolve naturally rather than being artifically constructed from an abstract theory or blueprint. Conservatism rejects the goal of equality achieved by social engineering, believing that the differences which exist between people are natural and should not be tampered with. Conservatism is often equated with nationalistic sentiments, seeking to safeguard domestic values and the way of life against foreign incursions.

Conservative thought developed in the eighteenth century and was especially influenced by the events of the French Revolution. Conservatism in the United Kingdom was considerably influenced by *Reflexions on the Revolution in France,* written by Edmund Burke in 1792. Although he had initially been sympathetic to the French Revolution, he subsequently turned against it when the scale of the destruction of the established order became apparent. He explained this alteration in the direction of his thought by providing a summary of the 'British way' which constituted a classic statement of conservatism. He argued that an Englishman's freedom was a national inheritance which was most effectively secured by government which balanced democracy, aristocracy and monarchy. His defence of traditions and institutions was coupled with the advocacy of evolutionary change. He accepted that change would sometimes be necessary, but advocated that this should be minimal and should seek to preserve as much of the old as was possible. In France, Joseph de Maistre contributed to conservative thought by providing a defence of established authority against revolutionary ideas and emphasizing the need for order.

In practice, conservative parties are often pragmatic, that is, they show a willingness to fashion policies in order to respond to pressing problems rather than seeking to advance a specific ideology.

New right

The term 'new right' refers to a body of ideas that underpinned the policies pursued by a number of conservative parties in the 1980s, most notably in governments led by Margaret Thatcher in the United Kingdom and Ronald Reagan in America.

New right policies were based on two specific traditions. The first of these was termed 'neo-liberalism'. This version of economic liberalism was rooted in classical liberal ideas and sought to reduce the activities of the state whose frontiers would be 'rolled back' by the application of policies such as privatization and reduced levels of government spending on functions such as welfare provision. This aspect of new right thinking voiced support for private enterprise and the free market and led to Keynesian economics (which regarded unemployment as the key problem to be addressed by economic policy) being replaced by new economic methods such as monetarism (which identified inflation as the main social evil which would be reduced by controlling the money supply). It was argued that government intervention in the economy led to inefficiency but that economic growth, employment, productivity and widespread prosperity would be secured if it ceased its attempts to regulate wages and prices.

Privatization

One aspect of privatization entailed transferring an industry from the public to the private sector. In the United Kingdom this was referred to as 'denationalization'. This policy was pursued by a number of new right governments although their motives for embarking on it differed. In the United Kingdom a key concern was to extend a 'shareholding democracy' by selling shares in former nationalized industries to ordinary members of the general public. In New Zealand, however, shares were mainly sold to large multinational companies. Here, the aim of privatization was to benefit the tax payer both by ensuring that shares were purchased for high prices and as a consequence of economic efficiency which was presumed to be a consequence of the transfer of a state-owned industry to an existing major company.

The second basis of new right thinking was termed 'neo-conservatism'. This emerged in America in the 1960s and was endorsed primarily by liberals who were disillusioned by the inability of government action to solve social problems. It entailed a number of ideas which included social authoritarianism. This asserted that contemporary social problems such as crime, disorder, hooliganism, indiscipline among young people and moral decay were caused by the decline of 'traditional' values which were replaced by permissive attitudes and disrespect for authority. Many neo-conservatives apportioned the blame for these problems on the lack of commitment by immigrants to a country's established cultural values. It endorsed a 'law and order' response to social problems and demanded a return to traditional forms of authority such as the family.

Neo-liberalism and neo-conservatism are not necessarily compatible since the former emphasizes self-reliance which might result in selfish behaviour whereas the latter views individuals as citizens with a range of civic obligations to fulfil.

Fascism

Fascism is a political ideology on the right of the political spectrum which, although lacking a coherent body of beliefs, shares certain important features. These include opposition to communism, Marxism and liberalism (especially individualism, which they advocate should occupy a position subordinate to the national community). Fascism also opposes the operations of liberal democracy which it seeks to replace with a totalitarian political system in which there is only one party and, ideally, the complete identity of this party with the state. One consequence of this is that civil and political liberties are absent in fascist states.

Fascist parties utilize action and violence as key political tactics especially when seeking to secure power and they stress the importance of firm leadership to solve a nation's problems. Prominent leaders of fascist movements, such as Adolf Hitler in Germany, Benito Mussolini in Italy, Francisco Franco in Spain and Antonio de Oliveira Salazar in Portugal, made great use of their personal charisma to secure loyalty from those who followed them. Fascist movements also emphasize the importance of nation and race, the consequences of which included a desire for territorial expansion and the practice of racism and genocide.

Fascist movements appeal to persons of all social classes by using populist rhetoric to secure support. Successful fascist parties attract the lower middle classes when these feel threatened by social and economic changes occurring in a particular country. There was, however, wide variation in the ideas and policies put forward by individual fascist parties whose leaders cultivated support by opportunistically exploiting popular concerns, fears or prejudices. This meant that the success achieved by fascist parties was significantly influenced by events which were unique to particular countries: in Germany, for example, Hitler's rise to power was aided by factors which included a widespread feeling that the Treaty of Versailles was unfair, the prior existence of nationalist and anti-Semitic beliefs and the economic problems faced by the country after 1919 which resulted in both unemployment and hyper-inflation. In Italy fascism was aided by the weaknesses displayed by the pre-fascist ruling class.

Populism

Populism is not a coherent political ideology but encompasses a range of right-wing attitudes and opinions.

Populism advocates the pursuance of policies supported by majority public opinion. These concerns and the values which underpin them are not derived from any coherent set of political beliefs but are widely varied, although a common strand is that the concerns which are articulated in populist rhetoric are depicted as resting on 'common sense' assumptions. Typically populist politics directs its appeal to the masses over the heads of other established social and political institutions (such as the family, social class, political parties and trade unions) by focusing on a cause which can be depicted as harmful and contrary to the best interests of mass public opinion. This appeal is especially directed at those at the lower end of the social scale although the leaders of such movements tend to be drawn from higher up the social ladder.

Examples of populist movements include the America People's Party of the 1890s which voiced the concerns of farmers in the western and southern states and demanded the increased coinage of silver. Populism is particularly identified with Juan Péron, the President of Argentina 1946–55 and 1973–74. His power rested on his ability to mobilize the poorer elements in society against the institutions of the state. As with fascism, populism is often identified with the strong leadership of a charismatic figure and a distrust of representative institutions.

In western liberal democracies, populist politics are often identified with extreme right wing political parties which suggest that the problems of 'ordinary' members of the general public are due to the policies pursued by 'unrepresentative politicians' who have ignored the interests of the masses by pursuing policies such as immigration, and by adopting over-liberal attitudes in areas such as law and order and social policy. Support for such views is often cultivated by selecting a target (usually a weak and vulnerable group in society) which can be scapegoated and depicted as both the root cause and embodiment of the crisis allegedly facing society.

The ability to mobilize public opinion has been enhanced by technological developments such as the internet which enable the speedy formation of support for a populist cause. This may exert a significant influence on the conduct of political parties who feel they must follow the expressed views of the general public in order to secure their support.

Questions

1 Outline the major features of the ideology of any one political party with which you are familiar.
2 Outline the main differences between communism and socialism.
3 Undertake your own study of a conservative party, identifying the ideology which underpins its policies.

Taking it further

This chapter has drawn our attention to the importance of political ideas. These provide politicians with a vision of the society which they wish to create should they control the government of a country.

There are numerous books which deal with political ideas. A particularly good account is provided by Andrew Heywood, *Political Ideas and Concepts* (Basingstoke: Macmillan/Palgrave, 1994). Additionally, a detailed account of how political ideologies in Britain are considered is to be found in Robert Leach, *Political Ideology in Britain* (Basingstoke: Macmillan/Palgrave, 2002).

04

elections and electoral systems

In this chapter you will learn:

- the theory of the mandate
- the key features of different electoral systems
- the strengths and weaknesses of proportional representation

The significance of elections

What is the purpose of elections?

Those of us who live in liberal democracies will periodically be invited to vote. We may be asked to choose representatives for local, state or national office. Elections are the mechanism whereby the views of citizens are translated into political actions, providing them with an opportunity to play a part in the political affairs of their country. They enable public participation in key activities which include selecting the personnel of government and determining the content of public policy.

Elections further constitute the process whereby public office holders can be made to account for their activities to the general public. It is an essential feature of liberal democracy that sovereignty resides with the people living in each country. Governments must be accountable to the people for their actions. Those that lose the backing of public opinion will be replaced by representatives drawn from another political party at the next round of elections. Elections, therefore, provide an essential link between the government and the governed. They serve as a barometer of public opinion and ensure that the holders of public office, and the policies which they pursue, are broadly in accord with the wishes of the general public.

Non-voting

Are low levels of voter participation a problem for liberal democracies?

It is sometimes argued that the extent to which citizens exercise their right to vote is one indicator of the 'health' of a system of government. A high level of voter participation (which is sometimes referred to as 'turnout') might suggest enthusiasm by members of the public to involve themselves in the affairs of government in their country and, in more general terms, to express support for the political system which operates in that country.

In some liberal democracies voting is compulsory: this is the case in Australia and Belgium, for example. In others, however, it is optional. Where voting is optional, the level of voter participation varies. In 2001 the turnout for the UK general election was 59.4 per cent. In 2000, only 51 per cent of the American public voted in the presidential election.

Various reasons might explain non-voting. Factors such as social class, education and income may be influential forces in determining whether a person votes or abstains. Generally, low voting rates are found among persons from low socio-economic backgrounds. Voting laws and registration procedures may also influence turnout. In the UK, for example, local authorities actively seek to ensure that voters are registered. In America, the onus of registration is placed on the individual and low levels of voting are sometimes attributed to the complex registration procedures utilized in some states.

Registration to vote in America

In America citizens are required to register in advance of election contests in order to participate in elections. The criteria governing registration are controlled by the states and are subject to wide variation across America.

Additionally, political parties are required to display a stipulated level of registered supporters by a determined date before they can be entered on ballot papers. This may make it difficult for new national parties to enter the political arena and thus work in favour of the two established national parties. Low levels of voting are sometimes blamed on complex registration procedures.

There is debate as to the significance of low levels of voting. It might be argued that low turnouts result in public policy failing to represent the national interest. If public opinion is imperfectly represented, governments may be swayed to act at the bidding of organized minorities. Disinclination by the public to involve themselves in the government of their country may also pave the way for totalitarianism in which the public become frozen out of participation in government. Alternatively, however, it might be argued that low voting levels are not of great importance. Non-voting may indicate a general level of popular satisfaction with the way in which public affairs are conducted.

The cost of election campaigns

Election campaigns are extremely costly events. It was estimated that spending on the presidential election and Congressional contests in America amounted to $3 billion in 2000 with a further $1 billion being expended on state contests.

In some countries, limits are placed on the spending of individual candidates and political parties. In the United Kingdom, electoral laws impose an upper limit on the expenditure in constituency contests and the 2001 Political Parties Elections and Referendum Act capped the expenditure of political parties in such contests. In America, candidates for the office of president may accept public funding provided that they cease to raise their own finance. This reform was designed to limit the expenditure of candidates in presidential contests. In practice, however, it has failed to prevent excessive expenditure in these election campaigns as there are ways to avoid federal limits (for example, by donors giving money to what are termed 'soft money' committees which escape federal limits).

The mandate

We often hear governments justify their actions by the claim that they have a mandate to carry out such actions. What does this mean?

Candidates for public office are usually selected by political parties. At election contests they generally put forward a statement of the principles or policies which will guide their future actions should they succeed in taking control of public affairs. In the United Kingdom this statement is termed an election manifesto and in America is referred to as a platform. A party which succeeds in gaining control of a public body through the election of its nominees claims to have a mandate to administer it in line with the statements contained in its election manifesto. Its right to do this has been legitimized by the process of popular election.

There are, however, several weaknesses associated with the concept of the mandate. This may lead us to conclude that while it is useful in a liberal democracy that parties should declare their policies to the voters at election time, it is unrealistic to expect that statements contained in election manifestos can give a thorough and complete guide to what a party will do when in control of public affairs. It is also inaccurate for a winning party to assert that the public has demonstrated support for the entire contents of its manifesto. The main problems associated with the mandate are considered in the following sections.

The influence of the mandate

How important is the concept of the mandate?

In some liberal democracies, such as the United Kingdom, it is influential. It forces a political party to declare the policies which will determine its subsequent actions if it gains control of a public authority. But it can also claim the right to carry out such policies on the grounds that the public has endorsed them.

In other countries, this concept may be of less importance. In America, for example, factors which include the nature of bicameralism and the separation of powers, tended to reduce the significance of electoral mandates, one consequence of which was that voters tended to look back and cast votes retrospectively rather than seeking to evaluate the merits of proposed future actions by candidates and parties. Nonetheless, candidates for public office usually put forward a statement of future intentions and since the 1990s the mandate has assumed greater importance. In the 1994 presidential election, for example, the Reform Party candidate, Ross Perot, sought a mandate from the voters to initiate changes in America's system of government.

The emergence of issues following an election

It would be unrealistic for us to expect that a party could include every item of policy which it intended to carry out over a period of several years in a single document prepared for a specific election. Issues emerge, unforeseen when the manifesto was prepared, which have to be responded to even though the public lack the opportunity to express their views on them. People in the United Kingdom, for example, were not invited to vote on their country's involvement in the attacks mounted against Yugoslavia by NATO in 1999.

We accept, therefore, that once installed into office governments need to exercise a certain amount of discretion to respond to pressing problems when they arise. This capacity to act without consulting the general public is referred to as trusteeship.

Voters endorse parties rather than their policies

A party's right to carry out all its promises on the grounds that the public expressed support for them is also a flawed argument. Electors are unable to pick and choose between those policies in a manifesto which they like and those of which they disapprove. It is a question of supporting all or nothing. It is also the case that voters support a party for reasons other than the policies which it advances. Factors such as social class may determine a voter's political allegiance. In extreme circumstances this may mean that parties secure support in spite of, rather than because of, the policies they put forward.

Voting may be influenced by negative factors

A party or its candidates may secure support for negative rather than positive reasons.

It was argued that the outcomes of both the 1992 American presidential election and the 1997 UK general election were heavily influenced by public disillusionment with the record of the previous administrations. Support obtained for negative reasons makes it difficult for parties to claim they have a mandate to carry out their policies.

Why do we vote the way we do?

The study of voting behaviour is termed psephology. Models of voting behaviour which were developed after 1945 drew heavily on American political science. The aim of a model is to provide an explanation for voting behaviour which holds good for a significant proportion of the electorate and, additionally, applies from one generation to the next when a large number of citizens become eligible to vote for the first time, replacing former voters who have died. The Michigan model was influential and suggested that the basis of voting behaviour was an attachment formed between voters and political parties. It was perceived that an individual's association with a political party was determined by the influences encountered in his or her social relationships. Of these, the major factor was the family.

There are a number of possible factors which may constitute the underpinning of political parties, providing them with their core support. These include religion, local and regional influences. Examples of the last include the Italian *Lega Nord*, the Scottish National party, *Plaid Cymru* in Wales, the *Parti Québécois* in

Quebec, Canada, and the Catalan Republican Left and Basque National parties in Spain. Gender and race may also influence party affiliation. The African-Caribbean vote is an important constituent of the support enjoyed by the United Kingdom Labour Party and the American Democratic Party.

Social class may also influence a voter's choice of political party. This dominated explanations of voting behaviour in the United Kingdom from 1945 until 1970 when partisan and class dealignment gave rise to new models of voting behaviour. These included issue voting, which suggested that specific topical events or policies influenced a person's political behaviour. A further model, the consumer model of voting behaviour built upon the concept of issue-based voting, suggested that a person's choice of political party was similar to a shopper's choice of goods in a supermarket.

The first-past-the-post electoral system and its variants

How does the first-past-the-post electoral system operate?

The first-past-the-post system is used in countries which include the UK, the United States, Canada and India.

Under this system, to be elected to a public office it is necessary for a candidate to secure more votes than the person who comes second. But there is no requirement that the winning candidate should secure an overall majority of the votes cast in an election. It is thus possible for a candidate to be victorious under this system despite having secured a minority of the votes cast in an election.

Elsewhere systems of election have been devised that seek to adjust the workings of the first-past-the-post system. These are the second ballot and the alternative vote. Neither of these constitutes a system of proportional representation although they do attempt to put right some of the injustices which may arise under the first-past-the-post system.

The first-past-the-post system – an example

Let us look at an example of the manner in which the first-past-the-post electoral system operates.

In the United Kingdom parliamentary constituency of Folkestone and Hythe at the 2001 general election the following result was obtained:

Conservative	20,645
Liberal Democrat	14,738
Labour	9,260
Others	1,212

The Conservative candidate was returned, although he obtained only 45.2 per cent of the vote cast in that constituency.

The second ballot

The second ballot is used in France, both for legislative and presidential elections. The process is a two-stage affair. It is necessary for a candidate to obtain an overall majority of votes cast in the first-round election in order to secure election to public office. In other words, if 50,000 people voted in a constituency it would be necessary for a candidate to secure 25,001 votes to be elected. If no candidate obtained this required figure, a second-round election is held in which the candidate with most votes is elected. This system seeks to ensure that the winning candidate gets the endorsement of a majority of the electors who cast their votes in the second election.

For presidential contests the second ballot is between the top two candidates from the first round. For elections to the National Assembly, any candidate who obtains 12.5 per cent of the vote in the first round may enter the second ballot. In practice, however, parties of the left and right have often agreed in advance to rally behind one candidate for the second ballot.

A variant of the second ballot is the supplementary vote system, which is used to elect the Mayor of London. Under this system voters select candidates in order of preference. If no candidate obtains an overall majority (50 per cent +1 of the vote cast) there is no second ballot. Instead, the top two candidates remain in the contest and the votes of those who are eliminated are redistributed to determine the outcome of the contest.

The alternative vote

The alternative vote is used in Ireland for presidential elections and for by elections to the lower house, the *Dáil*. It is also used to select members for the Australian House of Representatives. As with the second ballot a candidate cannot be elected without obtaining majority support from the electorate (namely 50 per cent + 1 of the votes cast). Unlike the second ballot, however, there is no second election.

Voters number candidates in order of preference. If, when these votes are counted, no candidate possesses an overall majority, the candidate with least first-preference votes is eliminated and these are redistributed to the candidate placed second on that candidate's ballot paper. This process is repeated until a candidate has an overall majority composed of his or her first preference votes coupled with the redistributed votes of candidates who have been eliminated.

Proportional representation

What is the objective of proportional representation and how might this be achieved?

Proportional representation indicates an objective rather than a specific method of election. It seeks to guarantee that the wishes of the electorate are arithmetically reflected in the composition of public bodies such as legislatures and local authorities. This is achieved by ensuring that parties are represented according to the level of popular support they enjoy at an election contest. Various forms of proportional representation are used widely in countries within the European Union. This section will consider two of these – the single transferable vote and the party list system.

The single transferable vote

When used for elections to legislatures, the single transferable vote requires a country to be divided into a number of multi-member constituencies (that is, constituencies which return more than one member to the legislative body). When electors cast their votes, they are required to number candidates in order of preference. They may indicate a preference for as many, or as few, candidates as they wish. To be elected a candidate has to secure a quota of votes.

The single transferable vote system ensures that each successful candidate is elected by the same number of votes. It is used in Ireland for elections to the *Dáil* and for the majority of seats in the upper chamber (the *Seanad*). Of the 60 members 49 are elected in this fashion. This system is employed in Northern Ireland for the election of members to the European Parliament and the Northern Irish Assembly. It may also be used for elections to the Australian Senate.

The 'Droop quota'

Under the single transferable vote, a candidate is required to secure a quota of votes in order to be elected. This quota (which is termed the 'Droop quota', after its nineteenth-century 'inventor', Henry Droop) is calculated by the following formula:

$$\left(\frac{\text{Total number of valid votes cast in the constituency}}{\text{Total number of seats to be filled} +1}\right) +1$$

Thus in a constituency in which 100,000 electors voted and in which there were four seats to be filled, the quota would be 20,001. Any candidate who obtains the necessary number of first-preference votes is declared elected. Further first-preference votes cast for that candidate are then redistributed to the candidates listed second on that candidate's ballot paper.

If, when the count is complete, no candidate obtains the necessary number of first-preference votes, the candidate with fewest is eliminated and these are redistributed to the candidates listed as second choice on the eliminated candidate's ballot paper. This process of eliminating candidates with fewest first-preference votes is continued until the requisite number of seats are filled.

The party list system

The other main system of proportional representation is the party list system. Its main objective is to ensure that parties are represented in legislative bodies in proportion to the votes which were cast for them. Political parties are responsible for drawing up lists of candidates which may be compiled on a national or on a regional basis.

There are several versions of the party list system. In a very simplistic form (in what is termed a 'closed party list') candidates are ranked in order of preference by political parties. When the votes are counted a party's representation in the legislative body arithmetically reflects the proportion of votes which it obtained. Thus a party which obtained 20 per cent of the total national poll would be entitled to 20 per cent of the seats in the legislative chamber. If this chamber contained 300 members, this party would be entitled to fill 60 places. The actual nominees would be those numbered 1–60 on that party's list. In an 'open party list', which is used in Finland, voters determine the ranking of candidates put forward by the individual parties. The *panachage* or 'free party list system' is used for elections in Luxembourg and Switzerland. A particular feature of this system is the 'mix-in' whereby voters are not confined to selecting candidates from one party's list but may support candidates nominated by different parties. This is termed a 'free party list'.

A number of formulas exist to determine the electoral quotas used in party list systems. A popular one in Europe is the *D'Hondt* system which is used for national elections in Belgium, the Netherlands, Portugal and Spain. This uses the 'highest average' formula which seeks to ensure that the number of votes required to win a seat is the same for each party. An alternative formula is the *hagenbach-bischoff* quota which divides the total vote by the number of seats to be filled plus one. This system is used for elections to the Greek parliament.

The United Kingdom 1999 European Elections Act provided for members of the European Parliament representing England, Scotland and Wales to be elected by the party list system. Electors were given one vote which they could cast for a candidate or a party.

The additional member system

The additional (or mixed) member system of election blends the first-past-the-post system with proportional representation. In Germany, for example, both systems are used concurrently in order that minority parties who fare badly under the former system can be compensated under the latter. Under this country's additional member system, electors have two votes in Parliamentary elections. The first (*erste Stimme*) is for a constituency candidate, elected under the first-past-the-post system. The second (*zweite Stimme*) is for a party list drawn up in each state (or *Land*). The Niemeyer system is used to allocate additional members according to the following formula:

Total votes obtained by a party x number of seats available
Total number of votes of all parties getting above 5 per cent

This last method serves as a 'top up' seeking to ensure that there is a degree of proportionality between the parties. This system gives electors the opportunity of 'split ticket' voting: that is, they can support a constituency candidate of one party and the party list of another. This is a growing feature in German elections.

In 1993 a referendum in New Zealand narrowly supported changing the electoral system from first-past-the-post to a mixed-member system, whose main features are similar to the electoral system used in Germany. This was first used in the 1996 general election. Elections to the Scottish parliament, the Welsh Assembly and Greater London Assembly also use the additional member system. In Scotland and Wales the additional members are selected from regional party lists drawn up by the political parties and in London from one London-wide party list.

The first-past-the-post electoral system analysed

Strengths

Easy to understand
The system is relatively easy to understand. Voting is a simple process and it is easy to see how the result is arrived at. The winner takes all.

Executive strength
The failure of this system to ensure that the composition of the legislature arithmetically reflects the way in which a nation has voted often benefits the party winning most votes nationally. This is of particular importance in parliamentary systems of government such as the UK where the executive is drawn from the legislature since it may provide the executive with a large majority thereby enhancing its ability to govern.

An aid to party unity
The manner in which this system treats minorities may serve as an inducement for parties either to remain united or to form electoral alliances in order to secure political power. This is a particular advantage in countries with parliamentary forms of government since its support within the legislature is likely to be durable.

Enhancement of the link between the citizens and legislators

The first-past-the-post system may strengthen the relationship between members of the legislative branch of government and their constituents. In the UK, the House of Commons is composed of members elected from 659 single-member constituencies which aids the development of a close relationship between individual legislators and their constituents. This may also enhance the extent to which legislators can be held accountable for their actions. Local relationships are of great significance to the conduct of American politics.

'Strong government' in the UK

In countries with parliamentary forms of government, the winner-take-all aspect of the first-past-the-post system is greatly to the benefit of the executive branch of government.

In the 2001 general election in the UK, a Labour government was returned. Although this party obtained only 40.7 per cent of the votes cast by the electorate, the workings of the first-past-the-post system gave it 412 seats in the House of Commons (62.5 per cent of the total number). This majority guaranteed the government the ability to govern for a full five-year term if it wished to do so.

Weaknesses

Distortion of public opinion

It has been suggested that the purpose of elections is to ensure that public office holders and the policies they pursue are reflective of public opinion. A main problem with the first-past-the-post system is that it distorts public opinion by failing to ensure that the wishes of the electorate are arithmetically reflected in the composition of the legislative or executive branches of government. This may thus result in public policy being out of line with the views or wishes of the majority of the general public.

There are further difficulties arising from the tendency of the first-past-the-post system to distort public opinion. It may produce extreme changes in the composition of the legislatures which do not reflect the political views of the electorate. Major political parties can be virtually wiped out by such a system. An extreme example of this occurred in the 1993 Canadian general election when the ruling Conservative Party was reduced from 157 seats to 2 in the House of Commons. Violent changes in the composition of the legislature or executive result in the loss of experienced personnel and may create a system of adversarial politics. Parties have less incentive to co-operate when the electoral system may translate them overnight from a minority to a majority.

Unfair treatment of minority parties

A second problem arising from the operations of the first-past-the-post system is the manner in which it treats minority parties. In the United Kingdom, the Liberal Party/Liberal Democrats have, for much of the century, been under-represented in parliament as the electoral system has failed to translate that party's national vote into seats within the legislature. Although in both the 1997 and 2001 general elections this party fared far better than in previous contests as its support was concentrated in certain areas rather than being evenly spread across the country, its share of the national poll in 2001 (18.3 per cent) entitled it to 121 seats rather than the 52 it won.

Expressing this figure another way, in 2001:

> It took 26,031 votes to elect a Labour MP.
>
> It took 50,337 votes to elect a Conservative MP.
>
> It took 92,554 votes to elect a Liberal Democrat MP.

This clearly contravenes the principle of 'one vote, one value'.

Discouragement to voter participation

A further problem with the first-past-the-post system is that it may discourage voter participation. Areas may be considered 'safe' political territory for one party or another and this may discourage opponents of that party from voting on the grounds that if they do so their vote is effectively 'wasted'.

The downplaying of ideology

The first-past-the-post system may discourage parties from fragmenting and thus promote the conduct of politics within the confines of a two-party system. However, this may result in ideology becoming diluted, obscured or played down in order for the parties to serve as vehicles capable of attracting a wide range of political opinions. The absence of a distinct identity may result in voters becoming disinterested in the conduct of politics. The consequence of this is low turnouts in elections and the utilization of alternative ways (such as pressure group activity and various forms of direct action) in order to bring about political change.

Attainment of the benefits of the first-past-the-post system

We must finally analyse whether the theoretical advantages of the first-past-the-post system are actually realized in practice. To do this we shall examine the situation in the UK.

In the UK the executive branch of government comes from the majority party in the legislative body. However, strong governments (in the sense of the executive having a large parliamentary majority and thus being in a position to ensure the enactment of its election manifesto) have not been a consistent feature of post-war politics. Sixteen general elections have been held between 1945 and 2001: in six of these (1950, 1951, 1964, February 1974, October 1974 and 1992) governments were returned with a relatively small (and in one case – February 1974 – no) overall majority in the House of Commons. Governments in this position cannot guarantee to stay in office and carry out their policies. On one occasion (between 1977 and 1978) the Labour and Liberal Parliamentary Parties concluded a pact which had the effect of sustaining what had become a minority Labour government. Thus the first-past-the-post electoral system does not always deliver the benefits which advocates claim this systems possesses.

The strengths and weaknesses of proportional representation

To what extent do the disadvantages of proportional representation outweigh its advantages?

Advantages

The main advantage of proportional representation is that the system addresses many of the defects of the first-past-the-post system. It ensures that minorities are fairly treated. Legislative bodies throughout Europe contain members drawn from parties such as the Greens and thus provide an inducement for such groups to operate within the conventional political system. Outside Northern Ireland (where members of the European Parliament have been elected by the single transferable vote since 1979), this inducement was traditionally absent in the UK (where, for example, the 15 per cent of the poll obtained by the Greens in the 1989 European elections failed to secure the return of any members to the European Parliament) until proportional representation was introduced for these elections in 1999. Proportional representation may also induce parties to co-operate (especially in cases where the executive is drawn from the legislative body) and this may, in turn, divert politics away from extremes.

Disadvantages

Let us first consider the following example. In 1986, President Mitterrand of France introduced proportional representation (in the form of the party list system) for the French legislative elections in order to dilute the strength of the dominant conservative forces in the country (the RPR and the UDF). One consequence of this was the election of a number of representatives from the *Front National*. This party obtained 10 per cent of the vote and secured 35 seats. In 1988 the second ballot was restored by the Prime Minister, Jacques Chirac, and the *Front National* was virtually eliminated as a legislative force. This episode illustrates two problems which might be associated with proportional representation which are discussed in the sections that follow.

Furtherance of vested interests

First we should note the association of this reform with political vested interests in this example – it was not viewed as a progressive reform which would improve the relationship between government and the governed, but was instead designed to aid the political fortunes of those who enacted it.

Representation given to political extremists

Second, this example suggests that proportional representation may facilitate the representation of the political extremes which, once established within a legislative body, gain respectability and may enjoy a growth in their support. Some countries which use this system seek to guard against this problem by imposing a requirement that a party needs to secure a minimum threshold of support in order to secure any representation. In Denmark this figure is 2 per cent and in Germany 5 per cent or, alternatively, three seats secured from the *erste Stimme* constituency contests. In the 1998 German national election, this threshold figure enabled the Greens and communists to secure representation in the *Bundestag* but denied it to parties on the extreme right of the political spectrum.

There are further problems associated with proportional representation.

Multiparty systems
The tendency for proportional representation to aid minority parties to obtain representation in legislative bodies may promote the development of a multiparty system. This is of particular significance for those countries with parliamentary forms of government whose executives are drawn from the legislative body. In these cases, multiparty systems may make it difficult for the electorate to determine the composition of the executive or the policies which it pursues. Executives may consist of a coalition of parties which are often depicted as being weak and unstable.

Complexity
Critics of proportional representation argue that the system is difficult in the sense that it may not be obvious how the eventual result has been arrived at. This is especially the case with the single transferable vote which requires a process of redistribution (either of the surplus votes of an elected candidate or of the redundant votes of one who has been eliminated). Such votes are not randomly redistributed and electors may not fully understand the manner by which this process is carried out. A danger with this is that if the process by which the result is arrived at is not fully understood, the result itself may be deprived of popular legitimacy.

Enhancement of position of party leadership
Proportional representation has been accused of enhancing the power of the party leadership. This is especially the case with the party list system which may give regional or national party leaders the ability to place candidates in order of preference and thereby improve the chances of loyal party members being elected ahead of those who are regarded as dissentients. This objection is, however, mitigated by the ability of electors to vote for individual candidates in many countries which utilize the party list method of election.

Proportional representation and minor parties

Opponents of proportional representation assert that minor parties may secure a role in a country's political affairs that is out of all proportion to their levels of support. The relatively small Free Democratic Party in Germany enjoyed participation in government between 1969 and 1998 as it held a pivotal position between Christian Democrats and Social Democrats. It could keep either out of office by siding with the other. The outcome of New Zealand's first national election using proportional representation in 1996 gave the New Zealand First Party (which had obtained 13 per cent of the vote and 17 seats in parliament) a place in a coalition government headed by the National Party and following the 1997 general election in Ireland the small Progressive Democrat Party was able to enter into a coalition government with *Fianna Faíl*.

Impact on legislator and constituent relationships

It might be argued that proportional representation weakens the link between legislator and constituent, which in countries such as the UK and America is regarded as a crucial political feature. This problem arises from the large size of multi-member constituencies. But this is not necessarily the case. The multi-member constituencies used for elections to the *Daíl* in Ireland are small: 41 constituencies returning 166 members. There are at least three MPs to each constituency whose average population is between 20,000 and 30,000. The ability of electors to express support for individual candidates under some versions of the party list system may also serve to enhance the relationship between constituent and representative.

Coalition government assessed

Proportional representation does not necessarily result in coalition government. The single transferable vote did not prevent the dominance of *Fianna Faíl* over Irish government for many years, while in Sweden, the Social Democrats were able to govern alone for most of the period between 1930 and 1970 despite the existence of a multiparty system. Neither (as we will discuss in Chapter 5) should we uncritically accept the argument that proportional representation is the cause of multiparty systems. However, we first must analyse whether coalition governments are actually an undesirable political phenomenon.

Absence of popular choice

It might be argued that the formation of a coalition government and the determination of the policies which it will pursue are not conducted in a democratic manner. Although separate political parties can enter into pacts or alliances prior to an election contest, coalition governments are frequently formed after an election has taken place allowing party leaders to conduct negotiations. These discussions may be lengthy and drawn out and the electorate is not consulted concerning the composition of the executive or the choice of policy it pursues.

Ineffective accountability

Effective accountability may be impaired by coalition government. When several parties are involved in government it may be difficult for the electorate to know who has been responsible for making decisions and to make them answerable for their actions.

Instability

Coalition governments are also accused of being unwieldy. A minor party may desert the government and the whole structure tumbles down. The downfall of the Berlusconi government in 1994 (due to the desertion of the Northern League) and the downfall of the Reynolds government in Ireland in the same year (following the desertion of the Irish Labour Party) are examples which can be used to justify the argument that coalition governments are unstable. Italy has had in excess of 50 post-war governments compared to 16 in the UK between 1945 and 2001. The belief that this situation arose from proportional representation prompted Italian voters to move away from this system. Following a referendum in 1993, new election rules were introduced under which 75 per cent of the seats in the Chamber of Deputies were subject to the first-past-the-post system of election. The remaining seats were allocated by the party list system.

We should observe, however, that coalition governments are not inevitably weak and unstable. A coalition of the Christian Democrats, the Christian-Social Union and the Free Democrats provided Germany's government between 1982 and 1998. This coalition was confirmed in office in the 1990 'all-German' election and held onto power in the 1994 *Bundestag* elections. In 1998 a coalition government composed of the Social Democrats and Greens was formed under Gerhard Schröder, which was re-elected in 2002. The existence of local authorities in the UK in which no single party possesses an overall majority (termed 'hung councils') has in some cases forced political parties to co-operate and may help legitimate coalition government in a country in which this has previously been resorted to in times of emergency (1915, 1919, 1931 and 1940).

Result of the 2001 UK General Election		
Seats	**Votes**	
Labour	10,724,895 (40.7%)	412
Conservative	8,357,622 (31.7%)	166
Liberal Democrat	4,812,833 (18.3%)	52
Others	2,473,448 (9.3%)	29

In total 26,365,192 electors (59.1 per cent) of the total voted. The election was of particular significance in Northern Ireland where a much higher turnout of 68.0 per cent occurred. The Ulster Unionist Party lost 3 seats to the more extreme Democratic Unionist Party and Sinn Fein outpolled the more moderate Social Democratic and Labour Parties and won 1 more seat. This situation had considerable consequences for the Northern Irish peace process as it heightened tensions between Unionist and Nationalist politicians, thus making it hard for them to work together. This resulted in lengthy suspension of the Northern Ireland Assembly in October 2002 and the reimposition of direct rule.

Questions

1 Assess the level of public involvement in a national election which can serve as your own case study. What factors influence why some people vote and others choose not to do so?

2 'Government should only pursue policies for which they obtained a mandate at the previous election'. List points for and against this statement.

3 Based on the evidence presented in this chapter, do you think that the benefits of the first-past-the-post system are outweighed by its disadvantages?

4 Using sources such as newspapers, textbooks and journals, make a study of one country which uses a system of proportional representation. Based on this study, indicate the main strengths and weaknesses of this system for the conduct of government in that country.

Taking it further

This chapter has drawn attention to the wide variety of ways in which citizens in liberal democracies elect our political leaders. A detailed discussion of different electoral systems is to be found in David Farrell, *Comparing Electoral Systems* (Hemel Hempstead: Prentice Hall/Harvester Wheatsheaf, 1997).

Liberal democracies frequently consider whether their electoral system should be reformed. A detailed account of what an electoral system is designed to achieve can be found in Michael Dummett, *Principles of Electoral Reform* (Oxford: Oxford University Press, 1997). In the United Kingdom, the main organization seeking electoral reform is the Hansard Society. This body publishes regular discussion papers of issues related to reform. Further information may be obtained from this organization whose address is St Philips Building North, Sheffield Street, London, WC2A 2EX. The website address is www.hansard-society.org.uk.

05

parties and party systems

In this chapter you will learn:
- the functions served by political parties
- the factors influencing the development of political parties
- the contemporary problems facing political parties

Objectives and key characteristics

What are the main features of political parties in liberal democratic political systems?

We are familiar with political parties. They are especially prominent at election times. But what do they do?

The main aim of a political party is to secure power and exercise control over government. This may be at national, state, regional or local level. It seeks to determine the composition of government and the policies that it carries out. To achieve this objective a party may operate independently or it can co-operate with other political parties.

We tend to regard political parties openly competing for power as the hallmark of a liberal democracy. However, political parties often exist in countries which do not possess a liberal democractic political system. The ability to inaugurate meaningful change within society is thus an important qualification required by political parties in a liberal democracy. They should be able to carry out their policies without hindrance from other state institutions.

A party possesses a formal structure which involves national leadership and local organization. The main role of the latter is to contest elections and recruit party members. This organization is permanent although it may be most active at election times. The relationship between a party's leaders and its membership varies quite considerably, especially the extent to which a party's leaders can be held accountable for their actions by its rank-and-file supporters. Policy making is frequently the preserve of the party's national leadership which may also possess some degree of control over the selection of candidates for public office.

Dominant party systems and one-party states

We might believe that it is essential in a liberal democracy that office should alternate between political parties. However, in some countries one party frequently wins national elections. This was so for *Fianna Faíl* (which held office in Ireland for 37 of the 43 years between 1932 and 1973) and for the UK Conservative Party which won four successive general elections held between 1979 and 1992. In Germany, Helmut Kohl's Christian-Socialist-dominated government was in power from 1982 until 1998.

However, in all these countries the replacement of the party holding office is theoretically possible and it is the potential of change which separates a one-party state (in which opposition parties are not allowed openly to exist) from one in which a single political party is dominant but which could be replaced through the process of free elections.

Factions and tendencies

The term faction denotes the existence of a minority group within a larger body which takes issue with the majority over the leadership of that body or the policies that it advocates.

A faction is frequently defined as a group which exists within a political party. It consists of a group with formal organization and a relatively stable membership and is effectively a 'party within a party'. The Italian Christian Democrats and Japan's Liberal Democrats are essentially coalitions of several factions.

Factions need to be distinguished from tendencies. These also exist with a political party and consist of persons who share common opinions. Unlike factions, however, they lack formal organization. During Margaret Thatcher's period of office as Prime Minister in the United Kingdom (1979–90) the 'Wets' were a tendency within the Conservative Party opposed to many of her policies. Towards the end of the 1990s a further tendency emerged within that party, the Eurosceptics. These were opposed to any further moves towards the pooling of sovereignty and political integration within the European Union and in particular opposed the goal of the 1991 Maastricht Treaty of economic and monetary union. In 1995, Eurosceptics supported the leadership challenge mounted by John Redwood to the then Conservative party leader and Prime Minister, John Major.

In the United States the term faction is closer in meaning to its eighteenth-century definition of 'party'. Key provisions contained in the American Constitution, including the separation of powers and the system of checks and balances, were devised to prevent a majority faction seizing control of the government and riding roughshod over minority interests. James Madison (1751–1836) exerted considerable influence over these provisions of the Constitution, believing that factions were derived from the unequal distribution of wealth.

The role of political parties

What advantages do political parties bring to the workings of liberal democratic political systems?

Political parties perform a number of roles. In this section we consider the major functions they fulfil and explain their importance to liberal democratic political structures.

Views of party

Political parties are now an accepted way for political affairs within liberal democracies to be conducted. But political parties have not always been accepted as helpful political mechanisms.

The American Constitution contained no provisions for party government and in his farewell address to the nation in 1796 President Washington bemoaned the 'baneful effects of the spirit of party'. In France, the development of political parties was checked by the belief that they tended to undermine the national interest.

However, parties became an accepted feature of political life in both these countries. The 1958 Constitution of the Fifth French Republic specifically acknowledged their existence.

Selection of candidates and political leaders

Parties are responsible for selecting candidates for public office at all levels in the machinery of government. Having selected a candidate, the role of the party is then to secure electoral support for its standard bearer. In particular, a country's national leaders emerge through the structure of political parties. Parties provide the main method for selecting a nation's political elite.

This function is an important one. In the nineteenth century monarchs frequently exercised their powers of patronage to select members of their country's government. But with the gradual extension of the right to vote, the composition of governments became the subject of popular choice which was aided by the operations of political parties.

The selection of candidates

There are a variety of procedures which parties might use to select candidates. The choice might be made by the rank-and-file supporters of a political party. The American system of primary elections opens the choice of candidate to a wide electorate. These elections enable registered party supporters to select candidates for public office.

Elsewhere, party activists at local level might choose candidates, possibly subject to the approval of the central organs of that party. This is a more restricted electorate, being confined to party members. Such is the practice in the UK in which a key role is played by the constituency organizations in the selection of candidates for elections at all levels of government.

Finally, the central party organization might select candidates, perhaps taking local views into consideration. The party list electoral system may encourage the selection of candidates to be made in this fashion.

Organization of support for governments

Parties ensure that governments are provided with organized support. This is especially important in parliamentary systems of government in which the executive is drawn from the legislative branch of government. In the UK the party whip system in the House of Commons ensures that governments have the necessary backing to implement their policies. The whip consists of written instructions indicating how the party leadership wishes its members to vote. Members who disobey such instructions may have the whip withdrawn. This entails expulsion from their parliamentary party and their replacement with an alternative party candidate at the next election. Without the support of party and its accompanying system of party discipline, governments would be subject to the constant fear of defeat. This organization is also adopted by opposition parties which are thus able to step in and form a government should the incumbent party be defeated.

However, while parties aid the operations of liberal democratic political systems, they are not indispensable to it. In America, for example, candidates for public office often promote themselves through personal organizations, even if they latterly attach themselves to a political party. Neither is membership of a major political party essential for those seeking national office. In the 1992 presidential election an independent candidate, Ross Perot, secured 19.7 million votes. This showed that many Americans were willing to endorse as that country's leader a person who had no association with either of the major political parties.

Further, although governments usually rely on the organized support afforded by a political party (or a combination of parties) there are exceptions to this. In 1995 the Italian President, Oscar Luigi Scalfaro, appointed a banker, Lamberto Dini, to be Prime Minister and head a non-party government. Although this government was seen as a temporary, stop-gap expedient it does illustrate that governments can be formed without the initial backing of established political parties. It possessed sufficient vitality to survive a vote of 'no confidence' in October 1995 designed to force an early general election. Dini resigned at the end of that year and subsequently headed a caretaker administration.

Stimulation of popular interest and involvement in political affairs

Political parties are also beneficial to liberal democracies because they stimulate popular interest and facilitate public participation in political affairs. They perform this function in a number of ways. Parties need to mobilize the electorate in order to win votes and secure the election of their representatives to public office. This requires the party 'selling' itself to the general public. In theory, therefore, a party puts forward its policies and seeks to convince the electorate that these are preferable to those of its opponents. The electorate thus becomes better informed concerning political affairs.

Second, parties enable persons other than a small elite group of public office holders to be involved in political activity. Members of the general public can join political parties and engage in matters such as candidate selection and policy formulation.

Crucially, parties are a mechanism whereby those who hold public office can be made acccountable for their actions. Although elections provide the ultimate means to secure the accountability of public office holders, parties may subject these officials to a more regular, day-by-day scrutiny, possessing the sanction of deselecting them as candidates for future elections if they fail to promote party policy.

Promoting national harmony

Political parties simplify the conduct of political affairs and make them more manageable. They transform the demands which are made by individuals and groups into programmes which can be put before the electorate. This is known as the 'aggregation of interests' which involves a process of arbitration in which diverse demands are given a degree of coherence by being incorporated into a party platform or manifesto. One consequence of this is to transform parties into 'broad churches' which seek to maximize their level of support by incorporating the claims of a wide cross section of society.

Such activity enables parties to promote national harmony. Numerous divisions exist within societies, based among other things on class, religion or race. But to win elections, parties have to appeal to as many voters as possible. In doing this, they may endorse policies and address appeals which transcend social divisions. Thus parties might serve as a source of national unity. For example, the UK Labour Party needs to secure support from a sizeable section of the middle class in order to form a government. Thus it may put forward policies to appeal to such voters. In doing so it bridges the gulf between the working class (whose interests it was formed to advance) and the middle class. One political party thus becomes the vehicle to further the claims of two distinct groups in society.

Providers of patronage

Political parties serve as important sources of patronage. They are able to dispense perks to their members. The party in charge of the national government is in the best position to do this. The chief executive can make ministerial appointments and thus the party becomes the vehicle through which political ambitions can be realized. Party supporters can also be rewarded. In the UK this includes paid appointments to public bodies (quangos) and the bestowal of a range of awards through the honours system.

Problems associated with political parties

Do parties perform a crucial role in contemporary liberal democratic politics?

In this section we consider some of the problems affecting political parties which question the contribution they make to liberal democratic politics.

Electoral support for parties

In theory, electors vote for a party following a dispassionate examination of the policies which are put forward during an election contest and a calculated assessment as to which set of policies they deem to be the most preferable. But this is rarely the case. Most of us support a political party for reasons other than the policies that it puts forward. Factors such as our traditional loyalty to a party or its association with social class are likely to be more important than party policy when we decide how to vote.

Political education

Parties may not seek to educate the public in any meaningful manner. Election campaigns may be conducted around trivia rather than key issues. Parties may be more concerned to denigrate an opponent than with an attempt to convince electors of the virtues of their own policies. Or they may decide that the wisest course of political action is to follow public opinion rather than seek to lead it. Thus ideology or policy that is viewed as unpopular might be abandoned by a party in an attempt to win elections.

Popular involvement

We may also question the extent to which parties enable widespread involvement in political affairs. Parties do not always have a mass membership. In America, voters do not 'join' a party as they might, for example, in the UK. However, even in countries where individuals can join a political party they do not always do so in large numbers. French and Irish political parties, for example, lack a tradition of mass membership and tend to be controlled by small elitist groups.

Neither are those who do join a party guaranteed a meaningful role in its affairs. The Italian Christian Democrats, for example, has a mass membership but this has little say on matters such as party policy. The formal accountability of party leaders to rank-and-file activists through mechanisms such as annual party conferences is often imperfectly achieved in practice due to the domination which leaders often exert over their parties.

Divisiveness

Political parties do not always seek to promote harmony. Some may seek to make political capital by emphasizing existing divisions within society. The French *Front National* has sought to cultivate support by blaming that country's economic and social problems on immigration, especially from North Africa. The scapegoating of racial or religious groups, depicting them as the main cause of a country's problems, is a common tactic of the extreme right and which serves to create social tension rather than harmony. Racial tension in Germany in the late twentieth and early twenty-first centuries led some politicians to suggest banning the far-right National Democratic Party.

Self-interest

The role of parties as dispensers of patronage may result in accusations that they are mainly concerned to award 'jobs for the boys'. This may result in popular disenchantment with the conduct of political affairs with politics being associated with the furtherance of self-interest rather than with service to the nation.

The funding of political parties

Political parties commonly secure their income from a variety of sources. These may include sponsors (who make regular donations to party funds) and donors (who make 'one-off' gifts). Commercial activities undertaken by political parties may contribute towards party funds and parties such as the United Kingdom's Labour Party derive income from the trade unions particularly at a general election. Subscriptions paid by party members also constitute a source of funding for some political parties.

A major problem with donations from private or business sources is a perception that those who give money to parties will expect something in return for their outlay. This may include influence over the content of party policy or its leadership.

In some countries political parties are funded by the state. It is vital in Spain and Portugal where the late transition to liberal democratic politics in the 1970s meant that political parties were unable themselves to raise adequate finance. State funding also occurs in Germany (where parties represented in the *Bundestag* receive finance based on the level of their popular support) and in the USA (where since 1976 public funding has been available to candidates contesting the office of President provided that they accept an overall capping on their total spending).

There are several reasons for state funding of political parties. This avoids perceptions that wealthy people or organizations are able to buy influence over the operations of a political party in return for their financial support. State funding may also place a ceiling over political expenditure, especially at election times. This last objective was one reason for the introduction of federal funding for presidential candidates in America. However, a danger with state funding of parties is that these become perceived as organs of the state which have little incentive to recruit a mass membership.

Determinants of party systems

What factors influence the way in which political parties and party systems are formed, function and develop?

Considerable differences exist within liberal democracies concerning the nature of party systems. Some countries such as Britain, America and New Zealand have relatively few political parties. Scandinavia, however, is characterized by multiparty systems. In order to explain these differences we need to consider what factors influence the development of political parties and party systems.

The basis of party

The degree of homogeneity (that is, uniformity) in a country is an important determinant concerning the formation and development of political parties. Basic divisions within a society might provide the basis of a party, reflecting its key divisions. These might include social class, nationalism, religion or race. Any of these factors are capable of providing the basis around which parties are established and subsequently operate. Some form of partisanship in which groups of electors have a strong affinity to a particular political party is crucial to sustain a stable party system.

Let us consider some examples of this.

Social class
In the UK, social class was a key factor that shaped the development of political parties in the nineteenth and early years of the twentieth century. The landed aristocracy was identified with the Conservative Party, the industrial bourgeoisie with the Liberal Party and the working class with the Labour Party.

Religion
In France, Italy and Germany religion played an important part in providing the underpinning for political parties. In nineteenth-century France, the basic division was between clericals and anti-clericals. Today the vote for left-wing parties is weakest where the influence of the Catholic Church is strongest, although by the 1960s social class began to play an increasingly important role in determining party affiliation. In Italy, the Christian Democrats initially relied heavily on the Catholic vote, while in Germany the coalition between the Christian Democrats and the Christian Social Union represented a religious alliance between Catholics and Protestants in opposition to the Social Democrats who were viewed as representative of the secular interests within society.

The Irish party system

Political parties may emerge when key social divisions are absent. This is the case in Ireland. Here a party system developed in the early twentieth century in a country that was relatively unified in terms of race, religion, language and social class. The key issue that divided the country was a matter of policy – support or opposition for the 1921 Anglo-Irish Treaty which accepted the partitioning of Ireland whereby six Irish counties remained part of the United Kingdom.

In response to this situation, two parties emerged – *Fine Gael* (which supported the treaty) and *Fianna Fail* (which opposed it).

However, as the treaty issue became irrelevant to the conduct of Irish politics, the parties remained as permanent interests. In this sense it might be argued that the parties became the cause of divisions in Ireland rather than reflections of them.

Regionalism and nationalism

Regional and national sentiments may provide the basis of party. These may arise from a perception that the national government pays insufficient regard to the interests of people living in peripheral areas and is often underpinned by cultural factors. Regional or national autonomy is frequently demanded by such parties. Examples include the Italian *Lega Nord*, the Scottish National party, *Plaid Cymru* in Wales, the *Parti Québécois* in Quebec, Canada, and the Catalan Republican Left and Basque National parties in Spain.

Political parties and social and economic change

It follows from the discussion so far in this chapter that fundamental changes to a country's economic or social structure might have a significant effect on its political parties. The decline in jobs in the French steel, coal and shipbuilding industries has been cited as one explanation for the reduced support for the Communist Party. Immigration may influence the growth of racist political parties.

Political parties and electoral systems

It is sometimes argued that the electoral system has a major influence on the formation or operation of political parties. The first-past-the-post system is said to encourage the development of a relatively small number of parties since third parties are discriminated against. However, proportional representation facilitates the representation of minor parties in legislative bodies and thus, it might be suggested, promotes a multiparty system.

But we must be wary of unquestioning acceptance of the argument that proportional representation results in the development of a multiparty system. If parties are based on factors such as social divisions within society, proportional representation may be used to ensure that a country's legislature mirrors these differences. But the electoral system was not responsible for creating them in the first place.

However, an electoral system may have some influence over the nature of the party system. The first-past-the-post system may encourage groups to align with a dominant political party in order to achieve their objectives. The UK Conservative and Labour parties and the American Republican and Democratic parties illustrate this process. Groups are further encouraged to stay attached to a major party rather than split off and form smaller parties. These might become consigned to political oblivion due to the way in which this electoral system often works against the interests of minor parties.

The decline of party?

What changes influence the support enjoyed by established political parties?

In this section we analyse the extent to which existing major parties have experienced losses in the level of support which they have traditionally enjoyed and suggest reasons why this has occurred.

In the UK 97 per cent of the vote cast in the 1955 general election went to the Labour and Conservative parties. In 1964 this figure had declined to 88 per cent. In 1992 it was further reduced to 76 per cent. In France a similar picture occurred. In the 1981 legislative elections the four main parties (RPR, UDF, PCF and PS) secured 93 per cent of the votes cast in the first round of elections. Subsequently, there has been a significant move away from the two-bloc, four-party system. In 1993 the four main parties obtained 68 per cent of the vote cast. Further, two million voters spoiled their ballots in the second round of the 1993 legislative elections rather than give their support to a major party candidate. In the 1993 legislative elections the support for the Italian Christian Democrats dropped to below 30 per cent.

Extreme right-wing parties have been beneficiaries of the decline in support for established political parties. Parties which include the *Front National* in France, the Progress Party in Norway, the Danish People's Party, the Swiss People's Party, the Italian Northern League and Vlaams Blok in Belgium have gained considerable support in the late twentieth and early years of the

The French party system

In France, the behaviour of political parties is influenced by the electoral system.

The second ballot system involves a number of second-round contests. Electors may be required to cast votes for candidates who do not represent the party of their choice. This, coupled with the emergence of the directly elected presidency as the key political prize and the traditional core distinctions between left and right, encouraged major parties and/or their supporters to co-operate. This was referred to as bipolarization.

Bipolarization emerged during the 1970s and involved the major parties of the right and those of the left co-operating to contest elections. A two-bloc, four-party system emerged. In the case of the parties of the left, electoral co-operation took the form of the formation of the Union of the Left which in 1974 narrowly failed to secure the election of François Mitterrand to the presidency. Although subsequent changes to the structure of the French party system have affected this development, in both 1986 and 1993 the main parties on the right presented a common programme for government.

twenty-first centuries. In parliamentary elections held towards the end of 1999 Austria's far right Freedom Party secured over 33 per cent of the vote. This resulted in the party forming a government in coalition with the conservative People's Party an outcome which was continued after the November 2002 elections in spite of a slump in support for the Freedom Party. In the October 2000 local elections in Belgium, Vlaams Blok secured 33 per cent of the vote in Antwerp, making it the second biggest political force in that country's second city. However, the most significant achievement of extreme right-wing parties occurred in France in 2002 when the *Front National* candidate defeated the socialist prime minister in the first round of the presidential election.

Explanations for the loss of support by established political parties

Dealignment
There are two aspects of dealignment – partisan dealignment and class dealignment.

Partisan dealignment means that a large number of electors either desert the party to which they were traditionally committed or identify with the party which they historically supported far more weakly. A number of factors may explain this phenomenon. These include increased education and political awareness of many members of the electorate (making them prone to basing their vote on logical as opposed to traditional considerations) and perceptions that the party normally supported by an elector does not reflect his or her own views on key isssues. For example, the loss of support experienced by the United Kingdom Labour Party in the early 1980s was attributed to the 'swing to the left' which occurred after the 1979 general election defeat causing what is termed an 'ideological disjuncture' between the views and values of the party and those of its supporters. Political crises may also influence partisan dealignment. In America, between 1958 and 1968 key political issues such as the Vietnam War and the civil rights movement resulted in an increased number of voters registering themselves as independents. In France in the same period, however, the perception that the Gaullist Party would defend economic development and political stability in the face of civil unrest resulted in enhanced voter identification with that party.

Class dealignment suggests that the historic identity between a political party and a particular social class becomes of reduced significance. In the United Kingdom this might be explained after 1970 by the reduced intensity of class consciousness which arose for a number of reasons, including the increased affluence of the working class (which is termed 'embourgeoisement'), the decline in the number of manual workers and the rise in the service sector of employment. This was perceived to have a particularly damaging effect on the electoral prospects of the Labour Party which failed to win a general election betwen 1979 and 1997.

The twin effects of partisan and class dealignment have two main consequences for the conduct of politics. It results in third parties obtaining increased levels of support, and makes the core support given to established major parties less consistent from one general election to the next. These factors make voting behaviour more volatile.

Realignment

Realignment entails a redefinition of the relationship between political parties and key social groups within society which has a fundamental impact on their relative strength. Partisan and class dealignment, which entail the loosening of traditional bonds attaching individuals and groups to particular parties, may be the prelude to realignment.

The formation of new relationships is usually confirmed in what is termed a 'realigning election' which is seen as the start of new patterns of political behaviour. In the United Kingdom, the 1918 general election evidenced the desertion of the working-class vote from the Liberal Party to the Labour Party. The 1932 American presidential election, which witnessed the birth of the 'new deal coalition', was a further example of realignment. This coalition was composed of union members, ethnic minorities, liberals and intellectuals and these newly established patterns of voter loyalties provided the Democratic Party with domination over Congress and the presidency for a number of subsequent decades. In both of these examples, however, the changes in voter loyalty which were evidenced at the realignment elections had been initiated earlier.

Subsequent examples of realignment have occurred. In America, the victories of Ronald Reagan in 1980 and 1984 were based on the existence of a new coalition. The preference of white male voters in the southern states of America for the Republican Party indicated a major shift in this group's political affiliation which had taken place earlier in the 1970s. In the United Kingdom, the era of Conservative Party dominance (1979–97) rested in part on the defection of relatively affluent members of the working class in south-eastern England (who were dubbed 'Essex Men' and characterized by working in the private sector and owning their own homes) to vote Conservative. However, neither of these changes has been sufficient to bring about a substantial era of political dominance for the parties which benefited from them. In America, the Democrats succeeded in winning the presidency from the Republicans in 1992 and in the United Kingdom the Conservative Party was voted out of office in the 1997 general election.

The continued vitality of political parties

Is the position of established political parties in jeopardy?

Although the position of established political parties in many liberal democracies is weaker than was previously the case, it seems likely that they will continue to carry out important roles within liberal democratic political systems. One reason for this is that parties are adaptable and have understood the importance of reform.

Reforms to restore the vitality of parties may take a number of forms. They include attempts to increase the number of citizens joining such organizations. In countries such as America, where local parties have often been controlled by 'bosses', initiatives to increase party membership have sometimes been accompanied by reforms designed to 'democratize' the workings of political parties and ensure that members are able to exercise a greater degree of control over key party affairs including the selection of candidates and the formulation of policy.

There have been problems associated with such developments. Increasing the membership of local parties has sometimes (although not consistently) resulted in accusations of extremists 'taking over' control of organization, which in turn makes it difficult for parties to appeal to a wide electoral base in order to win elections. What is termed 'coalition building' in America becomes difficult if a party is associated with extremist issues. Similar problems beset the UK Labour Party in the early 1980s which resulted in that party's disastrous showing in the 1983 general election in which it placed a manifesto before the electorate based on left-wing principles. These policies emerged as a result of reforms designed to democratize that organization by giving rank-and-file members a greater role in party affairs, principally the selection of party candidates and the party leader.

In this concluding section we examine in greater detail the initiatives that have been developed by American political parties to address the issue of decline.

Questions

1 With reference to the political parties in any country with which you are familiar distinguish between factions and tendencies, giving examples of each.
2 Conduct your own study of the operations of political parties in a country with which you are familiar. In your view, do parties aid or hinder the conduct of liberal democratic politics in this country?
3 Analyse the nature of the support obtained by the political parties in any country with which you are familiar.
4 With reference to any country with which you are familiar, analyse the evidence which suggests that the major political

parties are 'in decline'. Why has this development occurred, and what might such parties do in order to reverse this trend?

Taking it further

This chapter has discussed a number of matters in connection with the development of political parties and party systems. A more detailed account of the concerns raised in this chapter is found in Alan Ware, *Political Parties and Party Systems* (Oxford: Oxford University Press, 1996). Additionally, the *Journal of Party Politics* provides up-to-date information on contemporary issues affecting political parties throughout the world.

A more thorough understanding of the operations and contemporary developments affecting the political parties and party system in any particular country can be gained from specialist literature dealing with the politics of that country. A good book which specifically refers to the development of political parties in Great Britain is Paul Webb, *The Modern British Party System* (London: Sage, 2000). We may contact the political parties directly to gain information of this nature. In Great Britain the main political parties can be contacted as follows:

- Labour Party, 16 Old Queen Street, London, SW1H 9HP (www.labour.org.uk)
- Conservative Party, 32 Smith Square, London, SW1P 3HH (www.conservatives.com)
- Liberal Democrats, 4 Cowley Street, London, SW1H 3NB (www.libdems.org.uk)
- Scottish National Party, 107 McDonald Road, Edinburgh, EH7 4NW, Scotland (www.snp.org)
- Plaid Cymru, Ty Gwynfor, 18 Park Grove, Cardiff, CF10 3BN, Wales (www.plaidcymru2001.com)

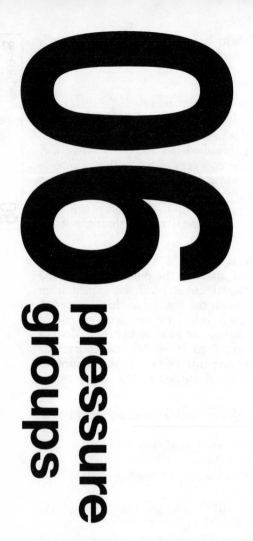

06 pressure groups

In this chapter you will learn:
- the role performed by pressure groups
- the methods used by pressure groups to influence policy-making
- the advantages and disadvantages of pressure group activity

Definition

What is a pressure group?

A pressure group is an organization with a formal structure which is composed of a number of individuals seeking to further a common cause or interest. These groups operate at all levels of society. Some seek to influence the activities of local or central government. Others exist within the workplace in the form of trade unions. The factions or tendencies found within some political parties are further examples of such organizations. Many groups perform functions which are not political, for example by providing benefits or advisory services either to their members or to the general public. For the purposes of our discussion, however, we shall concentrate on those seeking to exert influence over national government policy making.

Social movements

Many reforms are promoted by organizations termed 'social movements'. Examples include the peace movement, the women's movement and the environmental movement. But it is not easy to differentiate precisely between these and pressure groups.

Social movements tend to be loosely organized in comparison to pressure groups and their focus of concern is often broader. Rather than concentrate on one specific policy area, their concern is to instil new moral values within society. They may, however, embrace the activities of pressure groups whose specific aims are compatible with this overall objective. We would, for example, place the British Campaign for Nuclear Disarmament under the umbrella of the peace movement.

Social movements typically operate outside mainstream political institutions and their tactics are thus dominated by non-conventional forms of political activity. This is frequently carried out on an international stage rather than being confined to any particular country.

The environmental movement is an important example of a contemporary social movement. It has succeeded in bringing together a range of groups engaged in counter-cultural protest (such as new age travellers) and those opposed to hunting, live animal exports, motorway construction and pollution. These seemingly disparate, single-issue bodies are united by a social vision that rejects the culture of advanced capitalist society. All stand opposed to what they view as an alliance of developers, business, the construction industry and government. They have utilized tactics of protest and direct action to project an alternative vision to a modern industrial society which emphasizes environmental considerations over the pursuit of wealth and profit. All are concerned with man's damage to the planet and are opposed to materialism and consumerism.

The role of pressure groups

What activities are performed by pressure groups?

Pressure groups seek to influence policy makers. Their actions are thus directed at politicians, civil servants and, in some cases, the general public. The complex and lengthy nature of the policy-making process provides wide scope for group activity.

A major concern of pressure groups is to persuade policy makers to consider their views and then to act upon them. This involves inducing policy makers either to adopt a course of action which they did not initially intend to embark upon or to abandon a measure which they had originally decided to introduce. If a group succeeds in getting its views acted upon it may also become involved in further stages of the policy-making process. These include participating in the formulation of policy to achieve the objective(s) which the group successfully placed on the political agenda. Pressure groups may also be concerned with the implementation of that policy and with monitoring it to ensure that the desired aims are achieved.

Pressure groups and non-governmental bodies

Our discussion of pressure groups is primarily concerned with their influence on central government policy making. However, pressure groups frequently direct their activities towards alternative targets, such as the practices adopted by commercial organizations. Indeed, a number of Greenpeace activists see business rather than politics as the best arena within which to further environmental aims.

One example of this was the activity mounted in 1995 by that environmental organization against the decision by the Shell Oil company to sink a disused oil rig, *Brent Spar*, in the North Atlantic. Adverse publicity coupled with boycotts against Shell's products organized by other environmental groups resulted in the company agreeing to examine alternative ways of disposing of their unwanted property.

Political parties and pressure groups

What is the difference between a political party and a pressure group?

The key words for us to consider here are 'control' and 'influence'.

Political parties normally seek control over the policy-making process. They may achieve this through their own efforts or in combination with other political parties. They contest elections in the hope of securing power so that they can carry out the policies contained in their election manifestos. Such policies cover all aspects of public affairs and the party seeks to exercise control over a wide range of issues.

Pressure groups, however, wish to influence those who control the policy-making process. They do not normally have an interest in the overall work of government but only in those aspects of its operations which are of concern to the group and its membership. In order to pursue their aims, groups usually possess a degree of autonomy from both government and political parties. Thus, while a pressure group seeks to exert influence over a relatively narrow aspect of policy making, a political party wishes to control the overall direction of public affairs.

One further distinction between political parties and pressure groups concerns the manner in which they seek to cultivate support. Political parties concentrate their activities on the general public, hoping to convince voters to support them in election contests. Although campaigns directed at the public may form one aspect of pressure group campaigning, the tactics at their disposal are more diverse. Influence may be sought at all levels of the decision-making process.

Classification of pressure groups

How can we distinguish between the wide range of pressure groups which operate within liberal democracies?

Various ways may be adopted to classify the pressure groups which are to be found within liberal democratic political systems. One method is to differentiate according to the relationship which exists between the objective put forward by the group and its membership. This provides us with two broad categories into which groups might be placed.

Sectional groups

These are groups in which the members have a vested interest in the success of their organization. They stand to benefit materially if the aims of the group are adopted by policy makers. Such organizations are sometimes referred to as 'interest' or 'economic' groups. The membership of sectional groups tends to be narrow and restrictive, drawn from people with similar backgrounds. In the UK, examples include employers' associations (such as the Confederation of British Industry), professional bodies (such as the British Medical Association) or labour organizations (such as the Transport and General Workers' Union). American examples include the American Bar Association and the American Medical Association.

Promotional (or cause) groups

These are organizations in which the members are united in support of a cause which does not necessarily benefit them directly. They tend to view the work of the group as a moral concern and their aim is to change social attitudes and values. The aims of promotional groups may be designed to benefit specific groups (especially minorities whose needs are often ignored by policy makers) or to be directed at an issue affecting society as a whole. Membership of promotional groups is open to all who share its objectives: members are typically drawn from a wide range of social or occupational backgrounds and are united solely by their common support for the cause advocated by the organization.

Bodies other than pressure groups

Pressure group activity is not confined to organizations which are specifically established to advance an interest or a cause. It may also be performed by bodies whose existence is concerned with other functions but which may, on occasion, act in the capacity of a pressure group and seek to exert influence within the policy making process.

The Catholic Church in Ireland is an example of a body which sometimes acts as a pressure group. The Roman Catholic bishops played a prominent role in the 1995 referendum campaign opposing a change in the Irish Constitution to permit divorce.

In Britain, chief constables and senior members of the judiciary have sometimes made public pronouncements designed to influence the approach adopted by policy makers to the operations of the criminal justice system, and in America the Pentagon sometimes performs a role akin to that of a pressure group on behalf of the military establishment.

The activities of pressure groups

How do pressure groups seek to exert influence on policy makers?

Pressure groups operate throughout the machinery of government. In this section we examine the main areas which form the focus of group activity.

The executive branch of government

This consists of both ministers and civil servants. Some pressure groups have the ability constantly to liaise with, and be consulted by, these key policy makers.

The relationship between groups and the executive branch of government may be constructed in a number of ways. Some have a permanent relationship with government departments. Members representing a group may be appointed to joint advisory committees which are mechanisms through which the concerns of a pressure group can be made known to the relevant government department. In France, the access of some groups to government departments is institutionalized through advisory councils. These are composed of representatives of interest groups, technicians and prominent personalities appointed by the government and are attached to individual ministries. Alternatively, some pressure groups enjoy regular access to civil servants and they may also be involved in discussions on appointments to bodies which are responsible to a department. In some countries, contact is secured through the 'old boy' network, in which former ministers or civil servants secure jobs in organizations which may benefit from the contacts in government possessed by such former public officials.

Groups in this position are termed 'insider' groups. This denotes the close relationship which some groups enjoy with key members of the policy making process. It is a desirable position to occupy in a country such as the UK where political power is centralized in the executive branch of government although it is of equal importance in some federal countries such as Australia. The relationship between the UK National Farmers' Union and the Ministry of Agriculture, Fisheries and Food is an example of such an 'insider' relationship.

Other groups may secure influence through their relationship with the political party that forms the government. This was the case in the UK between 1964 and 1970 when leading trade unionists were frequently invited to Downing Street to discuss industrial affairs over 'beer and sandwiches'. This politically fashioned link with the ministerial component of the executive is not permanent and may alter when the government changes. This was the case in the UK after 1979 when Conservative administrations adopted a more hostile attitude to the trade unions than had been the case when Labour governments were in power.

The legislature

There are a number of ways whereby pressure groups may seek to exert influence over the legislature. A major mechanism is that of lobbying. This describes communication between someone other than a citizen acting on his or her own behalf and a government policy maker with the intention of influencing the latter's decisions.

Lobbying was originally directed exclusively at legislators but has subsequently extended to the executive branch where politicians and bureaucrats are made the subject of this activity.

Its aim is to ensure that law makers are fully briefed and are thus in a position to advance the interests of the pressure group when issues which are relevant to it come before the legislature for discussion or resolution. The importance attached to this activity is much influenced by the independence of action which legislatures possess. Pressure groups may devote relatively little attention to such bodies if they believe them to be dominated by the executive branch of government.

Much lobbying is carried out by pressure groups. Some employ full-time lobbyists to promote their interests while others hire lobbyists on a temporary basis when they wish to advance, or secure the defeat of, legislation that is relevant to their interests. The influence that they are able to exert over policy makers is derived from their being regarded as an important source of information. In the United Kingdom parliamentary lobbyists (or parliamentary consultants) provide political advice and analysis which may be sought by commercial companies or by other governmental organizations. The most influential lobbyists are those who have established regular contacts in the legislative or executive branches of government and in this sense they act as a conduit to power.

Iron triangles

In America, some pressure groups enjoy considerable power from the relationship that they have constructed with both the executive and legislative branch of government.

The term 'iron triangle' has been used to describe the close links (governed by ties of interdependent self-interest) that exist between an interest group, the government department or agency concerned with the interests espoused by that organization and the Congressional committee charged with responsibility for that policy area. Each element of the 'triangle' provides services, information or policy for the others.

This arrangement provides some groups with a powerful position from which its interests can be advanced. In 1997 a representative of an American consumer group alleged that the Food and Drugs Administration (which regulated the American food industry) was so closely associated with the biotech/pharmaceutical/agri-business complex that it could be described as their Washington branch office. Although a close working relationship between an agency and groups representing industries does not necessarily constitute improper influence, iron triangles have also been argued to be responsible for decentralizing and fragmenting the policy-making process to the detriment of the exercise of central control by the executive and legislative branches of government. In more recent years, the autonomy of such 'sub-governments' has been challenged by alternative centres of power (such as issue networks).

Lobbying consists of a variety of activities, ranging from personal approaches to policy makers to bribery. However, it remains small-scale in Britain compared to America where it is big business: in 1998 corporate (that is, business and commercial interests) in America spent approximately £700 million a year to field 14,000 official registered lobbyists in Washington DC. This amounted to 27 lobbyists for each member of Congress. By comparison the British lobbying industry had earnings of around £70 million a year.

Pressure groups may voice their concerns to the legislature through ways other than lobbying. In the Fourth French Republic (1946–58) some groups such as the trade union and farmers' associations enjoyed permanent membership of specialized legislative standing committees. In both the UK and America investigations conducted by the legislature provide a mechanism for the articulation of group interests, while in Germany the committee system utilized by the *Bundestag* secures pressure group influence over legislation.

The judiciary

Pressure groups may turn to the courts to secure the adoption of their aims, usually by challenging the legality of legislation. This approach was crucial to the American civil rights movement. Organizations such as the National Association for the Advancement of Colored People used this mechanism in their fight against segregation practised by a number of the southern states. A landmark in education was reached in 1954 when the Supreme Court ruled (in the case of *Brown* v. *Board of Education of Topeka*) that segregation in schools was unconstitutional and thus illegal throughout the entire country. In more recent years, American consumer and environmental groups have turned to the courts to advance their concerns.

Rules governing the operations of a country's judicial system have a major bearing on the ability or willingness of pressure groups to use the courts to further their objectives. In Australia, for example, the rules of *locus standi* have made it difficult for pressure groups to initiate legal actions since it is necessary for plaintiffs to demonstrate a personal stake or material interest in a case. In America, however, interests groups are permitted to present arguments to courts directly.

The role of the courts is less prominent in countries such as Britain and New Zealand, where judicial challenge to national legislation is precluded by the concept of parliamentary sovereignty, but pressure groups may utilize the courts and launch test cases or challenge the legality of the way in which the law has been implemented.

Political parties

Pressure groups may forge close links with political parties and use them to further their aims. Parties may incorporate aspects of a group's demands within their own policy statements. The American AFL-CIO is associated with the Democratic Party while the French CGT has close ties with the Communist Party. The relationship that exists between pressure groups and political parties may be organizational or financial. In the United Kingdom leading trade unions are affiliated to the Labour Party while the Conservatives receive funding and support from the business sector.

Pressure groups and public opinion

Pressure groups often take their case 'to the streets' and seek to mobilize public support for their objectives. Demonstrations are a frequently used tactic. In doing this they seek to influence policy makers by demonstrating the extent of public support for their views.

In the UK, for example, protests organized by animal welfare groups such as Compassion in World Farming occurred at ports and airports during 1995. These were directed against the export of British calves for the continental veal trade.

Direct action, which is discussed next, is a tactic which may be used by an organization to secure the support of public opinion for its views.

Direct action

Direct action is a form of extra-parliamentary politics which seeks to advance a cause through some form of physical action. The tactics of direct action are varied, ranging from mainly non-violent methods, such as civil disobedience, sit-ins, blockades and occupations, to actions involving considerable use of force and violence associated with terrorist organizations (which may arise when those who conduct activities that a group opposes are the target of a physical sanction). The objectives sought by direct action are broad and include promoting local concerns, seeking to alter the direction of government policy, or repudiating the political system.

Direct action is frequently practised by social movements and pressure groups. These may seek to remedy social problems through their own efforts (for example, the United Kingdom's squatting movement which initially emerged in 1946 sought to deal with homelessness by occupying empty property) or they may seek to make the general public the focus of attempts to further their cause. This may involve educating the public to support the views of the group but it may entail the use of tactics designed to inconvenience or even intimidate the public in the expectation that public opinion will exert pressure on the government to change its policy.

Direct action occurs in all liberal democracies, although the importance attached to it as a means of securing change varies and is influenced by each country's political culture. In France, for example, direct action is frequently used as a method of first resort by groups wishing to alter government policy, whereas in the United Kingdom such methods have traditionally been used as a last resort, perhaps when other ways to influence the content of public policy have failed. The growing interdependence of nations (especially the growth of supranational bodies such as the European Union) may induce the wider use of direct action. In 2000, for example, French fishermen blockaded the Channel ports in protest against high fuel prices. This action succeeded in forcing the government to reduce the tax on fuel and resulted in the blockade of fuel distribution points in the United Kingdom by protesters with a similar objective.

The international arena

Pressure groups do not confine their activities to one country but increasingly operate on a world stage. They may be international organizations seeking the universal adoption of standards of behaviour throughout the world. Groups such as Amnesty International (which is concerned with human rights) is an example of such a body. Alternatively groups may be formed in one country seeking influence over policy making in another. The Greek Animal Welfare Fund, for example, is a London-based organization which seeks to alter the official and public attitudes towards the treatment accorded to animals in Greece.

Pressure groups have also adapted to the development of supranational governmental organizations. The policy makers of the European Union (principally the Commission and Council of Ministers) are subject to pressure group activity. Organizations within individual countries may co-ordinate their activities with similar groups in other countries in order to secure overall influence on European Union policy. For example, an umbrella body (COPA) was established to co-ordinate farming policy at the European level to ensure that farmers and their families obtained income and living conditions which were compatible with those in other sectors of the economy. Similarly, UNICE was set up to provide a European business perspective on behalf of all the national business organizations and sectoral federations. Pressure groups may also establish permanent machinery to further their interests within supranational bodies such as the European Union. An example of this is the Brussels Office of the Confederation of British Industry, which monitors developments in the European Union and seeks to influence the direction of European legislation to the benefit of its membership.

International institutions, such as the United Nations Human Rights Committee and the European Court of Justice, have also been used by pressure groups which seek to question the actions undertaken by individual governments. In Britain, for example, groups opposed to motorway construction have exercised their right to complain to the European Commission that the government failed adequately to implement the procedures of the 1988 Directive concerned with Environmental Impact Assessments. If the Commission decides that there is a case to answer the government can be taken to the European Court of Justice for contravening European law.

Pressure group influence

What factors determine whether a pressure group is likely to be successful in furthering its aims?

The previous section discussed various tactics a pressure group might utilize to further its aims. The extent to which these tactics succeed in influencing policy makers depends on a range of factors which we now consider.

The ability of a group to mobilize support

The level of support enjoyed by a group may be one determinant of its strength. Successful groups need to represent all who adhere to a particular interest or a specific cause. The fragmentation of French labour organizations into a number of competing federations has tended to weaken their influence over policy makers and is in contrast to the organizational unity of business interests (whose trade associations are linked by the umbrella organization, CNPF). The strength of American labour organizations is reduced by the low affiliation rate of workers to trade unions. The cause of animal welfare in Britain may be impeded by the existence of a wide range of organizations, which include the Royal Society for the Prevention of Cruelty to Animals, Compassion in World Farming, the Animal Liberation Front and the International Fund for Animal Welfare.

Pressure group strength

One development designed to enhance group strength is the banding together of bodies with similar objectives under the auspices of an umbrella organization. Examples of such 'associations of associations' include Britain's Trade Union Congress and Confederation of British Industry and Australia's National Farmers' Federation.

Expertise commanded by a group

A further factor that may affect the influence groups exercise over policy making is the expertise which they are able to command. Governments may be reliant upon such bodies for advice on the technical and complex issues that surround much contemporary public policy and may further be reliant on a group's goodwill or support to implement policy. Such considerations had a major bearing on the influence possessed by the British Medical Association following the establishment of the National Health Service in 1946.

Resources possessed by a group

The resources which pressure groups are able to command may also determine the success or failure of a group. Economically powerful groups possess the ability to publicize their objectives and also to resist sanctions that may be deployed against them. Employer organizations are often influential for such reasons. By contrast, consumer groups have traditionally suffered from lack of resources which may help to explain their difficulties in securing influence over the actions of policy makers. Some governments, however, (such as the French) and supranational bodies (such as the European Union) have contributed towards the funding of pressure groups which offsets weaknesses that derive from lack of funds.

Sanctions available to a group

The sanctions which an organization is able to deploy may be a factor in its ability to influence policy making. Investment decisions or strikes may be used as weapons by business groups or trade unions to influence the conduct of policy makers. Consumer boycotts may influence the practices of the private sector. Groups involved in the implementation of public policy possess the ability to withhold their co-operation and thus prevent the progress of policies to which they object.

The strengths and weaknesses of pressure group activity

The role performed by pressure groups is said to be beneficial to the operations of liberal democratic political systems. Why, therefore, are their activities sometimes criticized?

To answer this question we need to examine the benefits which pressure groups bring to liberal democratic political systems and then to assess the disadvantages which may arise.

Benefits of pressure groups

The main benefits associated with the activities of pressure groups are discussed in the following sections.

Popular involvement in policy making

Pressure groups ensure that the policy-making process is not monopolized by politicians or senior civil servants. The control which they are able to exercise is to some extent offset by the operations of pressure groups. Additionally, these organizations aid the participation of members of the general public in policy making whose role in political affairs is thus not merely confined to casting a vote in elections.

Political education

The need for pressure groups to 'sell' their case to secure influence may aid the process of public education in political affairs. Groups may need to explain what they believe in and why they endorse the views that they hold. Groups who oppose government policy may engage in activities such as investigative journalism, which results in enhanced scrutiny and popular awareness of government activity.

Promote reform

Pressure groups may raise matters which the major political parties would prefer to ignore either because they do not consider them to be mainstream political issues, which generally dominate election campaigns (such as the economy or law and order), or because they are internally divisive to the parties. The emergence of women's issues and environmental concerns onto the political agenda owed much to the activities of presssure groups.

However, pressure groups do not always perform such a progressive role. The stance taken by the American National Rifle Association towards gun control in the 1990s demonstrated the negative role which groups sometimes perform in resisting reform proposals which they view as contrary to the interests of their members.

Put forward minority interests

The workings of liberal democratic political systems may also benefit from the ability of pressure groups to advocate minority opinions or concerns. Liberal democracies tend to pay most heed to majority opinion. There is thus a risk that minorities get ignored. Pressure groups provide a vehicle whereby minorities can articulate their needs and encourage policy makers to pay heed to them. In the 1960s the British group Campaign Against Racial Discrimination sought to voice the opinions of ethnic minority communities. This group's activities was one factor that led to the passage of the 1965 Race Relations Act.

Disadvantages of pressure groups

Let us now consider the main problems associated with the operations of pressure groups.

Inequality

One problem associated with pressure groups is that all are not given the same degree of attention by policy makers. The influence they are able to command is considerably influenced by factors including the resources at the group's disposal and the relationships they have constructed with government departments. There are two diametrically opposed problems that arise from the inequality which exists between groups.

First, this situation may result in worthy minority causes making little impact on public policy as they are relatively ignored by the bureaucrats, ministers, political parties, the media and public opinion. Members of groups in such a position may become frustrated and resort to violence, seeking to coerce when they are denied opportunities to persuade.

Second, factors such as resources and sanctions may result in some groups occupying a powerful position within the policy-making process. The ability of some groups to command considerable economic resources and be in possession of powerful sanctions which it can deploy to further its interests may result in them being in a position not merely to influence but to dominate the policy-making process. The power of large American corporations has for a long time provided them with a wide degree of autonomy in their dealings with government. In its most extreme form confrontation may result between the group and the government when the issue is, effectively, one of 'who governs?'.

Internal democracy

A further difficulty which we encounter with the workings of pressure groups is the extent to which the opinions or actions of the leadership faithfully reflect the views of the membership. The belief by UK Conservative governments that trade unions, for example, sometimes endorsed political activity which was not genuinely supported by the rank-and-file resulted in a number of pieces of legislation being enacted during the 1980s designed to ensure that such organizations were responsive to their members' opinions. These measures included requirements for compulsory secret ballots to be held before the commencement of strike action and the periodic election of union leaders. However, most pressure groups are not subject to such internal regulation and are thus susceptible to domination by their leaders. In this situation pressure groups fail greatly to extend the degree of popular involvement in policy making.

Methods used to secure influence

Concern has been expressed within liberal democracies regarding the expenditure of money by pressure groups in order to achieve influence. The purposes of such spending may go beyond political education and extend into activities which are perceived to approximate bribery or corruption. Lobbying has been a particular cause of concern and has led some countries to introduce measures to regulate these activities. In America, for example, lobbying activities directed at the federal government are regulated by the 1995 Lobby Restrictions Act (which replaced the 1946 Federal Regulation of Lobbying Act). This legislation requires lobbyists to register with the clerk of the House of Representatives and the secretary of the Senate within 45 days of having been hired. Lobbyists are required to file reports and list the issues on which they have lobbied and the institutions which they have contacted. In Germany, lobbying is regulated by the 1977 Members of Parliament Law and in Canada by the 1988 Lobbyists Registration Act. In the United Kingdom, however, the relationship between lobbyists and members of parliament is controlled by rules drawn up by the House of Commons.

Political action committees (PACs)

In America, political action committees were established in 1974 as a mechanism through which groups can direct funds into the individual campaign funds of candidates who supported their aims. PACs are set up by pressure groups and registered with the Federal Election Commission. This procedure permits groups to collect money from their members which is then donated – via the PAC – to political campaigns. The number of such bodies has risen dramatically – from about 600 in 1974 to almost 4,000 in 1988.

The support that can be given to individual candidates has been limited by subsequent amendments to the 1974 Federal Election Campaign Act, but PACs are able to inititiate independent political action. One form this may take is to campaign against the election of candidates to whom they are opposed. PACs have also been accused of weakening the role of local party organization by reducing the importance of its fund-raising activities and thereby reducing the level of public participation in election campaigns. In an attempt to combat this problem, new legislation enacted in 1979 allowed state and local parties to raise and spend money for 'party-building' activities.

The corporate state

A final problem which is associated with pressure groups arises when a relatively small number become incorporated into a state's decision-making machinery. The content of public policy may be heavily influenced by leaders of key pressure groups (especially employer and labour organizations) if they are accorded privileged access to ministers and civil servants through formal institutionalized arrangements. The term 'corporate state' is applied to such political arrangements.

Policy makers frequently consult with pressure groups in liberal democracies. In France, the Constitution requires the government to consult with the Economic and Social Council on socio-economic legislation. This body contains civil servants, trade unions, farmers' organizations, business associations and professional groups. The nature of the political system changes, however, if these consultations preclude the involvement of other parties and lead to consensual decisions being taken which cannot be meaningfully discussed in other forums. Elections cease to enable the public to exert influence over the content of policy while legislatures may be relegated to bodies which rubber stamp decisions taken elsewhere but over which they possess little or no control. An additional concern is the lack of accountability of policy makers in such corporate structures. Meetings involving pressure groups, ministers and civil servants are conducted in secret, away from the public gaze. It is difficult to ascertain precisely where power resides and who can be held responsible for particular decisions.

Pluralism and hyper-pluralism

Power in a pluralist society is dispersed. Policy emerges as the result of competition, consultation, bargaining and conciliation conducted between groups who are accorded relatively equal access to the policy-making arena. This process is overseen by the government which is viewed as a neutral arbitrator. Pressure groups thus perform a crucial role in policy making.

A problem may arise, however, in a society in which a very wide range of groups emerges, some of which hold diametrically opposing views. The processes of consultation, bargaining and conciliation may be long and drawn out. The decision-making process may stagnate and governments find it difficult, or impossible, to take any decisions. This situation (which regards all interests as being on an equal footing) is known as 'hyper-pluralism'. However, the tendency for powerful groups (including the government) to dominate the policy-making process serves to reduce the likelihood of such stagnation occurring in many liberal democracies.

Questions

1 Carry out your own study of pressure groups by listing four examples and indicating the goals which these organizations seek to further.

2 In connection with your own study of pressure groups, identify whether the groups you have selected are cause or interest groups. Explain how you have reached your decision.

3 What do you understand by the term 'direct action'? Why is this activity often used by pressure groups to further their aims?

4 Based on your reading of the section in this chapter, do you think that the disadvantages of pressure groups outweigh the advantages they bring to the operations of liberal democratic systems of government?

Taking it further

This chapter has highlighted the impotant role performed by pressure groups to influence the content of public policy. There are many books which provide informative accounts of the operations of these bodies. A good (although dated) discussion of pressure groups in 12 western liberal democracies (including the United Kingdom, America, France, Germany and Italy) can be found in Clive Thomas (editor) *First World Interest Groups: A Comparative Perspective* (Westport, Connecticut: Greenwood Press, 1993).

There are numerous books concerned with the workings of pressure groups in particular countries. In connection with the United Kingdom these include Bill Coxall, *Pressure Groups in British Politics*, Wyn Grant, *Pressure Groups and British Politics*, (Basingstoke: Macmillan/Palgrave, 2000). A good account of pressure groups in America is found in Anthony Newnes, *Pressure and Power – Organised Interests in American Politics* (Boston, Massachussetts: Houghton Mifflin, 2001).

07

the media

The role of the media in a liberal democracy

What is understood by the term 'media' and why do the media perform an important role within a liberal democracy?

The media are mechanisms of communication: historically the media consisted mainly of newspapers, but today they are more diverse and include journals, radio, television and newer means of communication using computer technology. The internet is one example of the latter. This consists of networks of computers linked by the international telephone system through which information can be disseminated. It is developing into a major mechanism of international communication and is becoming widely utilized as a source of information regarding political affairs and also to organize extra-parliamentary political activities on a global basis.

We now consider the importance of the functions performed by the media in the operations of a liberal democratic political system.

A source of information

The media are a source of information concerning internal and international events. By reading, listening to or viewing the media, members of the general public are informed about events of which they have no first-hand knowledge and thereby become more politically aware. One advantage of this is that public participation in policy making is facilitated. Public opinion is able to exert pressure on governments over a wide range of matters which, but for the role of the media, would be confined to the knowledge of a relatively small, elite group of rulers. The problems facing minorities can be made more widely known in this manner.

Scrutiny of government

The media act as a watchdog and scrutinize the activities performed by governments. The electorate has information placed at its disposal with which it can judge the record of governments: in particular the shortcomings or errors committed by individual ministers or by the government as a whole may be exposed. Investigative journalism has especially aided this role whose impact was spectacularly displayed in the downfall of President Nixon in 1974 in connection with the Watergate episode (which was concerned with a break-in at the Democratic National Committee headquarters in 1972 and the subsequent attempt to cover up White House involvement). In this manner, the media perform an important function by ensuring that governments can be held effectively accountable to the electorate.

The 'fourth estate'

The term 'fourth estate' is often used to describe the role of the media as guardians of a country's constitution and its liberal democratic system of politics. This implies, however, that the media possess autonomy and are independent of the state, the institutions which comprise it (including the political parties) and the economic interests which underlay it.

Problems posed by the media

Why are the operations of the media frequently subject to criticism?

While it is generally accepted that the media are important to the functioning of liberal democracy, their operations are frequently subject to adverse comment. In the next sections we consider the major criticisms which have been made concerning the manner in which the media operate.

Partisanship

The first problem is that of partisanship. Although in countries such as the UK and Ireland, radio and television are subject to legislation which is designed to prevent programmes favouring one politician or political party at the expense of another, other sections of the media, especially the press, are politically biased: they may support one party which they portray in a favourable light while seeking to belittle its political opponents.

Press bias is primarily effected through analysis: that is, newspapers do not simply report events, but seek to guide the public to a particular interpretation of those occurrences and the manner in which problems might be resolved. One way this is done is by blurring fact and opinion. This results in a story which is slanted towards the political perspective that the newspaper wishes to advance.

Partisanship is not necesarily a problem: if a country possesses a press which is diverse, a relatively wide range of political opinion will be presented. The biases of one newspaper, for example, can be offset by another presenting a totally different report or analysis of the same issue. Most members of the general public, however, do not read a wide range of newspapers and thus secure such a balanced view. We tend to be selective in our choice of newspaper and thus may be influenced by the interpretation which it puts forward.

Further, newspapers rarely reflect the wide range of political views and opinions found within a particular country. In the United Kingdom, for example, the bulk of national newspapers support the Conservative Party. In Germany, they tend to articulate a moderate conservative political position. This problem of bias has been compounded by recent developments in the concentration of ownership. In many liberal democracies a number of newspapers are owned by one individual which may restrict the diversity of views expressed in that nation's press. Examples of such 'press barons' include Silvio Berlusconi in Italy, the Springer Group in Germany and Rupert Murdoch whose worldwide interests cover Europe, Asia and (following the acquisition of Direct TV in 2003) North and Latin America.

Selective coverage of events

A second criticism which is sometimes levelled against the media concerns the process by which events are selected for coverage. It is argued that stories which appear in our newspapers or on our television screens are chosen not according to their importance but, rather, their presence is determined by the criterion of 'newsworthiness' applied by media owners or editors. This may mean that stories which are sensational get media coverage at the expense of worthier events which lack such 'glamour'. Thus war coverage or an inner city riot may get coverage at the expense of events such as famines, simply because editors believe that the spectre of a tenement block being bombed or a police car being burned is more likely to attract readers or boost listening or viewing figures than is a story of quiet and resigned suffering which lacks such drama.

This criticism suggests that the media do not fulfil their role of educating the public since they are selective in the information provided and how this is presented. This is especially of concern if media owners or editors concentrate on trivia at the expense of key issues of national or international concern.

Privacy versus the 'right to know'

A third criticism which has been directed against the media is concerned with editorial freedom: should the media be free to publish any story which they believe is of interest to the general public or should limits exist to prevent publication under certain circumstances? Censorship is regarded as anathema to a liberal democratic system of government. This is suggestive of state control and implies that the media function as a propaganda tool of the government, as was the case, for example, in the former communist state of East Germany. Written constitutions in liberal democracies frequently incorporate provisions to guarantee the freedom of the press: the first amendment to the American Constitution contains such a statement and this principle is also enshrined in the German Basic Law.

However, restrictions on the media exist in all liberal democratic systems of government. For example, it is a requirement that reports should be truthful. Those which are not might be subject to actions for slander or libel. A more contentious restriction concerns state interests. Legislation (such as the United Kingdom's 1989 Official Secrets Act) is designed to protect the state against subversive activities waged by foreign governments. In Ireland, the 1939 Offences Against the State Act or the 1960 Broadcasting Act may be used to prohibit media coverage of illegal organizations.

However, state interests are difficult to define precisely. Should the term cover such activities performed by a government in the name of the state which it might find politically embarrassing if revealed to the general public or to world opinion? This issue arose in the former state of West Germany in the 1960s in connection with the 'Spiegel Affair'. It led to an amendment of the criminal code of the former state of West Germany in 1968 whereby the press could be punished for revealing secrets which were clearly and unambiguously a threat to the state's external secrecy.

Another contentious area is that of individual privacy. The media's watchdog function may involve publishing information which infringes on the personal life of a public figure. Such information may be obtained in dubious ways including the use of telephoto lenses or bugging devices. This reveals an important dilemma: where does the public's 'right to know' stop and a public person's 'right to privacy' begin?

This issue is often determined by the media themselves who may perhaps operate some form of code of practice. However, accusations that the United Kingdom media, and especially the newspaper industry, have unduly infringed on the privacy of members of the Royal Family and leading politicians have led to calls for the enactment of legislation (in the form of a privacy law) to impose restrictions on the activities of the media which would make intrusive behaviour by newspapers a specific criminal offence.

This issue became one of public debate following the circumstances surrounding the death of Diana, Princess of Wales, in Paris in 1997. The car in which she was travelling crashed while engaged in avoiding the attention of freelance photographers (termed 'paparazzi'). Although such persons were not employed by major media outlets, the willingness of the tabloid press to buy photographs from them effectively encouraged their work. Accordingly, a revised code of practice designed to provide greater protection to members of the public against intrusion by newspapers and magazines was drawn up and came into force in the United Kingdom on 1 January 1998. However, the effectiveness of this reform is doubted, a particular problem being that stories which appear in the press sometimes seem to confuse the concept of 'public interest' with a broader notion of 'what interests the public'.

Media regulation in the United Kingdom

There are a wide range of formal and informal mechanisms to regulate the media. Public morality is safeguarded in legislation which includes the 1959 Obscene Publications Act, the 1984 Video Recordings Act and also through the work performed by the Broadcasting Standards Council which was established on a statutory footing in 1990 governing both radio and television.

State interests are safeguarded by the 1989 Official Secrets Act: however, governments have a range of other means at their disposal to influence the conduct of the media. These include the D-Notice system (which is a procedure designed to stop the reporting of security matters). The political concerns of a government may be furthered through the provision of information to selected journalists through the 'lobby system'. Allegations have also been made that appointments to bodies such as the British Broadcasting Corporation and the Independent Television Commission may be used in a partisan manner.

A privacy law

The main alternative to media self-regulation is through privacy legislation which would enable the courts to award damages when such rights were violated. Privacy legislation exists in a number of European countries: a right to privacy is recognized in both French and German law while in Denmark unauthorized photography on private property is forbidden. This issue is regulated by state governments in America and most have some form of privacy law. However, privacy legislation to regulate the media in the United Kingdom has been fiercely resisted on the grounds that it would interfere with their ability to act as a public watchdog.

However, the effectiveness of privacy legislation is limited in those countries which have it by broader considerations. In France, for example, the civil damages awarded are usually low and the sanction of the total stoppage of a publication is rarely used. In Germany, privacy is balanced by Article 5 of the 1949 Constitution which specifically protects the freedom of speech and of the press. The main objections to a specific privacy law in the United Kingdom have been that it would be very complicated to draft and would encounter key problems, including the precise legal definition which could be accorded to 'privacy', thereby possibly preventing the reporting of issues such as corruption in government by investigative journalists.

The debate concerning a specific law of privacy in the United Kingdom has been influenced by beliefs that other legislation concerning open government and human rights, which was put forward by the Labour government after 1997, could also safeguard privacy and effectively secure the enactment of a privacy law 'through the back door'. This argument rested on the ability of judges to develop a common law right of privacy derived from their interpretation of this new legislation. This consisted of the following.

Data protection legislation

Data protection introduced in Italy in 1996 has been used to restrict media coverage. In 1998, the UK's Labour Government enacted the Data Protection Act to implement a European Directive designed to protect the individual's rights to privacy. It gave the public the right to inspect personal information held on them in computer files and other databases and insisted that such personal data could not be used without the subject's consent.

Human rights legislation

In 1998, the government's Human Rights Act incorporated the European Convention of Human Rights and Fundamental Freedoms into United Kingdom law. This prospect alarmed the press which feared that Article 8 (concerned with asserting an individual's right to privacy in connection with his or her relationship to state authority) would be applied to them and that used in conjunction with the Data Protection legislation and the new offence of harassment, their ability to investigate, report and comment on matters of public interest would be curtailed.

The government's response to such fears was to deny their intention to provide for privacy legislation in this indirect manner. The legislation included an explicit statement that the courts should give higher priority to freedom of expression (embodied in Article 10 of the European Convention of Human Rights) when it clashed with respect for private life and required the courts to take into account the public interest of any disputed published item coupled with a judgement as to whether the newspaper had acted 'fairly and reasonably' within the provisions of the Code of Practice of the Press Complaints Commission. This situation still gave judges a wide discretion which might aid them developing a law of privacy.

In America, the determination of the boundary between freedom of speech and the right to privacy is left to the judges who deal with the matter on a case-by-case basis. The increased involvement of the United Kingdom judiciary in matters affecting privacy was viewed sceptically by the media in the belief that judges are likely to adopt a hostile attitude towards them. This view is justified by the negative stance frequently adopted by the judiciary towards the disclosure of information whether state or private interests were concerned. The ability of journalists to protect the sources of information is regarded by many as a key safeguard of press freedom. The judiciary, however, have frequently taken a different view of this situation and have compelled journalists to disclose the sources on which their stories were based.

The media and the conduct of politics

In what ways does the media affect the manner in which the political affairs of a nation are conducted?

In all liberal democracies the media exert a profound influence over the conduct of political affairs. In the nineteenth century, the only way members of the general public could see a leading politician was physically to attend meetings which they addressed. It followed, therefore, that oratory was a prized political skill in that period. But this is no longer the case. Initially, the popular press made it possible for politicians to put their case to a wider audience than was able to attend a political meeting. Then the radio and now television enabled leading politicians to address us directly in our own living rooms. This has had a significant influence over the conduct of national election campaigns.

Election campaigns

Election campaigns may fulfil one of three roles: they may reinforce a voter's existing loyalty to a political party, attempt to activate its existing supporters to turn out and vote on election day or seek to convert members of the general public and thus gain new sources of electoral support for the party.

Political meetings are now a less important feature of election campaigns. Campaigns at national level now utilize technology and market research techniques. Computerized mailing lists, opinion polls and advertising are commonly utilized in an attempt to 'sell' candidates to the general public. Politicians seize opportunities offered by the media to project themselves to the electorate: the photo opportunity, the walkabout, the press conference, televised debates and political broadcasts have diminished the importance of the old-style political meeting. The role of the media is especially enhanced in countries such as America in which it is possible for politicians and political parties to buy air time.

Television, in particular, has had a number of consequences for the conduct of national elections. This provides candidates with an opportunity to address large audiences and 'head-to-head' televised debates are common in countries with directly elected presidents. This is especially the case in America, where the televised debates in the 1960 presidential election contest (between Richard Nixon and John F. Kennedy) became a feature of all subsequent contests. In the 1980 presidential election an estimated audience of 81 million people watched the Jimmy Carter–Ronald Reagan debates.

Even in countries with a parliamentary form of government such as the UK, television has tended to focus attention on party leaders and thus transform general elections into contests for the office of prime minister. In such countries, national elections have become 'presidentialized'. Central control over party affairs has been enhanced by this development which has also tended to reduce the importance of activities performed by local party members in connection with the election of candidates to public office.

Additionally, television has placed emphasis on presentation: major political events such as campaign rallies are carefully orchestrated so that viewers are presented with an image of a united and enthusiastic party. Leading politicians are carefully schooled in television techniques since the ability to perform professionally on television has become an essential political skill. Advertising companies play an ever increasing role in 'selling' political parties and their leaders. The danger with such developments is that content may be of secondary importance to what advertisers refer to as 'packaging'.

However, the influence of the media over the conduct of politics is not confined to national elections. The role performed by legislatures may also be adversely affected. Investigative journalism may provide more effective scrutiny of the actions of the executive than a legislator's speeches or questions. An appearance by a legislator in a brief televised interview will reach a wider audience than a speech delivered within the legislature. One response to the latter issue has been the televising of the proceedings of legislative bodies. The Australian parliament, for example, voted to televise the proceedings of the Senate, House of Representatives and their committees in October 1991.

There have also been disadvantages associated with this development, however. It has been argued that MPs 'play up' to the cameras, perhaps tailoring their speeches to include words or phrases which are likely to get reported. These are referred to as 'soundbites'.

The UK House of Commons and the media

Legislatures may respond to arguments that the media have taken over their traditional functions by using them to publicize their activities. In 1989, the House of Commons allowed its proceedings to be televised. The main benefit intended from this course of action was to make government more visible to members of the general public who would thus understand the importance of the work performed by parliament. Although the viewing public of live proceedings is not substantial, snippets of broadcasts are utilized in the more widely viewed news programmes.

Soundbites

Soundbites consist of a short, self-contained phrase or sentence through which a politician seeks to communicate views, opinions, attitudes or personality traits to the general public. The term was first used in America in the 1960s but has subsequently been applied on both sides of the Atlantic.

Soundbites may be used to provide the public with a brief statement which encapsulates a politician's or political party's stance on a particular policy issue or which seeks to provide the public with an image associating a politician or political party with a particular course of action. In this case they are similar to an advertising jingle. An example of a soundbite with this intention was the statement in 1993 by the then United Kingdom Home Secretary, Michael Howard, that 'prison works'. This was intended to convey the impression of a government that intended that a tough line on crime should be taken involving the use of imprisonment rather than non-custodial forms of punishment.

Soundbites may also be used by politicians to summarize their personality traits which they believe might enhance their popular appeal. An example of this was the statement made by the then Prime Minister of the United Kingdom, Margaret Thatcher, in 1980 that 'the lady's not for turning' in response to suggestions that her economic policies should be adjusted to combat increasing unemployment and deepening economic recession.

The use of soundbites has been especially prompted by the role played by the media (especially television) in political affairs. The time given over to political affairs is limited and it is thus essential that politicians use the time at their disposal to maximum effect.

Their use has additionally been encouraged by a perception that the attention span of the general public is extremely limited and that anything beyond a brief statement will not be absorbed.

A major problem with soundbites is that complex political issues become abbreviated into catchy words, slogans or catchphrases designed to cultivate public support without seeking fully to explain to the public the rationale for the course of action proposed.

Ministers have also been accused of 'planting' questions: this involves a MP from the government party tabling a question of which the minister has prior knowledge. This is designed to make the minister appear an effective parliamentary performer thus enhancing both minister's and government's reputation.

The political influence of the media

How are the media able to influence activities such as policy making and the outcome of election contests?

Issues such as ownership and bias are regarded as important in liberal democracies as it is assumed that the media possesses considerable ability to determine the course of political events. In this section we consider various arguments concerning the influence of the media on political affairs.

Agenda setting

It is argued that the media have the ability to 'set the political agenda': that is, the media may publicize a particular issue in the hope of concentrating the attention of their readers, listeners or viewers on this topic. Whether this is a good or a bad development much depends on the motives that lie behind the media's attempts to influence public perceptions. A beneficial aspect of this activity is that the media may lead public opinion in a progressive direction, perhaps securing action on a social problem which would otherwise have been ignored. In the United Kingdom, a television programme shown in 1966, *Cathy Come Home*, had a significant impact on publicizing the plight of Britain's homeless and aided the growth of the organization Shelter.

Alternatively, however, the media may be guided by partisan motives. Attention may be directed at an issue in order to secure support for a course of action favoured by its owner or by the political interests which the owner supports. This may involve whipping up public hysteria to persuade governments to act in a manner advocated by the media or the interests which lay behind it.

'Moral panics'

Moral panics occur when the media concentrate on a particular problem which is exaggerated and blown out of all proportion. This problem is depicted as being typical of a wider social malaise which threatens social tranquillity. It frequently involves groups being scapegoated and blamed for all the ills facing society. In undertaking such activities the media are accused of acting at the behest of the powerful interests in society who are threatened by this underlying crisis.

Moral panics often form an aspect of law and order policy, in which the police and courts will be urged by the media to take tough action against a problem, frequently identified with youths. The consequence of moral panics is to produce a more heavily regulated society. This activity is consistent with a Marxist interpretation of the role of the media: it holds that the media are ideological tools which operate in the interests of the powerful and thereby help to sustain their position within society.

Reinforcement or change?

Agenda setting is, however, only one aspect of media influence. It is sometimes argued that the media have the ability to determine not merely the policies which governments adopt but, more fundamentally, their political complexion. This accusation implies that the media have a significant influence over voting behaviour at election times. There are two basic schools of thought concerning the ability of the media to influence how we vote. The debate centres on the extent to which the media merely reinforce existing political behaviour rather than being able to act as the agent of political change.

Those who argue that the media reinforce existing political activity suggest that the power of the media over politics is limited since most members of the general public have preconceived political opinions. They will either read, listen to or view material which is consistent with these existing ideas or ignore contrary ideas should these be expressed. Further, as the media know the tastes of their clientele, they will cater for these opinions and not run the risk of losing readers, listeners or viewers. The reinforcement theory thus suggests that issues of media bias are of no significant political importance even at election times.

A contrary opinion to the reinforcement theory suggests that the media have a profound influence over political activity such as voting behaviour. It is suggested that many people are unaware of the political biases of the media to which they are subject and may thus be influenced by the manner in which they portray events, especially when such exposure takes place over a long period of time.

This may be especially important when the gap between the leading parties for political office is small: in the United Kingdom the Conservative Party's election victory in 1992 has been attributed to the influence exerted by the Conservative tabloid press on working class voters, and Silvio Berlusconi's victory in the 1994 Italian elections has been explained by the impact of his three television channels on voting behaviour. The perception that the United Kingdom Labour Party needs to convert Conservative supporters in order to win elections considerably affected this party's stance towards the tabloid press, especially that owned by Rupert Murdoch.

Media influence over political events

It is alleged that the role of the media extends beyond merely influencing the outcome of elections: it also may promote major political episodes.

In the United Kingdom it was alleged that the Social Democratic Party (formed in 1981) was a media creation. This argument suggested that the heavy emphasis placed in the media on ideological divisions within the Labour Party was a major factor in inducing a number of social democrats to form a new political vehicle to advance their views.

The initial successes enjoyed by that party were also attributed to media interest in that party's affairs – an interest that waned when the Falklands War commenced in 1982.

The extent to which the media influence political affairs is thus open to debate. It is one social agency among several others (which include the family, the workplace or the neighbourhood) which may affect political conduct. Those without established political views or loyalties (who are described as 'don't knows' in opinion polls) may be most susceptible to media influence.

The suggestion that the media can influence the political behaviour of at least some members of the general public thus implies that issues such as ownership and political bias are important in a liberal democracy. It may mean that some parties have an unfair advantage.

Spin doctors

The important role played by the media in determining the outcome of political activities makes it essential that parties undertake measures to ensure that they are favourably projected. Those who undertake this work are termed spin doctors.

A spin doctor is concerned with ensuring that the policies of a political party are effectively presented to the electorate in order to ensure their maximum popular appeal. The term was first used in America in the 1980s and the United Kingdom Labour Party's success at the 1997 general election was heavily influenced by the manner in which spin doctors were able to manage or manipulate the reporting activities of the media, particularly the newspapers, so that their policy and criticisms of the Conservative government received favourable coverage. Following Labour's victory at the 1997 general election, a number of spin doctors were employed in order to secure governmental control of the media's agenda so that journalists would be placed in the position of responding to government initiatives rather than putting forward proposals of their own. The main advantage of this for the government was that it gave it the appearance of being in control of situations.

The position occupied by spin doctors as middlemen between politicians and the electorate provides them with considerable power, since to perform their functions effectively they are required to exercise much control over political affairs and in particular a party's media relations. This may have disadvantageous consequences for the operations of liberal democracies. Spin doctors might feel it necessary to dominate elected politicians to the extent of devising policy proposals which they deem to have popular appeal or imposing censorship on the media. If a spin doctor acts for a party which is in government, this may take the form of seeking to control media activities by bullying journalists into favourably reporting the activities of the government or denying access to government sources to journalists or publications which adopt a critical stance to it. Further, the emphasis which they place on presentation and image may become a substitute for policy so that the attention of electors becomes diverted from the contents of government proposals and is instead focused on issues such as delivery, appearance or image. The role of spin doctors may also accelarate a trend whereby official pronouncements on government policy are made in the media rather than in legislative bodies whose work thus becomes devalued.

Cross-media ownership

What does 'cross-media ownership' mean and why is this relevant to politics?

Traditionally media operations were discrete: a 'separation of media powers' existed in many liberal democracies whereby ownership of the print media was divorced from other major forms of communication such as radio and television. While it became increasingly common in the twentieth century for newspaper ownership to be concentrated in relatively few hands by a process of mergers, such processes were conducted within the print media. But this is now changing. Increasingly, media owners have financial interests in various forms of communication including newspapers, journals, radio and television. This is what we mean by 'cross-media ownership'. In the remainder of this section we consider why this development occurred and what problems might arise as the result of it.

The development of cross-media ownership

The role of the private sector in ownership of television companies has had a profound influence on this development. In many European countries television was initially viewed as a form of public service. It was operated by the state (sometimes using the mechanism of public corporations as is the case in the United Kingdom) whose main duty was to ensure that news was reported in an impartial fashion: objectivity and balance were the guiding principles of public service broadcasting. This situation was different from that in the United States where broadcasting organizations were privately owned.

The monopoly enjoyed by public service broadcasting was eventually challenged by the private sector which sought to make a profit from this form of communication. This gave rise to commercial television which was exclusively funded by advertising revenue (unlike public service broadcasting which was mainly funded by its users paying a licence fee, sometimes – as in the former state of West Germany – topped up by income derived from advertising). The costs involved in establishing a television channel made it essential that established business and commercial interests involved themselves in commercial television. In many countries, however, commercial broadcasting was initially subject to state supervision. This was justified on the grounds that the frequencies available for transmission were limited in number and so the state had to regulate the use of this scarce commodity.

However, more recent developments concerned especially with cable and satellite television have facilitated a massive growth in the number of television channels which can be transmitted within any one particular country. Although these may also be subject to some degree of state supervision, these innovations have served to further increase the role of the private sector in broadcasting.

Problems associated with cross-media ownership

Cable and satellite channels are attractive to the private sector whose role in broadcasting has been further facilitated by the process of deregulation: this occurred in Italy and France during the 1980s and is likely to happen in America following the relaxation of media ownership rules in 2003. Many of these commercial and business interests were already engaged in other aspects of media activity such as newspapers and radio. The ability of an individual or a commercial company to have interests in a wide range of media outlets has considerable political significance.

One major problem is that such media owners possess a considerable degree of power: as we have already described, they may seek to place ideas on the political agenda or to influence the manner in which members of the general public think or act. Their ability to do so may be enhanced by a situation in which a wide range of media outlets hammer out a common political line.

Cross-ownership may further erode the diversity of the media which is regarded as essential in a liberal democracy. It is important that the media articulate a wide range of opinions in order for members of the public to become politically educated. A similarity of views expressed in various media forms may be more reminiscent of a one-party state than of a society which flourishes on the expression of a variety of opinions.

A further difficulty with cross-ownership is that commercial concerns dominate the content of newspapers or programmes. A major fear is that stories or programmes will cater for the lowest common denominator: the practices of the United Kingdom tabloid press, for example, will become the standard form of activity. While this problem may seem confined to media operating on commercial lines it has serious implications for public service broadcasting. If they lose viewers to commercial television companies their case for receiving all, or any, of a licence fee paid by the public is undermined.

However, it would be incorrect to assume that all developments in the media have undesirable consequences for the conduct of politics. Innovations which include desktop publishing, cable and satellite broadcasting theoretically facilitate a diversity of opinion which is beneficial to a healthy liberal democracy. The key consideration is the extent to which companies taking advantage of these developments are able to remain independent. Developments in the mid-1990s in connection with the information superhighway have tended to promote takeovers and mergers resulting in the formation of large companies with diverse media interests. If small companies are taken over or driven out of business by larger concerns, with interests in a range of different forms of communication, the benefits which could be derived from technological innovations will be lost. It is this concern which has prompted the enactment of national or state legislation to limit the extent of cross-media ownership.

Mergers in the media industry

In January 2000 the American company Time Warner announced a merger with the world's biggest Internet Service Provider, America Online. This $350 billion deal created the world's fourth largest corporation, called AOL Time Warner. It was described as the world's first fully integrated media and communications company and united a wide range of news and entertainment outlets (including a major cable television network) with a major online service provider.

Questions

1 Using examples of your own, assess the importance of the role performed by the media in liberal democratic political systems.
2 Discuss the case for and against introducing a privacy law which is designed to curb the reporting activities of the media.
3 Assess the way television has influenced the way in which political activities are conducted.
4 What do you understand by the term 'cross-media ownership' and what problems might affect the conduct of political affairs as the result of it?

Taking it Further

This chapter has considered the diversity of the media and the vital role which it performs in the operations of contemporary liberal democratic systems of government. More detailed discussion of matters raised in this chapter is provided in John Street, *Mass Media, Politics and Democracy* (Basingstoke: Macmillan/Palgrave, 2001) and Mark Wheeler, *Politics and the Mass Media* (Oxford: Blackwell, 1997).

The issue of media manipulation was an important issue which was referred to, and a more detailed examination of this topic is to be found in Nicholas Jones, *Soundbites and Spin Doctors: How Politicians Manipulate the Media – and Vice Versa* (London: Cassell, 1995).

08

constitutions

In this chapter you will learn:
- why states have constitutions
- the distinction between codified and uncodified constitutions
- the process of constitutional reform in the UK

Definition

What is a constitution? Why do states have them?

As students of politics we need to know how a country's system of government operates. For example, we may wish to ascertain what power is possessed by head of state. Or we may be interested in the relationship between the executive and the legislature or between the government and its citizens. We would turn to a constitution to discover information of this nature.

A constitution sets a framework within which a country's system of government is conducted. It establishes rules which those who exercise the functions of government have to obey. All future actions performed by the executive and legislature, for example, must be in conformity with the country's constitutional provisions.

There is usually one document which contains information concerning the manner in which a country's system of government operates. Examples of such codified documents include the American Constitution which was drawn up in 1787, the Irish Constitution of 1937 and the French Constitution of 1958. The provisions of codified constitutions have a superior status to ordinary legislation and provide a key point of reference whereby the activities performed by the executive and legislative branches of government and subordinate authorities such as state or local government can be judged. Actions which contravene it may be set aside by the process of judicial review. Britain and New Zealand, alternatively, are examples of countries which do not have codified constitutions.

However, it would be impossible to include all the material relevant to the government of a country in one single document. Codified constitutions are supplemented by several additional sources to provide detailed information concerning the operations of a country's system of government. A constitution sometimes establishes broad principles of action whose detailed implementation is left to legislation. Such statutes constitute a further source of information concerning the manner in which government functions. Other sources include declarations made by judges whose work may involve interpreting the constitution. These written sources are supplemented by the adoption of practices concerning the way in which government works. These are usually referred to as conventions.

Conventions

The manner in which a country's system of government operates is often determined by unwritten customs or practices rather than by specific constitutional enactment. Such constitutional conventions may fundamentally alter arrangements contained or implied in a country's constitution.

The 1958 French Constitution gave the National Assembly the power to dismiss prime ministers. However, their willingness to accept that they could be dismissed by the president, even when enjoying the support of the legislature, facilitated the extension of the president's power. The American Constitution envisaged that Congress would be the main source of legislation. In practice, however, the president subsequently assumed a major role in initiating legislation.

Codified constitutions are traditionally drawn up following some major political event or crisis which necessitates the reconstruction of the apparatus of government. There is a widely felt need to 'start afresh'. In America, new arrangements for government were required when this country secured its independence from the United Kingdom in the late eighteenth century. A similar situation required an Irish Constitution to be written following the First World War. In Italy and the old state of West Germany, defeat in war and the collapse of fascism necessitated the construction of new governing arrangements. In France, the Algerian war provided the occasion for the drafting of a new constitution in 1958, thus bringing the Fifth Republic into being.

The role of a constitution

What do we learn from studying a country's constitution?

A constitution provides a student of politics with a wide range of important information which is outlined in this section.

The key features of government

A constitution describes the essential features of a country's system of government. A constitution contains a formal statement of the composition of the key branches of government – the legislature, executive and the judiciary – and refers to the role which each of these plays in the machinery of government.

A constitution further informs us of the relationship between the branches of government. The American president, for example, is required to deliver a state of the union address to Congress periodically and may put forward legislative proposals for that body's consideration.

The composition of American government

The American Constitution provided for a legislature which is termed 'Congress'. It consists of two chambers – the House of Representatives and the Senate. The Constitution allocated the executive function to the president while the judicial function was ascribed to a Supreme Court and a range of subordinate courts. This Constitution further stipulated the qualifications required for membership of the House of Representatives and the Senate and laid down conditions governing the presidency, including eligibility to serve in that office and the length of that official's tenure.

The functions of each branch of government were also discussed in this document. A key role given to Congress was that of levying and collecting taxes. One key duty allocated to the president was to be commander-in-chief of the country's armed forces. The federal judiciary was charged with upholding federal law, including the Constitution, and arbitrating disputes between two or more states.

Civil rights

In liberal democracies we usually find statements contained in constitutions concerning the relationship between the government and its citizens. Such documents typically contain safeguards against arbitrary conduct by a government which are designed to safeguard individual freedom. The German Constitution, for example, contains a prominent statement of basic rights which guarantee its citizens a range of personal freedoms. The omission of such provisions was regarded as a major weakness of the American Constitution. Accordingly ten amendments (collectively known as the Bill of Rights) were incorporated into this document in 1791.

The American Bill of Rights

The first ten amendments to the American Constitution list a range of personal freedoms. These include the freedom of religion, speech and assembly and the right to petition for the redress of grievances. The Constitution safeguards the right of all citizens to possess arms. Provisions concerning the manner in which citizens or their property can be searched are incorporated into this document which also establishes the right of an accused person to a speedy and public trial.

Similar provisions are found in many other constitutions. In Ireland, personal rights such as the equality of all citizens before the law, the right of *habeas corpus* and the freedom of expression (including the right to criticize government policy) are embodied in the Constitution. In Italy, the right to join a political party or a trade union is enshrined in the Constitution.

Traditionally, such freedoms focused on the conduct of political affairs and the operations of the criminal justice system. They were designed to prevent governments acting in an overbearing fashion towards their citizens. In the late twentieth century, however, other forms of rights have entered political debates. These include social rights such as the right to a job, the right to be housed, the right to enjoy a minimum standard of living or the right for a woman to have an abortion. Although legislation may sometimes remove impediments to prevent specific groups of citizens from exercising defined social functions, constitutions rarely contain a fundamental, all-embracing statement of social rights.

Guarantor of a federal system of government

In a federal country such as America or Germany, government is jointly exercised by national and sub-national units. The constitution will commonly establish the division of responsibilities which exists within that country between these units of government. The existence of these sub-national bodies is guaranteed by the constitution.

The balance of power between the federal and state governments in America, for example, is discussed in the Constitution, especially in the tenth amendment which stipulated that powers not expressly delegated to the federal government in that document or prohibited from being exercised by the states would be 'reserved to the states respectively, or to the people'. We shall discuss the changing nature of the balance between federal and state governments in America in Chapter 13.

Unconstitutional and anti-constitutional actions

An unconstitutional act is one which contravenes either the letter or the spirit of the constitution. The perpetrator usually contravenes one specific constitutional provision or convention. In the United Kingdom, a government refusing to resign following the passage of a 'no confidence' motion in the House of Commons would be accused of acting unconstitutionally.

An anti-constitutional action is one which displays a total disregard for the entire constitutional arrangements that exist within a particular country and may seek to overthrow them. The assassination of the Israeli prime minister, Yitzhak Rabin, in 1995 in order to try to alter the direction of government policy towards the Palestinians, was an example of an anti-constitutional action. Military intervention to overthrow a system of liberal democracy and impose a different form of government is a further example. The overthrow of Salvador Allende's government in Chile in 1973 and its replacement by a military regime headed by General Pinochet was an anti-constitutional action.

The embodiment of political values

A constitution will tell us about the political views, aspirations and values of those who wrote it. The Italian Constitution of 1947 reveals a desire on the part of its authors to organize that country's system of government in order to prevent the return of fascism. This was reflected in the widespread dispersal of political power and the absence of a provision for the direct election of the president. The French Constitution of 1958 displayed a commitment by its authors that strong, effective government was an essential guarantee of national security. They sought to secure this objective by strengthening the executive branch at the expense of the legislature. Parties such as the socialists who traditionally viewed a strong legislature as the essence of republicanism subsequently accepted the enhanced power of the presidency.

An examination of a constitution thus enables us to discover how theory is translated into practice and how the climate of political opinion at the time when that document was drafted subsequently influenced the conduct of a country's governing institutions. It thus embodies a statement of political theory and political history. We shall examine this situation more fully in relationship to the drafting of the American Constitution.

The principles of the American Constitution

The 55 delegates who assembled at Philadelphia in 1787 to draft the American Constitution were influenced by a variety of political ideas and priorities. These included John Locke's social contract theory and Montesquieu's concept of the separation of powers.

The separation of powers was advocated by Montesquieu in his work *De l'Esprit des Lois*, written in 1748. This held that tyranny was most effectively avoided if the three branches of government (the legislature, executive and judiciary) were separate. This implied that each branch would possess a degree of autonomy and its personnel should be different. This theory appealed to those who drafted the American Constitution. It was widely believed that George III's unreasonable treatment of the American colonists had triggered the War of Independence in 1775. The monarch embodied all three functions of government and was thus prone to tyrannical action. Accordingly, the Constitution placed the legislative, executive and judicial functions of government into the hands of different bodies.

However, one difficulty with the separation of powers is that if it were strictly followed each branch of government would be accountable only to itself. This might result in insufficient restraints being imposed over their actions, enabling each the potential to act in an arbitrary (that is, unreasonable or dictatorial) fashion. The American Constitution thus sought to avoid this situation from occurring by providing for the fragmentation of political power through a system of checks and balances whereby the key functions and operations performed by one branch were subject to scrutiny by the others. Thus the president's power to appoint members of the executive branch of government is restricted by the requirement that senior appointees are subject to the approval ('confirmation') of the Senate. This principle extended to the relationships within the branches of government so that, in the case of Congress, the actions of one of its two Houses could be restrained by the other. The American system of government has thus been described as one of 'separated institutions sharing powers'.

The main problem with a system of checks and balances is that can result in inertia – the involvement of numerous people in decision making may result in nothing being done as one group effectively cancels out the work of another.

Codified constitutions as living documents

How do codified constitutions survive over long periods of time?

Codified constitutions are designed to be enduring documents. The process of drafting and ratifying (that is, approving) a constitution is a lengthy one. No country can thus afford the luxury of frequently rewriting its constitution.

The question we need to address, therefore, is how a document written at one specific point in time can endure for many years after. In particular we shall consider how a constitution can adjust to subsequent social, economic and political changes which may have a significant impact on the role and operations of government and how it might respond to eventualities which were not perceived when the document was originally drawn up.

The process of amendment

Constitutions generally contain provisions whereby additions or deletions can be made to the original document. The process of amendment, however, is subject to great variation. Flexible constitutions are those which can be amended by the normal law-making process. The uncodified British constitution (discussed later) is a good example of a flexible constitution, but the German constitution can also be altered by the normal law-making process.

Usually, however, constitutions can be amended only by a process which is separate from the normal law-making process utilized in a particular country. These are known as rigid constitutions.

Amendment of the German Constitution

Changes to the German Constitution are constrained by two factors. One is that they must secure the support of at least two-thirds of the members of both the *Bundestag* and the *Bundesrat*. The other is that certain elements of the constitution may not be amended. These concern the key principles governing the operations of the state, including its 'democratic and social' nature, the ability of the people to exercise political power through the process of voting in elections and the functioning of government through legislative, executive and judicial organs. The role performed by the states (*Länder*) in the process of government may also not be altered.

Amendments provide one obvious way for a constitution to be kept up to date. Those made to the American Constitution include civil rights issues such as the abolition of slavery, the right of women to vote and the universal introduction of votes at the age of 18. The power of federal government was enhanced by the amendment which authorized Congress to levy income tax.

Rigid constitutions – Ireland and America

Amendment of the Irish Constitution requires a referendum to be held to determine popular support or rejection for any constitutional change put forward by parliament (the *Oireachtas*). Examples of amendments which were made using such a procedure include two in connection with Ireland's membership of the European Union (in 1972 and 1987).

The American Constitution can be amended in two ways. The manner which is usually utilized requires two-thirds of the members of both Houses of Congress to approve a change, following which it is submitted to state legislatures or ratification conventions organized at state level. A proposal needs the support of three-quarters of the states in order to be incorporated into the Constitution. The alternative method enables the states rather than Congress to initiate the process of reform.

Generally, amendments are most easily secured to flexible constitutions. When the amending process is lengthy and drawn out, changes become more difficult. There have only been 26 amendments made to the American constitution since 1789. Well-supported changes (such as the Equal Rights Amendment in the 1970s) failed to secure sufficient support to be incorporated into that document. One potential danger with rigid constitutions is that they fail to keep abreast of social changes.

Judicial review

A second way whereby constitutions can be adapted to suit changed circumstances is through the process of judicial review which is performed by the judiciary. This entails assessing when a contemporary issue or problem is compatible with the letter or spirit of the constituion, enabling judges to strike down actions which, in their view, contravene a country's basic law. In performing this function judges may draw solely on their legal expertise or they may, as in the case in Germany, consider submissions from interested parties before reaching a judgement. Judicial review enables the courts to inject contemporary views and values into a country's constitution when they are required to deliver judgement on a specific issue which comes before them. Judicial review may extend the scope of state activity or it may affect a citizen's civil rights. The American Supreme Court's decision (in *Roe* v. *Wade*, 1973) that under certain circumstances a woman had a right to an abortion is an example of judicial interpretation of the constitution.

There are two dangers with the process of interpretation. The first is when the core values enshrined in this document lose their appeal because broader social changes make them unfashionable. In such circumstances, the constitution may lose its authority and under extreme circumstances may have to be replaced by a new document.

The second problem is that an acceptance that the constitution is a document whose meaning can be determined by judicial interpretation may result in the loss of its ability to restrain the actions of government. The ability to adjust a constitution in this manner may result in sanction being given to any action which the government wishes to undertake, especially when the latter has the ability to appoint judges. In these circumstances, the constitution does not meaningfully limit the operations of government or force it to subscribe to any basic standard of behaviour. It thus ceases to be an independent source of power, which is essential if it is to act as an impartial arbitrator.

The United Kingdom's uncodified constitution

Where can information concerning the United Kingdom's constitution be found?

Britain possesses an uncodified constitution. With the exception of the Commonwealth period, 1649–60, there has been no political revolution or fundamental political crisis to justify the writing of a constitution. The processes of government have been subject to evolutionary adjustments enabling them to accommodate major changes, including the agricultural and industrial revolutions in the eighteenth and nineteenth centuries and the expanded role of the state after 1945. There is thus no one document that provides a basic store of knowledge concerning the operations of the branches of government or the rights and liberties of the subject in the United Kingdom. Instead, information of the type normally contained in a constitution is dispersed. There are a wide range of written and unwritten sources to the United Kingdom's constitution.

The sources of Britain's constitution

The main sources of Britain's uncodified constitution are as follows:

Statute law

There are numerous examples of acts of parliament that govern the way in which Britain's system of government operates. Examples include the 1911 and 1949 Parliament Acts (which concern the relationship between the House of Commons and the House of Lords and which specify the powers of the latter chamber) and the 1971 Courts Act (which established the present system of crown courts). Devolved government for Scotland, Wales and Northern Ireland was provided in the 1998 Scotland Act, Northern Ireland Act and the Government of Wales Act and the 1998 Human Rights Act set out the fundamental rights possessed by citizens in the United Kingdom.

European law

Britain's membership of the European Community in 1972 involved the incorporation of the European Convention, the Treaties of Rome and 43 volumes of existing European legislation into United Kingdom law. These provisions and subsequent European legislation perform an important role in determining the operation of the United Kingdom's system of government.

Judicial interpretation

Traditionally, the doctrine of the sovereignty of parliament prevented the United Kingdom courts from declaring parliament's statutes null and void on the grounds that their contents contravened provisions of the constitution. The process of judicial review was solely concerned with determining whether powers derived from statute had been correctly applied by the executive branch of government or by lower tiers of government, such as local authorities. However, the United Kingdom's membership of the European Union involves the courts determining whether parliament's legislation is compatible with European law, which has precedence, and the 1998 Human Rights Act enables judges to assess whether other legislation is compatible with the principles of this legislation.

Common law

Common law derives from historic customs and traditions and from the decisions made by judges when required to interpret the precise meaning of legislation. Many of the liberties of the subject (such as the freedoms of assembly, speech, movement and privacy) are rooted in common law.

Conventions

Many matters concerning the operations of government are governed by practices which have become the accepted way of behaving. One example of this concerns ministerial responsibility, which governs the relationship between the executive and legislative branches of government. One advantage of a convention is that it can be disregarded if circumstances justify this course of action. Harold Wilson's suspension of the principle of collective ministerial responsibility during the referendum campaign on Britain's continued membership of the European Economic Community in 1975 was an example of political expediency overriding normal constitutional practice. This enabled the Labour government to avoid having to take a decision which would have had damaging repercussions for the unity of the Labour Party.

Constitutional reform in the United Kingdom

What constitutional changes have been introduced in the United Kingdom since 1997?

The lack of a codified constitution is of profound significance. With the exception of European legislation there is no constitutional enactment superior to ordinary statute law. Other sources of the constitution are ultimately subordinate to this. Accordingly, the constitution is whatever parliament decrees it to be. This has significant implications for the conduct of government. The actions taken by parliament (and the government which exercises control over it) is limited only by adherence to popular conceptions as to what is correct behaviour. The restraints

---

Ministerial responsibility in the United Kingdom

There are two types of ministerial responsibility. Individual ministerial responsibility concerns the relationship between ministers and the departments they control. As the political head of a department, ministers are expected to be accountable for all actions which it undertakes. If a serious error is committed by that department, the minister may be subject to the parliamentary sanction of having his or her salary reduced, which would result in resignation. This convention does not apply to ministers who resign (or who are forced to resign) as the result of some form of personal indiscretion. It is solely concerned with the formal role which they occupy within a department.

Collective ministerial responsibility embraces the relationship of the entire executive branch to the legislature. It is assumed that major issues of policy, even if associated with one specific department, have been discussed at cabinet level and thus constitute overall government policy. There are two consequences of this. First, ministers are collectively accountable to the House of Commons for all items of government policy. Theirs is a 'one out, all out' relationship. A vote of 'no confidence' in the government requires the resignation of all of its members. Second, while a minister has the right to voice opinions on an issue discussed within the cabinet, once a decision has been reached it is binding on all its participants. A minister who is not in agreement with what has been decided should either resign or 'toe the line' and be prepared publicly to defend the outcome that has been reached.

which Britain's constitution imposes on the workings of government are thus spiritual rather than legalistic.

The constitutional reforms of the 1997 Labour government

The Labour government which was elected in 1997 enacted a number of measures designed to secure constitutional reform. The main changes are discussed below.

Devolution

Devolution measures designed to bring government and the people closer together were contained in three measures enacted in 1998 dealing with Scotland, Wales and Northern Ireland.

The 1998 Scotland Act provided for the creation of a Scottish parliament of 129 members serving a fixed term of four years. This body appointed a first minister who in turn chose other ministers who were responsible to the first minister. The Scottish parliament was able to make laws on all domestic matters including health, education and training, law and home affairs, economic development and transport, local government, environment, agriculture, fisheries and forestry, and sports and the arts. It was financed by the Scottish block grant (which in 1997 was £14.3 billion), supplemented by the 'tartan tax'. This enabled the Scottish parliament to raise some of its own money by slightly varying the standard rate of income tax applied to all who had lived in Scotland for more than half of the year. It was estimated that the revenue from this was £450 million in 1998.

A wide range of matters (including the UK constitution, foreign affairs, fiscal, economic and monetary policy, defence and national security, medical ethics, social security and employment) were reserved to the Westminster parliament. Additionally, the Scottish secretary was empowered to overrule the Scottish parliament and halt legislation believed to be inappropriate and to ensure that the UK's international treaties were implemented in Scotland. The Scotland Act repealed the requirement (currently provided for in 1986 legislation) regarding the minimum number of Scottish MPs at Westminster.

The 1998 Government of Wales Act provided for an assembly of 60 persons. The body chooses a first secretary (*Prif Ysgrifennydd y Cynulliad*) who selects other assembly secretaries. Powers administered by the Welsh Office were transferred to this new body, thereby subjecting them to accountability. The assembly possessed no law-making or independent tax-raising powers and remained totally reliant on the block grant (which in 1997 totalled 6.9 billion pounds). This system thus provided for a system which democratized existing administrative arrangements as opposed to devolution.

The 1998 Northern Ireland Act provided for an assembly of 108 members. The executive was composed of 12 ministers. The first minister and deputy minister were elected by the assembly and the ministers were chosen by a formula designed to ensure that the assembly's executive committee reflected the strength of the parties in the assembly.

The electoral arrangements for these devolved structures of government also reflected the desire to bring government and the people closer together. The Northern Irish assembly was elected on the basis of the single transferable vote. In Scotland and Wales the electoral system was a mixture of the first-past-the-post system topped by additional members elected by the regional party list system.

The 1998 Human Rights Act

The Labour government introduced legislation in 1998 which placed the European Convention for the Protection of Human Rights and Fundamental Freedoms (which was initially drawn up in 1950) into UK law.

Human rights

Human rights consist of the basic entitlements that should be available to all human beings living in any society. Unlike civil rights (which are specific to individual countries) human rights are universal in application.

Human rights developed from the tradition of natural rights which sought to establish boundaries to protect an individual being interfered with by other citizens or by the government and were thus intimately associated with the objective of liberalism that government should be limited in its actions, which was an important aspect of liberal thought. These rights were thus essentially negative, seeking to impose restraints on actions that others might wish to undertake. The English political philosopher, John Locke, suggested that human rights embraced 'life, liberty and property' while the American statesman Thomas Jefferson indicated that they included 'life, liberty and the pursuit of happiness'. These were rights to which all persons were entitled simply as a consequence of being a human being and which no government could take away since to do so would constitute a denial of their humanity.

The European Convention asserted the right to life, liberty, security, the right to respect private and family life (including the right to marry and found a family), the right to a fair trial, the right to freedom of thought, conscience, religion, expression and assembly and prohibited torture, inhuman and degrading treatment, slavery and enforced labour, all forms of discrimination and asserted that there should be no punishment without law. Protocols to this declaration affirmed the right to participate peacefully in processions and the right to education.

Under this legislation, contravention of these rights would constitute an offence: the high court would be empowered to grant damages to plaintiffs whose complaints were upheld. The new law made it illegal for public authorities (including the government, courts and private bodies discharging public functions) to act in contravention of these designated human rights and required public authorities to act positively to defend the rights included in the legislation. The role played by the judiciary in adjudicating human rights matters considerably added to its powers.

In some countries (such as Canada) human rights legislation empowers judges to strike down any legislation which conflicts with such basic principles. This is *not* the case in United Kingdom (save in the case of legislation passed by the Scottish and Welsh parliaments). Under human rights legislation, judges are empowered to declare a law passed by parliament to be 'incompatible with the convention', thus upholding the concept of the sovereignty of parliament. Although it was assumed that declarations of this nature by the courts would induce the government and parliament to introduce corrective measures speedily to bring such complained-of legislation into line with the Convention of Human Rights, there was nothing to prevent either of these bodies from ignoring such rulings. This might induce an aggrieved person to refer the matter to Strasbourg, thus suggesting that the Act has failed substantially to improve the present situation regarding the defence of human rights.

Questions

1 With reference to any country with which you are familiar, give three examples of constitutional conventions, outlining why these are important for the conduct of government in that country.
2 Analyse the key functions which are served by codified constitutions.
3 Based on the discussion in this chapter, outline the key differences between codified and uncodified constitutions.
4 Using newspapers or journals to provide you with examples, assess the impact which the 1998 Human Rights Act has had on the defence of civil liberties in the United Kingdom.

Taking it further

This chapter has examined the importance of constitutions in providing a kind of organizational chart concerning the operations of a country's system of government.

Particular attention has been devoted to the process of constitutional reform in the United Kingdom since the 1997 general election, in particular concerning the devolution of government and human rights. An interesting account of a wide range of constitutional reforms enacted since 1997 is provided by Peter Riddell, *Parliament Under Blair* (London: Politicos Publishing, 2000).

Further information concerning the operations of the devolved governments can be found at:

- Northern Ireland Assembly, Parliament Buildings, Stormont, Belfast, BT4 3XX, Northern Ireland (www.niassembly.gov.uk)
- Scottish Parliament, George IV Bridge, Edinburgh, EH99 1SP, Scotland (www.scottish.parliament.uk)
- National Assembly of Wales, Cardiff Bay, Cardiff, CF99 1NA (www.wales.gov.uk)

Some coverage of the debates of these bodies is also provided by the BBC's *Parliamentary Channel*.

This chapter has argued that human rights are universal in application. Various pressure groups seek to uncover violations of these rights across the world. A particularly influencial organization is Amnesty International which regularly publishes reports into human rights issues. It can be located at 99–119 Rosebery Avenue, London, EC1R 4RE, and its website address is www.amnesty.org.uk.

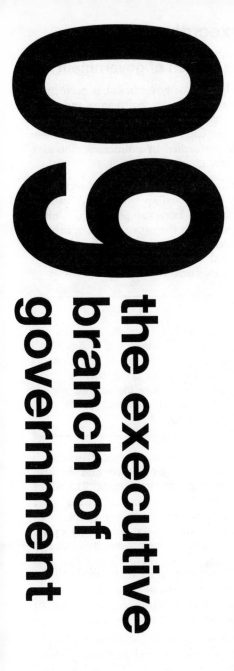

09 the executive branch of government

In this chapter you will learn:
- the functions of the executive branch of government
- the role of chief executives
- the features of presidential and cabinet government

The role of the executive branch

What is the executive branch of government?

The work of the executive branch of government is performed by two distinct sets of people. These are politicians and paid, permanent officials. As we will consider the workings of the latter, termed 'bureaucracy', in Chapter 10, the discussion here will concentrate on the role performed by politicians who give leadership to the executive branch of government.

The political control of a state's affairs is under the direction of a broadly constituted group of political appointees. We usually refer to these as 'the government'. For example, in the United Kingdom the government consists of the prime minister, cabinet and junior ministers. In America it is composed of the president and the cabinet. Within liberal democracies, governments tend to be either parliamentary or executive.

The core executive

The term 'core executive' refers to those bodies, agencies or procedures that are responsible for co-ordinating policy and managing conflict within national government. In the United Kingdom, the core executive includes the prime minister, the cabinet and cabinet committees, the treasury, the cabinet office, government departments and informal meetings which are frequently centred on the prime minister.

In a parliamentary system of government the executive branch of government is drawn from the legislature and is also collectively accountable to this body for its actions. The office of head of state is separate from the chief executive, the latter being the leader of the largest political party (or coalition of parties) commanding support in the legislature who is called upon by the head of state to form a government. Its tenure in office is dependent on retaining the legislature's support, and chief executives typically possess the ability to recommend the dissolution of the legislature to the head of state which triggers a general election. Countries which have this form of government include the United Kingdom and Germany.

In the United Kingdom, the prime minister, members of the cabinet and junior ministers are members of parliament (most being drawn from the House of Commons). The government operates with the consent of parliament and especially the

House of Commons which possesses the ultimate sanction, that of passing a motion of 'no confidence' in it which requires it to resign. In Germany, the chancellor is appointed from the largest party in the *Bundestag* (or the one which is able to construct a coalition which possesses a majority in that house). The chancellor possesses considerable power, which includes control over economic policy, defence and foreign affairs and the appointment of ministers who constitute the federal government.

Executive domination of the legislature often gives prime ministers considerable power in such systems of government. There are, however, limitations to this. A government with a small, or no, majority may have to rely on members drawn from other parties to sustain it in office. In this circumstance, the prime minister may have to agree to demands made by other politicians on whom the government is forced to rely or face the threat of defeat. Coalition government may further restrict a prime minister's power.

A presidential system of government is a political structure in which different personnel compose the executive and legislative branches. The executive branch is elected for a fixed term and also occupies the position of head of state. The legislature has no formal relationship with the executive branch of government other than its ability to remove the president through the process of impeachment and the president does not have the power to dissolve the legislature and call a general election. This system of government is found in both North and South America.

Collective ministerial responsibility

The mechanics of the process of collective ministerial responsibility vary. In the United Kingdom, a vote of 'no confidence' in the government by the House of Commons would usually result in the government's resignation and a general election. This happened in 1979 when the House of Commons expressed no confidence in the Labour government headed by James Callaghan.

To oust a government in Germany, however, the *Bundestag* is required to pass what is known as a 'constructive vote of no confidence'. This entails a vote of no confidence in the chancellor coupled with the selection of a replacement (who is required to obtain an absolute majority vote in the *Bundestag*). This process occurred in 1982 when Chancellor Schmidt was replaced by Chancellor Kohl following the decision of the Free Democrats to form a coalition government with the Christian Democrats.

Presidential powers are limited by the need to secure the legislature's support for certain executive actions. Thus one major problem faced by chief executives is how to mobilize the legislature to secure the attainment of their policy goals.

There are, however, hybrid systems which include elements of parliamentary and presidential systems of government. The French system of government is an example of this, which we now discuss in more detail.

The French system of government

In France the traditional division which exists between parliamentary and presidential systems of government has been obscured by the emergence of dual leadership within the executive branch of government.

The 1958 Constitution established the new office of president with powers additional to those normally associated with a head of state. The president was given a very wide range of functions and powers with which to perform them. These included acting as guarantor of national independence and protecting the functioning of public powers and the continuity of the state. Key duties included appointing the prime minister, presiding over the cabinet and acting as commander-in-chief of the armed forces. Special emergency powers could also be exercised by the president. The power and prestige of the presidency has grown, especially since direct election was introduced in 1962. The 'monarchical drift' of the office was acknowledged by the new president, Jacques Chirac, during the 1995 presidential election. The president serves for a period of seven years and the office is seen as France's key political prize.

The division of power between the president and prime minister is of central importance to an understanding of the operations of the French system of government. A major role of the president is to appoint (and dismiss) the prime minister. A newly appointed prime minister does not have to seek a specific vote of confidence from the national assembly although he or she is accountable to that body. In making such a choice, however, the president is constrained by the political composition of the National Assembly. It follows, therefore, that the power of the president is greatest when the president's party controls the National Assembly, when the prime minister is effectively a presidential nominee.

However, if the party affiliation of the president and the majority in the legislature differ, the president is forced to select a prime minister and a government who enjoy the support of the National Assembly. The prime minister is more likely to be assertive in such situations since he or she possesses a separate power base and is not totally reliant on presidential support to obtain or remain in office. This may thus reduce the president's power and occurred between 1986 and 1988 and between 1993 and 1995, when a socialist president (Mitterrand) was forced to coexist with a right-wing government dominated by the Gaullists. It occurred subsequently (between 1997 and 2002) when the Gaullist President Chirac was forced to appoint the socialist Lionel Jospin as Prime Minister following the latter's victory in the elections to the National Assembly.

In such periods of cohabitation, however, a president is far from impotent. Ultimately, it is possible to dissolve the legislature.

In September 2000, electors voted in a referendum to reduce the presidential term in France to five years. This reform would reduce future periods of cohabitation although potentially sacrificing the greater degree of stability provided when the president serves an elongated term in office.

Relations within the executive branch

How is power allocated within the government?

Leadership within the government is exercised by a chief executive. This person appoints other members of the government and usually exercises a pre-eminent position within it, being regarded as the nation's 'leader'.

Key functions of the chief executive
- The initiation of proposals for government policy. Often these derive from the party's election manifesto, although chief executives are also required to respond to unforeseen issues which require the government's attention.
- Overseeing the administration and execution of policy and the overall conduct of the government. The exercise of this strategic role may mean that the chief executive intervenes in the specific activities performed by individual government departments. As the result of such activities the work of government is given a degree of coherence.

- Mobilizing support for the policies of the government. This may involve liaison with members of the legislature or seeking to rally public opinion in support of government initiatives.
- Acting in times of crisis when decisive action is required. Firm leadership is usually best provided by a single person.
- Appointing (and dismissing) other members of the executive branch.

There are broadly two models which describe the manner in which political power is allocated within the executive branch of government. Power may be held by the chief executive alone. This is the case in America where the president is regarded as the main source of power within the executive branch of government. He is separately elected and can thus claim an electoral mandate to initiate recommendations concerning public policy. Alternatively, power may be held by a group of individuals who include the chief executive and other leading members of the government.

The American cabinet

The American Constitution made no reference to the concept of cabinet government. However, George Washington commenced the practice of holding regular meetings with senior members of his administration. Other presidents followed suit and the cabinet has now become an accepted institution of American political life. However, cabinet government (in the sense of a group of equals meeting regularly and making collective decisions concerning policy) has never assumed the importance attached to it in countries such as the United Kingdom.

The term 'cabinet government' is used to describe this latter situation and is more likely to be found in parliamentary systems of government.

The cabinet is recognized in Germany's Basic Law and given a number of powers. These include the right to introduce legislation and the power to veto laws that increase expenditure or decrease income. In the United Kingdom, there is a strong tradition of cabinet government. This suggests that political power is shared between the chief executive and other members of the government. Major issues of public policy are discussed by all members of the government as a team, presided over by the prime minister. In recent years, however, the nature of cabinet government in this country has been subject to debates which have questioned the ability of a small group of people to determine major issues of policy. It has been suggested that the United Kingdom's system of government has become 'prime ministerial' or 'presidential'. In the following section we examine these arguments in more detail.

How chief executives are chosen

The way in which chief executives are chosen varies widely as the following examples show.

In the United Kingdom, the chief executive is the leader of the largest party following a general election. This person is formally appointed as prime minister by the head of state, the monarch.

In Germany, the chief executive, or chancellor, is elected by the *Bundestag* from the ranks of the largest party or coalition of parties following a national election. It also elects a cabinet.

In the United States, the chief executive is technically directly elected, although this official is theoretically chosen by a body termed the 'electoral college'. Elections to choose the American president are organized by the states. Each of these is allocated a number of votes in the electoral college, which comprises the total number of representatives sent by each state to both houses of Congress. There were 538 electoral college votes for the 2000 presidential election. Popular vote determines which candidate wins a particular state and all of that state's electoral college vote is allocated for that victor regardless of the size of his or her winning majority (although state law in Maine and Nebraska permits the distribution of votes in accordance with the popular vote obtained by each candidate). The electoral college vote is physically cast in Washington by a slate of electors consisting of party officials chosen by the party whose presidential candidate wins the state. These electors are formally approved by each state legislature and are pledged to support the candidate who won their state (although in only 16 states are individual electors required by state law to cast their votes for that candidate). The votes cast in the electoral college are transmitted to the Senate, which counts them and formally declares the result of the presidential election.

Cabinet government in the United Kingdom

Why has it been alleged that the role of the cabinet has declined in modern government and how valid are these arguments?

The extent to which the cabinet operates as the decision-making body at the very heart of government, exercising general superintendence over policy and providing cohesion to its affairs, has been questioned. The following arguments have been put forward to explain the decline of cabinet government in the United Kingdom.

Ministerial pre-occupation with individual departments

It is argued that most members of the cabinet are preoccupied with the task of running their departments and thus lack the time or the inclination to involve themselves in affairs other than those with which they are directly concerned. Further, ministers in charge of departments may become parochial and seek to advance their department's interests, which may be to the detriment of concern for overall planning.

Government by clique

It has also been asserted that the extent of the work of contemporary government and its specialized nature means that decisions are made in forums other than at cabinet meetings which are usually held weekly. These alternative arenas of policy making include cabinet committees, which operate within the framework of the cabinet system. Alternatively, decisions may be made using more informal structures which may be divorced from the structure of the cabinet. These include liaison between ministers, or informal groupings centred on the prime minister which may comprise ministers and other advisers. It is thus asserted that the cabinet becomes sidelined and collective decision making is replaced by cliques centred on the prime minister.

> **Cabinet committees**
>
> These enable ministers or civil servants to examine issues in depth, perhaps reporting the conclusions of their deliberations to the full cabinet. There are two types of such committees, permanent and ad hoc, and these are serviced by the cabinet secretariat. Key committees are chaired either by the prime minister or the deputy prime minister.

Prime ministerial government

It is also argued that modern prime ministers dominate the proceedings of their governments. General elections tend to place considerable prominence on the party leader thus enhancing the status of that person should he or she become prime minister. The prime minister possesses the power to appoint and dismiss other members of the government and manages the workings of the cabinet through the control of the agenda and summing up its proceedings. The development of a prime ministerial office has further increased the power of this official by providing a bureaucracy which gives advice on major issues of policy. This ensures that the prime minister possesses much information on the key affairs of state. It is thus argued that the United Kingdom's government has become prime ministerial or even presidential in nature.

The continued vitality of cabinet government

However, the argument that cabinet government has declined in the United Kingdom is not universally accepted. The style or character of individual prime ministers has a bearing on the extent to which they wish to exercise initiative or resort to the teamwork of cabinet government to decide major policy issues. Further, prime ministers need to be wary of conduct that can be viewed as overbearing by their cabinet colleagues. Resignations can have a significant impact on the prime minister's hold on office. Sir Geoffrey Howe's resignation from Prime Minister Thatcher's government in November 1990 had a major impact on the vitality of her administration and her replacement by John Major later that year.

It is also alleged that although the role of the cabinet has changed, it retains an important role in the affairs of modern government. It provides a mechanism for leading members of the government to be made aware of key political issues and provides the semblance of a unified government involved in collective decision making. The cabinet may also act as a final court of appeal to arbitrate disputes between ministers.

The power of chief executives

What factors govern the ability of chief executives to achieve their political objectives?

It is often assumed that chief executives occupy a dominant position in the political system from which they are able successfully to advance initiatives designed to achieve their objectives or those of the government they head. In this section we consider the difficulties that chief executives in the United Kingdom and America may encounter when seeking to advance their political aims and which thus serve as constraints on their power.

The United Kingdom prime minister

It is frequently asserted that the prime minister possesses considerable control over the conduct of political affairs in the United Kingdom. However, while there are few formal restraints on this office, the prime minister is subject to a range of informal pressures which may greatly limit that person's power. These are discussed in the sections that follow.

Control of parliament

The parliamentary situation may restrict the ability of a prime minister to achieve political objectives. The prime minister is the leader of the majority party in parliament, which means that the chief executive's ability to exercise control over political affairs is potentially greatest when that party has a sizeable majority in the House of Commons. A government with a small, or no, majority may have to rely on members drawn from other parties to sustain it in the regular votes which occur. In this circumstance, the prime minister may have to agree to demands made by other politicians on whom the government is forced to rely.

Unity of the parliamentary party

A prime minister's power may also be affected by the unity of his or her parliamentary party. Internal divisions may exercise considerable influence on the composition of the government and a prime minister may be constrained to ensure that party balance is reflected in its make-up. A disunited parliamentary party may make it difficult for the prime minister to secure the passage of policies through the House of Commons. Discontented members may abstain, vote against their own party or even defect to the opposition. This may increase the government's reliance on other parties to secure parliamentary victory. While a prime minister may threaten to quell revolts by the threat of dissolving parliament and holding a general election, this is a double-edged sword and is rarely a credible sanction which can be deployed.

Public opinion

Public opinion may also affect the power of the prime minister. Prime ministers may find it easiest to assert themselves when there is a demonstrable degree of support from the electorate for themselves and the governments which they head. When the level of this support declines (tested in opinion polls, parliamentary by-elections or local government elections) a prime minister is in a weaker position. Accordingly, the ability to manipulate the media is of crucial importance to a contemporary prime minister. Margaret Thatcher's Press Secretary, Bernard Ingham, performed a major role between 1979 and 1990 in bolstering the power of the prime minister and, as Chapter 7 has argued, the Labour government, elected in 1997, subsequently made considerable use of 'spin doctors' in order to maximize the appeal of their policies.

Cabinet reshuffles

Cabinet reshuffles involve a prime minister sacking ministers when a government is experiencing unpopularity within the electorate. The implication of this action is that the ministers who have been dismissed are responsible for the government's difficulties and have been traditionally used by prime ministers in many liberal democracies in an attempt to increase the level of public support for themselves and the governments which they head. In September 1995, the French Prime Minister, Alain Juppé, dismissed 13 ministers in an attempt to reverse the decline in popularity experienced by his government.

The loss of public support may not necessarily affect the conduct of the prime minister. This to a large extent depends on that person's nerve as to whether to ignore the loss of support and continue with existing policies or whether to bow to public pressure and make changes in either the personnel or the policy of the government.

The American president

The American Constitution placed the executive branch in the hands of a president who is now directly elected. The president serves a term of four years and may be re-elected on one further occasion. The power exercised by a president depends to some extent on personal choice. Presidents may view themselves as an official who should merely enforce the laws passed by Congress, or they may see themselves as a dynamic initiator of public policy. These views are further flavoured by popular opinion.

The belief that American presidents should be strong and assertive in the conduct of public affairs was bolstered by the need for decisive presidential action to cope with the Depression in the 1930s. But this view has subsequently been revised by the perceived failings of strong presidents as revealed by the outcome of the Vietnam War (which was associated with presidential initiative) and the belief that strong executive action could lead to abuse of power, as was evidenced in Watergate and the subsequent forced resignation of President Nixon in 1974. Such factors have tended to make the public suspicious of presidents who wish to exercise dynamic leadership. Their ability to initiate actions was further weakened by the size of the budget deficit, which grew enormously during the Reagan–Bush years (1980–92) and served as a constraint on policies involving state intervention.

Such considerations have greatly affected the climate within which contemporary presidents operate. But even within such a climate, presidents retain a considerable degree of manoeuvre. They possess a range of formal and informal powers and may also exploit their position as the only national unifying force to secure the attainment of their objectives. We shall now consider a range of factors that have a bearing on the power of a modern president.

The president's mandate

The mandate that a president obtains in a general election may greatly influence subsequent behaviour. A president may feel it is legitimate to exercise the initiative in public affairs when the outcome of an election provides a clear statement of public support for a stated programme. When the outcome of an election is less clear (for example, the president fails to secure a majority of the popular vote) or it appears that the result was more concerned with the rejection of one candidate than with the popular endorsement of the winner, the president may find it more difficult to promote policy vigorously especially when this involves initiating radical changes. The initial power of President George W. Bush was undermined by the lack of a mandate. He secured victory in the 2000 presidential election by the very narrow margin of five electoral college votes. Not only did his Democratic rival in the 2000 presidential election, Al Gore, secure over 500,000 more popular votes nationwide, but considerable concern remained regarding the legitimacy of Bush's victory in the key state of Florida. However, a surge of patriotic fervour triggered by the terrorist attack in September 2001 and the determination of Bush to pursue military action against Iraq enabled the Republicans to regain control of both Houses of Congress in the 2002 mid-term elections and provided Bush with a mandate to pursue a right-wing policy offensive.

Clearly focused policy goals

Presidential success in initiating public policy may be most easily realized when policy goals are clearly focused. This suggests a limited set of key objectives which enable both Congress and public opinion in general to appreciate the president's fundamental concerns. It has been argued that President Carter (1977–81) put forward too disparate a range of proposals at the outset of his presidency, which presented a confusing statement of presidential objectives. Accordingly, President Reagan (1981–89) presented a programme which included fewer key issues. Subsequently, relations with Congress were fashioned around achieving these. The initial efforts of President Clinton (1993–2001) to focus on domestic policy issues was impeded by the emergence of defence and foreign policy issues (including the Bosnian crisis) which demanded attention at the expense of the original objectives.

Relations with congress

A president's relations with Congress have a fundamental bearing on that official's power. The president (unlike the United Kingdom's prime minister) has no direct connection with the legislature and Congress may not be inclined to follow the presidential lead. Congress has become more assertive since the

1970s which has been to the detriment of presidents seeking to exercise a dominant role in both domestic and foreign affairs.

In domestic affairs, legislation such as the 1974 Budget and Impoundment Control Act introduced innovations designed to enable Congress to compete with the president in the preparation of the budget. In foreign affairs (which had been traditionally dominated by the president) legislation such as the 1973 War Powers Act and the 1976 National Emergencies Act limited the scope of presidential initiative. Congress control over appropriations was used to stop aid to the Nicaraguan rebels in 1987. The end of the 'cold war' has further influenced Congressional involvement in foreign affairs, one example of this being the vote of both Houses of Congress in 1995 to overrule the president's policy of an embargo on the sale of arms to Bosnia.

Theoretically, the party system might secure a degree of support for the president from within Congress, but this does not operate in the same way as it does in the United Kingdom. Changes to the process by which presidential candidates are nominated and the manner in which presidential election campaigns are financed has been to the detriment of the relationship between a president and established party organization. Further, parochialism exerts considerable influence over the conduct of members of Congress. Thus, they may be more willing to follow the president's lead when they feel this will bring personal political benefits to them but be inclined to distance themselves from the administration if they feel that association with the president constitutes an electoral liability.

Thus, even when the president's party controls both Houses of Congress, this is no guarantee that all members of that party will support the president on every major policy initiative. President Carter, for example, did not construct good working relationships with his own party which controlled both Houses of Congress throughout his presidency. However, the position of the president is weaker when the opposition party controls either or both Houses of Congress. This is a position of 'gridlock' which post-war Republican presidents frequently had to endure and which President Clinton had to suffer for much of his presidency following the loss of Democrat majorities in both Houses in the November 1994 Congressional elections.

'Divided government' in America

In a situation of 'divided government' there is no onus on the Congressional majority to aid the passage of the president's programme and their own leadership might attempt to seize the initiative in policy making. In the period after November 1994 (when the Democrats performed badly in the mid-term Congressional elections) the Republican Speaker of the House of Representatives, Newt Gingrich, and the Republican majority leader in the Senate, Robert Dole, exercised a role in policy initiation which seemed to eclipse that exerted by President Clinton.

In this situation, presidents may seek to bargain with Congress in order to retain some influence over the legislative process. If Congress puts forward legislative proposals, the president is able to veto them. Although Congress may be able to override this veto, the threat or actuality of using it may trigger off a process of bargaining between the president and Congressional opposition. In 1997, co-operation between President Clinton and the Republican majority in Congress enabled the first nominally balanced budget to be achieved since the late 1960s.

However, divided government may result in neither side being willing to give way to the other. The inability of President Clinton and Congress to resolve disagreements on the budget in 1995 led to a shutdown in government in which federal employees were sent home when conditions attached by Congress for the approval of government expenditure were rejected by the president.

Conclusion – how presidents may achieve their goals

Contemporary presidents may seek to overcome the difficulties which impede the attainment of their goals in a number of ways. In situations of 'divided' and 'unified' government, a president is required to build coalitions within Congress to secure the passage of key legislation. It is a process which has been complicated by Congressional reforms initiated after Watergate, especially in connection with the committee system, which have tended to disperse power within Congress. This has made it harder for a president to manage this body through relationships forged with a relatively small number of senior, influential members of Congress.

This process of coalition building often involves securing support from politicians of different political allegiances by lobbying, persuading or even coercing them to support the president. The importance attached by presidents in working with their political opponents was evidenced in 2001 when President George W. Bush took the unprecedented step of addressing Democratic members of the House of Representatives at their private annual retreat. Presidents may need to construct coalitions on an issue-by-issue basis which has become a key feature of the so-called 'no win' presidency. Presidents such as Lyndon Johnson were able to conduct this 'wheeling and dealing' successfully especially in connection with his 'Great Society' programme. Others whose political experience was different (such as President Carter who was elected as an 'outsider' to Washington politics) were less successful coalition builders and found problems in persuading Congress to implement their programmes.

Relations with the media may also influence a president's power. A popular president is likely to find it easier to secure support within Congress for the administration's policies and traditionally presidents went to great lengths to ensure that they received favourable treatment by the media. However, in the post-Watergate period the media have become prone to subjecting the president to critical analysis. There are ways to counter this, in particular by seeking to ensure that the president's message is not mediated by the media but is heard (or received) directly by the people. This technique was particularly developed by President F. D. Roosevelt (1933–45) whose 'fireside chats' enabled him to address his message directly into the homes of the American people. Such tactics may enable a president to circumvent obstacles which threaten to impede the progress of key policies. Nonetheless, the ability of the media to subject the president to critical analysis is an important force which may weaken the president in the eyes of the population.

A president may also govern through the use of executive orders which enable the president to act without having to consult Congress. Executive orders cover a wide range of circumstances, which include implementing the provisions of the Constitution, to treaties and to statutes. They may also be used to create or modify the organization or procedures of administrative agencies. The president's power to issue such orders derives from precedents, custom and constitutional interpretation and particularly from discretionary powers embodied in legislation passed by Congress. The United Kingdom equivalent of executive orders is the use of the Royal prerogative, but its usage is more restricted.

The American vice-presidency

The American constitution provided for a vice-president who would take over on the 'death, resignation or inability' of the president. The circumstances under which this official would assume the office of president was subsequently expanded upon in the 25th amendment, passed in 1967. Otherwise the vice-president's main function was to act as president of the senate with the power to vote when there was a tie.

Traditionally, the office has not been highly regarded. When Lyndon Johnson considered Kennedy's offer of the vice-presidency in 1960, he contacted John Garner who had occupied this post under President Roosevelt from 1933–41. Garner reputedly informed Johnson that the office was not worth 'a pitcher of warm spit'. However, some recent presidents have given their vice-presidents a more significant role and initially the vast political experience of Vice-President Cheney, compared to the relative inexperience of President George W. Bush (particularly in Washington politics), resulted in the former playing a major role in political affairs in the early part of the latter's administration.

Service as vice-president is no guarantee of becoming president when the incumbent retires. In 1988 George Bush was the first serving vice-president to be elected president since Martin Van Buren in 1836, and in 2000 Vice-President Al Gore failed in his attempt to replace President Clinton when he had served his two terms in office.

The chief executive's bureaucracy

What is meant by the term 'chief executive's bureaucracy' and why is it needed by contemporary chief executives?

The scope of contemporary government requires those exercising control over it to possess detailed knowledge of complex and technical policy areas. Bureaucracies have thus been developed to serve the chief executive, enabling him or her to exert overall control within the executive branch of government. These fulfil a number of functions which include the provision of advice on policy matters. This gives the chief executive expertise which may provide leverage in dealings with the civil service employed elsewhere within the executive branch. Their role also includes performing functions designed to secure the success of policy initiatives put forward by the chief executive and may actually implement policy in certain areas.

Problems associated with chief executives' bureaucracies

While personalized bureaucracies give chief executives a greater ability to assert control over governments, we should note that there are problems associated with the role that these bodies perform. One major difficulty with such machinery is its size. As the number of staff which are employed within such bodies grows, it becomes increasingly difficult for the chief executive to maintain control over its work. This was a major problem for President Reagan whose personal reputation suffered in the 'Iran–Contra' affair. The President was held responsible for the actions of others that were undertaken in his name. A further danger is that such bureaucracies may insulate the chief executive from outside pressures to such an extent that they lose touch with the 'real world'. This may damage chances of re-election to office.

A final difficulty is that the role performed by the chief executive's advisers may eclipse that of departments headed by leading members of the government. President Nixon's national security adviser in his first term, Dr Henry Kissinger, had a national and international profile which surpassed that of the secretary of state. Leading politicians may resent being effectively sidelined by an entourage of unelected advisers and this friction may have damaging repercussions for the stability of the government. In 1989, the British Chancellor of the Exchequer, Nigel Lawson, resigned because of the influence exerted by Prime Minister Thatcher's adviser on economic affairs, Sir Alan Walters.

Examples of bureaucracies serving chief executives

In America, President Roosevelt established the Executive Office of the President in 1939. This contains three bodies – the National Security Council, the Council of Economic Advisors and the Office of Management and Budget. Their work is supplemented by the White House Staff which contains the key aides seen on a regular basis by the president.

The German chancellor has a personal department, the *Bundeskanzleramt*. This body is chiefly responsible for co-ordinating, planning and implementing policy and also ensures that the chancellor's policies are disseminated throughout the party and to the general public.

The French president has a presidential office, the General Secretariat of the Presidency, which includes a number of advisors. There is also the *cabinet du président* which contains personal presidential aides.

The British prime minister has the Prime Minister's Office. This contains a policy unit (sometimes referred to as the 'Number 10 Policy Unit') which gives advice, monitors and develops policy. The Prime Minister's Office gives the prime minister detailed knowledge of the affairs of government and enhances his or her ability to initiate policy and exert central control over the affairs of government.

Heads of state

What is a head of state, and what does this official do?

There is considerable variety within liberal democracies concerning the office of head of state. In countries such as Britain the head of state is a constitutional monarch, whose position is derived from birth. In other countries the head of state is elected. This may be direct election (as is the case in Ireland) or indirect election (as is the case in Italy where the president is elected by a college of 'grand electors' which includes members of both houses of parliament and regional governments). In most liberal democracies, the office of head of state is separate from that of chief executive, although in America the president occupies both roles.

A head of state performs important roles in the functioning of a liberal democracy. This official stands above party politics and constitutes the physical embodiment of the nation. This enables the head of state to provide a rallying point for national unity, which may be especially important in times of crisis or where national unity is undermined by separatist tendencies. Additionally, the head of state ensures that the system of government operates smoothly and efficiently. Many of the functions traditionally performed by a head of state are not controversial. These include receiving ambassadors from abroad or presiding over a range of official or ceremonial functions.

Typically, heads of state appoint chief executives or signify the formal approval of legislation. In most cases these are formal endorsements of decisions that have already been made, but the participation of the head of state to some extent neutralizes the party political dimension of the activity. The involvement of a head of state in selecting a chief executive, for example, seeks to suggest that this official serves the whole nation rather than the political interests which were responsible for securing the office for that person. A head of state usually possesses the ability to intervene in the conduct of political affairs. This intervention may seek to get a particularly contentious issue further examined, or the head of state may possess certain reserve powers (such as the ability to dismiss the government or dissolve the legislature) which serve to make the executive branch accountable to a higher authority for its actions. These powers are particularly important when there is an impasse in government.

An elected head of state may seek to use the authority derived from the position of an apolitical national leader into power and seek to exercise a major role in a country's political life. Mary Robinson used her tenure as President of Ireland (1990–1997) to promote radical politics which improved the position of the needy and remedied the perception of women as second-class citizens.

In the following section we consider the role of the constitutional monarchy in Britain and the Commonwealth countries.

The United Kingdom monarchy

The United Kingdom monarch is head of state and also head of the Commonwealth. Criticisms have been directed at this institution both from within the United Kingdom and also within the Commonwealth, most notably in Australia, where a referendum was held in 1999 that narrowly rejected establishing a republic.

Critics argue that the monarchy instils society with values that are inappropriate for a liberal democracy. It transforms 'citizens' into 'subjects' and, in particular, suggests that birth rather than merit is a key determinant of a person's social position. The monarchy has also been condemned on grounds of cost. This has been compared unfavourably with other European constitutional monarchies, for example in Spain or the 'bicycling monarchies' found in Scandinavia. A key issue concerns the costs of the court. In response to such criticisms it was announced in November 1992 that Queen Elizabeth would pay tax on her personal income and would assume responsibility for the payments made from the Civil List to most members of the Royal Family. But although the Civil List voted by parliament is a declining source of royal finance, public money is provided from other sources including government departments. In 2000, this amounted to approximately £30 million.

Further criticisms have been levelled against the monarchy for the role it performs in contemporary government. On the one hand, it is alleged that many actions performed by the monarch are ceremonial (such as the state opening of parliament) or are performed at the behest of others (such as granting royal pardons, which are determined by the home secretary). On the other, fears are sometimes voiced concerning the monarch's intervention (or potential involvement) in political affairs. The monarch's choice of prime minister in the United Kingdom is normally confined to the leader of the largest party following a general election. However, if third parties assume a more dominant role in future years, the monarch may be required to intervene more frequently in the conduct of political affairs as has been the case in Belgium and the Netherlands. This involvement may extend to decisions relating to the dissolution of parliament or the dismissal of a prime minister. Although no British prime minister has been dismissed by the monarch in recent years, the Australian Prime Minister, Gough Whitlam, was sacked in 1975 by the Queen's representative in Australia, the Governor-General, Sir John Kerr.

A final criticism relates to the alleged remoteness of the contemporary monarchy. The extent to which the monarchy

The royal prerogative

The existence of the monarchy justifies the continuance of the royal prerogative. This gives the British government the ability to act in a number of matters without having to consult with parliament. Declarations of war or the occasional use of troops in strikes are examples of actions undertaken by governments based on the use of the royal prerogative.

Although there have been reforms designed to introduce an element of accountability into the use of the royal prerogative (such as making the work of the intelligence services accountable to Parliament in the 1994 Intelligence Services Act) it is argued that it is essentially inconsistent with the operations of a liberal democratic political system since ministers may act without having to consult parliament.

understands the needs and expectations of its subjects in the late twentieth century was starkly questioned by events relating to the death of Diana, Princess of Wales, in 1997. Not only did the Princess possess a 'common touch' in her dealings with ordinary people in a wide range of scenarios far more diverse than the orchestrated 'walkabout', but the importance attached to protocol ensured that royal palaces (initially at Balmoral and latterly at Buckingham Palace) were the only major public buildings in the country not to lower their flags to half-mast as a gesture of respect when she died. Only when the Queen had left Buckingham Palace for the Princess's funeral was it felt possible to substitute the Royal Standard for the Union Flag which could be flown at half mast in accordance with protocol.

Arguments referred to in preceding sections have led to demands for a head of state who is politically accountable for his or her actions. Opinion polls, however, suggest that the monarchy continues to enjoy a relatively high level of public approval. Supporters will claim that much of the ceremony attached to the institution aids the tourist industry, while royal tours abroad help exports. The non-partisan nature of the monarchy may also be depicted as a source of strength enabling governments to receive impartial advice from a seasoned political observer, giving the nation a symbol to rally around. This may be important in times of national emergency, such as war, or on occasions of national rejoicing such as the VE and VJ celebrations held in 1995.

Reform of the monarchy

The 'Way Ahead' group of royal advisers was established in 1992 in an attempt to respond to criticisms of the monarchy. The role of this body is to review the state of the monarchy. It is presided over by the Queen and is attended by other senior members of the Royal Family.

The need for reforms became more pressing following the death of Diana, Princess of Wales, in 1997. Opinion polls revealed popular unease over the monarchy in the wake of the tragedy. An ICM poll in the *Daily Mail* on 18 October 1997 revealed that 70 per cent of Britons felt the Queen should consider retiring and handing over to a younger successor rather than delaying the issue of succession until after her death. This poll also indicated that 46 per cent of the nation felt that Prince Charles should succeed, but the high figure of 44 per cent believed he should step aside for his elder son. Concerns that the monarchy was remote from the public resulted in the appointment of a royal director of communications in early 1998. Suggestions were also put forward by the 'Way Ahead' group in 1998 to facilitate progress towards developing a 'people's monarchy'. These included restricting the future use of the title of 'His or Her Royal Highness' to children of the sovereign and the heir to the throne and abolishing the procedures of bowing and curtseying to members of the Royal Family.

Questions

1 Use examples from countries possessing presidential and parliamentary systems of government to examine what the main differences are between these two forms of government.
2 Assess the importance of cabinet government in any country with which you are familiar.
3 Based on the accounts of either the United Kingdom prime minister or the American president as given in this chapter, what do you consider to be the main factors which limit the ability of modern chief executives to secure their political goals? How might these limitations be overcome?
4 Consider the strengths and weaknesses of heads of state who are directly elected.

Taking it further

This chapter has concentrated on those who implement decisions, and has drawn particular attention to the American system of presidential government and the British tradition of cabinet government. More detailed studies of the workings of the executive branches of government in America can be found in David Mervin, *The President of the United States* (Hemel Hempstead: Prentice Hall/Harvester Wheatsheaf, 1993), Jon Roper, *The American Presidents* (Edinburgh: Edinburgh University Press, 2000) and Fred Greenstein, *The Presidential Difference* (Princeton, New Jersey: Princeton University Press, 2001).

The operations of the executive branch of government in the United Kingdom is discussed in works which include Roderick Rhodes and Patrick Dunleavy (editors), *Prime Minister, Cabinet and Core Executive* (Basingstoke: Macmillan/Palgrave, 1995), Simon James, *British Cabinet Government* (London: Routledge, 1999) and Dennis Kavanagh and Anthony Seldon, *The Powers Behind the Prime Minister: The Hidden Influence of Number 10* (London: HarperCollins, 2001).

An important debate in the United Kingdon centres on assertions that prime ministerial government is becoming increasingly presidentialized. This issue is considered in Graham Allen, *The Last Prime Minister – Being Honest About the UK Presidency* (London: Politicos Publishing, 2001).

The President of America has a website located at www.whitehouse.gov. In the United Kingdom, up-to-date information concerning the Prime Minister's Office can be found on the 10 Downing Street website at www.number-10.gov.uk.

10

the bureaucracy

In this chapter you will learn:
- what is meant by the terms 'bureaucracy' and 'bureaucrats'
- how civil servants influence policy making
- the key issues affecting the reform of the civil service

The role of the bureaucracy

Who are bureaucrats and what role do they perform in contemporary government?

This aspect of our study concerns the administrative arm of the executive branch of government. Here the work is performed by paid officials whom we term 'bureaucrats'. Many of these are categorized as civil servants. This means that key matters such as recruitment, pay, promotion, grading, dismissal and conditions of work are subject to common regulations which operate throughout the national government within which they work. Such common regulations are enforced centrally by bodies such as the American Office of Personnel Management or the United Kingdom's Civil Service Commission.

Civil servants perform a variety of roles in liberal democratic states, but there are two which have traditionally been emphasized: they give advice to those who exercise control of the political arm of the executive branch on the content of policy; they may also be responsible for implementing it. The implementation of policy is carried out at all levels of government and includes the delivery of a service to the public (such as the payment of welfare benefits).

Bureaucracies employ large numbers of people within government agencies and departments. Efficiency in administration requires rational organization. Max Weber suggested that the ideal bureaucracy would be organized according to a number of principles. He suggested that appointments should be determined on the basis of tests and not patronage, that bureaucratic decision making should be characterized by the impersonal application of established rules and procedures (the term 'red tape' being commonly used to describe the consequences of this method of operation), that the structure should be hierarchical with each bureaucrat occupying a defined place in a chain of command and that bureaucracies should operate on the basis of technical expertise.

The development of the bureaucracy differs from one country to another. Initially, jobs in government service were often allocated through the patronage system. Thus, people were employed on the basis of personal or family contacts rather than their ability to perform efficiently the tasks their job involved. This system, in which political loyalty was more important than personal competence, tended to promote inefficiency in the operations of the public sector. It was a problem which many countries addressed during the nineteenth century. In the following sections we briefly examine the experience of two countries – the United Kingdom and America.

Civil service reform in the United Kingdom

The major impetus to the reform of the nineteenth-century civil service in the United Kingdom was provided by a commission which included Sir Stafford Northcote and Sir Charles Trevelyan. This reported in 1854 and recommended that a distinction should be drawn between routine work and work that required intellectual ability. It was suggested that the latter should be carried out by appointees who were chosen on the basis of their performance in an examination of a literary kind, based on subjects studied at the universities. In 1855, three civil service commissioners were appointed to conduct such examinations, which in 1870 were made open to all suitably qualified members of the general public.

This report gave the United Kingdom civil service certain key characteristics. These were the generalist tradition of the higher civil service (in which the ability to implement decisions was given a higher priority than expertise in policy areas), permanence (which viewed the job as a career performed by servants of the Crown rather than a temporary position dependent on political patronage), neutrality (which derived from the permanence principle and suggested that a civil servant could serve any government impartially, regardless of its politican complexion) and anonymity (whereby ministers were publicly accountable for the actions undertaken by the government departments and civil servants traditionally remained silent on issues affecting public policy). The generalist tradition also facilitated movement of civil servants between government departments, thus fostering the concept of a unified civil service.

Civil service reform in America

Political patronage also influenced the appointment, promotion and dismissal of those employed in American federal public service for much of the nineteenth century. President Andrew Jackson played a key role in developing the 'spoils system' when he assumed office in 1829. This viewed public office as a legitimate prize with which politicians could reward their supporters. Only towards the end of that century did pressure exerted by bodies such as the National Civil Service Reform League succeed in promoting change. In 1883 the Pendleton Act established the Civil Service Commission (later renamed the Office of Personnel Management). This was a bipartisan board of three members which was charged with setting examinations that a candidate had to pass as a condition of appointment into certain civil service jobs. Initially, a relatively limited number of posts were affected by this reform, but the number expanded during the twentieth century. Today the bulk of civil service posts are covered by 'civil service rules' operated by the Office of Personnel Management. The main criterion for obtaining a job is merit displayed in a competitive examination.

A further characteristic of the American civil service is political neutrality. Under the provisions of the 1939 and 1940 Hatch Acts, civil servants are forbidden to take any active part in political management or political campaigns. However, this situation is offset by the situation that a considerable number of posts in the federal government's civil service remain at the disposal of a president. In 2001, President George W. Bush was able to appoint around 8,000 'patronage jobs' that change hands in Washington with the arrival of a new administration.

The machinery of government

How is the machinery of government organized?

The existence of government departments is sometimes determined by legislation. In Ireland, for example, the 1924 Ministers and Secretaries Act provided the legal basis for the establishment of the departments of state and the allocation of work between them. Chief executives may possess the ability to initiate reorganization to the structure of government by abolishing existing departments, creating new ones or reallocating the tasks of government between departments. However, political constraints frequently restrict the scope of such changes. This tends to mean that changes made by a chief executive to the structure of government are often of an incremental nature, marginally adjusting, but not radically overhauling, the organization which existed when the chief executive assumed office. We examine this proposition by considering the case of the United Kingdom.

The deployment of civil servants

The civil service is a hierarchical organization which utilizes common structures such as grades and classes to establish a chain of command and to differentiate work according to the complexity of the tasks involved. A key distinction exists between those who perform routine administrative or clerical duties and the higher civil servants who liaise with ministers and are the managers of government departments.

Civil servants working for national governments perform their work in a variety of bodies. Many are employed in government departments or in agencies which have a formal reporting relationship with departments. Political control over departments and their related organizations is exercised by a person appointed by the chief executive. This person is frequently termed a 'minister' or (in America) a 'secretary'.

The organization of the machinery of government in the United Kingdom

In this section we consider the organization of central government in the United Kingdom. We are using this country as a case study to examine the principles that have been applied by successive prime ministers to organize government departments. This entails allocating the tasks performed by government to specific departments.

Non-rational considerations, such as a prime minister's desire to emphasize a commitment to a particular policy area, the need to ensure that major responsibilities are evenly distributed between senior political colleagues and the preferences of pressure groups, play an important part in determining the way in which government departments are organized. Such political pressures may promote change or prevent it from occurring. Nonetheless, attempts have been made to organize the British machinery of government in a logical manner.

The expanded role of the state during the First World War prompted the Prime Minister, David Lloyd George, to appoint a Machinery of Government Committee, headed by Lord Haldane, to consider the organization of government departments. This committee reported in 1919. Haldane considered two alternative methods – organizing departments around a specific category of citizen whose needs were handled by a department (which was termed the 'client principle') or according to a particular service delivered by a department. His report recommended the latter method of organization which tended to justify the existence of departments whose range of policy was relatively narrow.

The increase of state functions during and after the Second World War thus resulted in the creation of a large number of separate government departments. As the ministers who headed them could not all be included in a prime minister's cabinet (since to do so would have created a body too large for decision making), this body's role as the co-ordinator of the entire work of government was placed in jeopardy. Various expedients were put forward in an attempt to remedy this problem. Churchill introduced the 'overlord system' in 1951 which involved the appointment of three co-ordinating ministers to represent at cabinet level the interests of a number of departments that retained their independent status. The blurred nature of responsibility between the departmental minister and the overlord led to the abandonment of this system in 1953. It was followed in the 1960s by physically merging departments whose responsibilities were related. In 1964, the Ministry of Defence was established, followed by the Foreign and Commonwealth Office and the Department of Health and Social Security in 1968. The term 'giant department' described the expanded policy areas controlled by these bodies.

The advantage possessed by giant departments was that they enabled a prime minister to ensure that all major areas of government activity were represented at cabinet level. However, the size of these departments (measured in terms of the staff they employed and the range of policy embraced within them) raised doubts as to whether effective managerial or political control could be exerted over them.

In 1970, the newly-elected Conservative government produced a white paper, entitled *The Reorganization of Central Government*. This proposed organizing the machinery of government according to what was termed the 'functional principle'. This principle was summarized by the assertion that 'organization should be the servant of policy' and implied that the machinery of government should be structured according to specific objectives which ministers wished to achieve. Its main benefit was stated to be that the planning and implementation of a programme would be in one set of hands rather than being shared between a number of departments with the inevitable problems of co-ordination and communication.

In practice, however, the white paper did not initiate any major departure in the manner in which government departments were organized. The two new organizations that were established (the Department of the Environment and the Department of Trade and Industry) were essentially giant departments in the mould of those created during the 1960s.

Subsequently, changes have been made to departmental organization with the creation of new departments (such as National Heritage in 1992 and Culture, Media and Sport in 1997), the division or abolition of existing departments and the reallocation of functions between them. A major change was the abolition of the Department of Employment in 1995 and the reallocation of its main functions between the Department of Trade and Industry and the renamed Department of Education and Employment which was subsequently renamed the Department for Education and Skills. But these alterations have not been based on any attempt to recast the structure of government according to any rational principle or formula.

Civil service influence over policy making

Do civil servants act as policy makers?

This question compels us to consider whether the theoretical division between politics and administration is a meaningful one. In theory, senior civil servants give advice to politicians but it is the latter who make decisions. The role of the civil service then becomes that of implementing these decisions. The key issue concerns the extent to which the provision of advice by senior civil servants enables them to dominate the policy-making process. It is argued that the role of civil servants sometimes goes beyond the mere provision of advice and entails the exertion of a considerable degree of influence over the content of public policy. Civil servants act both as policy makers and policy implementators.

The accusation that civil servants usurped (that is, took over without lawful authority) the role which ought to be fulfilled by politicians within the executive branch of government has been voiced in the United Kingdom in recent years. An extreme form of this argument has been that senior civil servants might conspire to prevent ministers from pursuing a course of action which they wished to embark upon. We examine this argument in greater detail in following paragraphs.

Minister–civil servant relationships in the United Kingdom

The aim of this discussion is to consider why and how civil servants might occupy a dominant position in policy making.

Civil servants are permanent officials with expertise (either of a policy area or of the workings of the administrative machine). Ministers hold office temporarily. They are 'here now and gone tomorrow'. Additionally, ministers may know little or nothing of the work of a department until they are placed in charge of it by a prime minister. Although they may employ a limited number of policy advisers, these are heavily outnumbered by permanent officials. In theory, therefore, civil servants are in a powerful position to overawe ministers, but in any case many will be voluntarily disposed to defer to the views or wishes of their permanent officials. Some ministers will by choice take little part in policy making and be content to legitimize decisions made on their behalf by their civil servants.

Delegated legislation

Civil servants in the United Kingdom may perform the task of law making through their ability to draft what is termed 'delegated legislation'. This arises when an act of parliament establishes broad principles whose detailed substance is left to civil servants who draft Statutory Instruments.

There are many advantages of this process. The ability of civil servants to draw up or amend delegated legislation means that the process is speedier than would be the case were parliament required to carry out this process. This means that the law can be speedily updated. Additionally, civil servants may be better equipped than politicians to devise detailed and technical regulations.

Nonetheless, parliament retains a scrutinizing role over delegated legislation. All statutory instruments must be referred to parliament and some require an affirmative resolution to be passed before they become law. A select committee was set up in 1944 to monitor delegated legislation and in 1973 a joint committee of both houses of parliament was established to perform such work.

The workload of a minister affects civil service involvement in policy making. A minister is also a member of parliament who needs to devote some time to constituency affairs. He or she is a leading member of a political party who is expected to perform activities to promote that party. A minister may additionally be a member of the cabinet and thus need to devote energy to the overall work of government. It would thus be physically impossible for a minister to supervise all aspects of a department's affairs. Thus ministers rely heavily on civil servants using their initiative to resolve unimportant or routine issues. These constitute the bulk of a department's work which does not, therefore, come before the minister for consideration. This gives the civil service the ability to make decisions over a very wide range of departmental activities in which the only political guideline might be that of 'knowing the minister's mind' – that is assessing how the minister would act were he or she available to deal with the situation personally.

These arguments suggest that ministers may acquiesce to civil servants playing a significant role in policy making. Problems arise only when ministers perceive civil servants acting improperly by seeking to control the policy-making process by manipulating or obstructing them.

Many ministers make decisions by selecting from options presented to them by the civil service. This gives the civil service ample opportunity to guide the minister in the direction in which they wish him or her to go. They may do this, for example, by producing an incomplete list of options designed to direct the minister towards the course of action favoured by the department. Alternatively they may attempt to 'blind a minister with science' that is, making an issue seem so technical that the minister, as a layperson, feels uncomfortable and thus disposed towards accepting the preferred view put forward by the civil service.

However, some ministers wish to exercise a more prominent role concerning policy making. They enter office with clearly defined policy objectives and an appreciation concerning how these goals should be acomplished. However, this does not guarantee that the civil service will follow the minister's lead. They may utilize an array of devices to stop, or slow down, the implementation of the minister's wishes. Such tactics include deliberately delaying the implementation of ministerial directives or mobilizing opposition to the minister's policy. The latter may involve the use of machinery such as interdepartmental committees (which are staffed by senior civil servants and from which ministers are excluded) to mobilize opposition to a minister's policy from civil servants drawn from a number of departments. Alternatively, civil servants might manufacture political pressure against a minister which is designed to secure the abandonment of the politician's preferred course of action. They may do this by appealing over the head of the minister to the prime minister or the cabinet, possibly utilizing the argument that the minister's intended actions are contrary or damaging to overall government policy. The success of such a tactic is considerably influenced by the minister's standing among his or her political colleagues.

However, the argument that civil servants conspire to dominate the policy-making process is not always accurate. Apparent attempts by civil servants to thwart the objectives of their ministers may indicate the existence of multiple accountabilities whereby civil servants acknowledge the authority of others within the machinery of government than his or her own minister. Additionally, although there may be occasions when ministers and their civil servants have clashed, the relationship between them is frequently harmonious. Each needs the other. The minister relies on the civil service for advice and the handling of routine business to ensure a manageable workload, but the civil service relies on the minister to promote the department's interests. This may involve defending the department when its interests or activities are scrutinized by the cabinet or within parliament. It may also involve performing an ambassadorial role to convince the general public that the department fulfils a vital role in civil affairs.

Ministerial advisers

Ministers may seek to offset domination exerted by civil servants by employing their own advisers. Towards the end of 2000 there were in excess of 70 of these appointments operating across all government departments.

There are, however, a number of difficulties with this situation. Ministerial advisers are employed as temporary senior civil servants and have thus been accused of politicizing the civil service even though they are appointed only for the lifetime of the government. Civil servants may resent the role of these 'outsiders'. Clashes between the Permanent Secretary at the Treasury, Sir Terence Burns, and the Chancellor of the Exchequer's special adviser, Ed Balls, resulted in the former vacating his post in 1998.

Political control of the bureaucracy

How can political control over the bureaucracy be secured?

There are various ways whereby the operations of the bureaucracy can be made susceptible to political control. Ministers may appoint their own advisers to offset the activities of civil servants. One problem is that if these advisers are outsiders they may effectively be 'frozen out' of the operations of a department by its permanent officials. In France, this difficulty is solved by ministers appointing existing civil servants to act as their advisers. These are located in the *cabinet ministériel*. They operate under the minister's direct control and usually revert to their previous posts when their service to the minister has ended.

Chief executives may also seek to exert influence over civil service actions. They may do this through involvement in the appointment, promotion and removal of civil servants. A major difficulty with these activities is that the civil service might become politicized. This means it becomes so closely identified with the policies of a particular political party that its neutrality (which is essential if it is to serve governments of other political persuasions) is questioned.

The legislature may also exert influence over the conduct of the bureaucracy. (This function is termed 'oversight' in America.) In the United Kingdom, special investigations may be launched by bodies such as parliamentary select committees into the operations of particular departments or agencies.

Civil service appointments in the United Kingdom

Political involvement in appointments became a particular issue in the United Kingdom during the 1980s when it was alleged that the Conservative Party subjected the higher echelons of the civil service to a considerable degree of political pressure to conform to the policies or working practices of the government. This was summarized in the phrase 'one of us' which allegedly was a test applied by the government to the promotion of civil servants to the post of permanent and deputy secretary.

In assessing the effectiveness of political control over the bureaucracy, however, we must be aware of a potential conflict between accountability and managerial freedom. Although those whose activities are financed by public money need to account for what they do, excessive accountability tends to stifle initiative and make civil servants operate in a cautious manner dominated by adherence to stipulated procedures. Ideally, therefore, agencies should be accountable for their results but given a degree of discretion as to how these are achieved.

We now go on to examine the manner in which the American bureaucracy is made subject to political influences.

Control of the American federal bureaucracy

In America, the control of the federal bureaucracy involves both the president and Congress. Their involvement is sometimes prompted by a belief that inadequate control results in waste and inefficiency. The president may seek to exert control over the bureaucracy in a number of ways. Commissions may be appointed to scrutinize its workings. Additionally, the president may install a number of political appointees into the federal bureaucracy to advance policy initiatives and install advisers, especially within the White House staff. Executive orders may be issued to agencies. During the 1980s, President Reagan further sought to use the Office of Management and Budget to ensure that agency regulations conformed to administration policy.

There are, however, a number of problems which impede effective presidential control over the federal bureaucracy. These include its fragmented nature. It is composed of a variety of departments, agencies, bureaux and commissions which possess varying degrees of autonomy. Presidential control may also be hindered by the relationship which such bodies are able to establish with Congress. Congress is required to approve proposals put forward by the president to reorganize government departments. Its opposition prevented President Nixon from amalgamating seven departments into four 'superdepartments' in 1971, and halted President Reagan's plans to abolish the Departments of Education and Energy during the 1980s. Further, the 'iron triangle' relationships which may be constructed between agencies, congressional committees and clients or interest groups may also prove impenetrable to presidential control.

Congress, however, may have its own reasons for wishing to exert control over the operations of the federal bureaucracy. It may seek to ensure that its policy goals are fulfilled by the federal bureaucracy. This is especially important in a situation of 'divided government' when Congress and the president may differ on the objectives which they wish the bureaucracy to achieve. There are a number of ways whereby Congress may seek to assert its control over the federal civil service. Control over funds is a key aspect of Congressional oversight which is asserted during the annual appropriations procedure. Some agencies or programmes are also subject to annual renewal which is based on an assessment by Congress as to whether their aims are being accomplished. Bodies such as the General Accounting Office and the Office of Technology Assessment help to procure information to aid the oversight function. Congress may also launch special investigations into particular government activities. An example of this was the examination of the Central Intelligence Agency conducted during the 1970s.

Congress and the bureaucracy

Congress has involved itself in the working practices of the bureaucracy. The exercise of discretion is governed by the 1946 Administrative Procedures Act and the 1990 Negotiated Rule Making Act.

The concern of Congress to secure efficiency and effectiveness within the civil service was displayed by the requirement in 1978 that all major agencies should appoint inspectors general, accountable to Congress (which was concerned with problems such as fraud and waste) and by the 1993 Government Performance and Results Act which introduced the practice of agencies (initially on a pilot basis) preparing annual development plans with measurable objectives to enable performance to be monitored.

The civil service as a ruling elite

To what extent are civil servants a ruling elite?

The description of senior civil servants as an 'elite' particularly refers to their social background. In many countries such officials derive from a middle- and upper middle-class background. The stereotypical British senior civil servant is middle-class, male, educated at public school and at Oxford or Cambridge University. A similar situation exists in France, where despite efforts by socialist adminstrations to broaden the recruitment base of such officials, a large number derive from socially exclusive backgrounds. There are, however, exceptions: in New Zealand, for example, the main source of recruitment into the civil service is secondary school graduates. Preference is given to internal promotions to fill higher level vacancies.

Concern has been expressed that senior civil servants are able to ensure that policy making is influenced by attitudes and values derived from their untypical social backgrounds. In some countries, however, the influence they possess extends throughout society and is not confined to the machinery of government. We now consider the case in France.

France: the administrators' state?

In France, an elite group of people trained as administrators occupy key positions in not only the civil service but also in political and commercial life in both the public and private sectors. Specialist training schools function as recruiting agencies for key areas of government activity. The most influential are the *École Nationale d'Administration* and the *École Polytechnique*. Their role is to recruit and train candidates for the higher-level civil service posts. Such training involves education and practical experience. Successful graduates are able to secure posts in the most prestigious areas of government activity. Additionally, however, their background and training enable them to move from the public to the private sector and occupy senior positions there or to occupy key positions in other aspects of public affairs.

Although the French administrative elite do not monopolize influential jobs throughout society, the dominant positions held by many from such a background have given rise to accusations that France is an 'administrator's state' in which people trained as civil servants are dominant in all walks of life.

Administrators and politics

Bodies such as the *École Nationale d'Administration* possesses considerable prestige. The administrative court system is dominated by graduates from this institution.

The absence of any requirement that civil servants should not participate in political activities further increases the likelihood of administrators playing an active part in politics. Leading politicians in the late twentieth and early twenty-first centuries including Jacques Chirac and Lionel Jospin were graduates of the *École Nationale d'Administration*.

Reform of the civil service

Why has civil service reform been pursued vigorously in a number of countries in recent years and what direction has this reform taken?

The growth in the role of the state in a number of countries after 1945 resulted in a large civil service. This was costly. Thus governments wishing to prune public spending cast a critical eye at the workings of the bureaucracy. The reform of the civil service has been advocated in many countries. In Ireland, the Devlin Report put forward reform proposals in 1969. In the United Kingdom, the Fulton Report in 1968 and the Ibbs Report in 1988 influenced significant changes within the civil service. In America this subject was considered by Al Gore's *National Performance Review* published in 1993. Governments influenced by 'new right' ideology have been especially interested in civil service reform in recent years. While it would be impossible to chart the directions which civil service reform has taken in various countries, there are certain developments which have occurred widely.

We consider some of these common themes in following sections.

New public management

New public management refers to a series of reforms which have sought to remodel the way in which public policy is implemented and has led to the fragmentation of government, with public policy being implemented by a range of agencies rather than being the preserve of bodies which are arms of the state. This approach is especially identified with the new right.

New public management embraces a number of key features. It is rooted in the new right's support for the free market, one consequence of which is to question the desirability of service provision by the public sector: this may require those agencies implementing public policy being required to prove which aspects of their work must remain in the public sector with the remainder being transferred to the private sector. It has sought to reorganize the operations of public sector agencies through the use of management techniques associated with the private sector such as performance indicators, business plans and a shift of emphasis towards the attainment of objectives at the expense of compliance with bureaucratic rules and procedures. It has emphasized the importance of value for money being provided by those who provide public services: this may be secured by a number of initiatives which include procedures to enable the private sector to compete for the right to deliver services which were formerly solely associated with the public sector through the process of contracting out.

The emphasis on efficiency, value for money and quality of service are integral aspects of new public management which seeks to transform citizens into consumers whose power rests not upon the political sanction of accountability but, rather, upon their ability to shop around and go elsewhere if a public service is being provided inefficiently. New public management is also identified with the twin forces of centralization and decentralization: this entails organizational goals being set by central government (whose attainment may also be measured by centrally set performance targets) while leaving their attainment to agency heads who possess considerable operational freedom but who must operate within a budget which is also centrally determined. The delegation of power downwards within organizations is a key aspect of new public management in America.

Efficiency and value for money

The objective of effective management has commonly been implemented by drawing on a number of management techniques utilized in the world of business by which efficiency can be monitored. These include the specification of departmental objectives and the preparation of performance indicators against which the attainment of objectives can be judged.

In the United Kingdom the concern for the elimination of waste and promotion of efficiency resulted in initiatives designed to establish accountable management within departments. This suggestion was made in the Fulton Report in 1968 and was pursued more vigorously following the 1979 general election when emphasis was placed on identifying the activities performed by units within a department in order for ministers to be more fully aware of that body's overall operations. Such an understanding paved the way for devolving managerial and budgetary responsibility to such units which could then more easily be held accountable by the minister for the performance of their duties.

During the 1980s the scrutinies conducted by Lord Rayner's Efficiency Unit, the introduction of the Management

Information System for Ministers (MINIS) into the Department of the Environment and the Financial Management Initiative were all concerned with the promotion of efficiency and value for money within central government.

Separation of policy planning and service delivery

A second direction which civil service reform has taken has been an attempt to redefine the role and organization of national bureaucracies. Typically, this involved the separation of policy planning from service delivery. There are two main advantages associated with this reform.

First, it gave key civil servants greater ability to engage in long-term planning by placing the day-to-day administration of services into the hands of bodies other than government departments. It has been argued that in the United Kingdom the senior civil service's preoccupation with administration rather than planning resulted in a dislike of change and innovation. This reform would enhance the capacity of senior civil servants to plan. Second, those responsible for implementing services (usually in 'agencies') would exercise a considerable degree of discretion and operational freedom. This would improve the morale and motivation of the staff employed in such work. Within the confines of policy objectives and a budget set by a government department, those who delivered services would be delegated a wide degree of authority as to how they achieved their set goals.

We briefly consider the progress of this reform in the United Kingdom in the sections that follow.

The 'Next Steps' Programme

In 1988, the Ibbs Report recommended that the national bureaucracy should be divided into a central civil service (which would advise ministers and be responsible for strategic planning within a department) and agencies (which would deliver the services within the framework devised by the department's central civil service). The rationale of this reform was to secure efficiency by freeing service delivery from what was perceived as the stultifying influence of traditional civil service working practices. Those who performed services were to be given a wide degree of discretion as to how they secured the results which were allotted to them. This recommendation was adopted by the government and became known as the 'Next Steps' Programme. The objective was for the executive functions of central government to be performed by agencies. These would be headed by a chief executive and staffed by civil servants.

Before an agency is set up ministers have to agree that the activity needs to be discharged by government. The alternatives of contracting out or privatization must first be considered. The relationship between departments and agencies are defined in a framework agreement. Innovations which were introduced included flexibility in recruitment, the development of pay and grading structures specific to agencies and the requirement that such bodies produce business plans and performance targets. Agency chief executives are appointed on fixed-term contracts and are paid bonuses to meet targets.

Agencies now dominate the central machinery of government. Over 60 per cent of all civil servants are employed by such bodies. and their total cost to the taxpayer exceeds £10 billion a year.

A number of criticisms have been made of the operation of agencies. It has been argued that they are insufficiently accountable for their actions. The convention of individual ministerial responsibility is harder to enforce when a wide range of operational decisions are made by civil servants who operate at arm's length from effective ministerial control. Further, such reforms tend to undermine the tradition of a unified civil service. The essence of this principle is that civil servants are able to move across departments and work anywhere within the bureaucracy. Such movement is less likely as the innovations referred to tend to promote the view that workers are agency rather than government employees.

Agencies and accountability

Ministers may use the existence of agencies to deny personal liability for the actions undertaken by civil servants.

In October 1995, for example, the then home secretary denied responsibility for day-to-day operational activities in the prison service. These were stated to be the concern of Derek Lewis, who had occupied the position of Director General of the Prison Service. Issues related to prison security such as the escape of prisoners were thus declared to be an agency matter for which ministers could not be held to account.

Privatization

A third direction which reform affecting the civil service frequently takes is for services to be delivered by private sector organizations. This is commonly referred to as privatization. These services may be contracted out (in which case the civil service is involved in drawing up contracts, which are subject to competitive tendering, and then in monitoring the performance of those to whom such contracts are awarded) or they may be divorced from government completely. Such reforms view competition as the main way to make services become responsive to public demand.

Contracting out was pursued in America during the 1980s and the *National Performance Review* (1993) urged that increased use should be made of service provision by non-governmental bodies. During the 1990s, 'market testing' was introduced by the United Kingdom government. This sought to establish the advantages of government departments contracting out a range of services to the private sector.

The progress of civil service reform

There may be problems when public policy is discharged by the private sector. Contracting out illustrates some of the difficulties which are involved. A full evaluation first needs to be undertaken to ascertain if it is appropriate for a service to be delivered by the private sector. If a service is contracted out it is essential that efficient monitoring procedures are put in place by departments to ensure that services are efficiently provided and to safeguard the interests of consumers. Such mechanisms involve cost but also may create tensions by seeking to evaluate the performance of those involved in commercial activities according to civil service standards.

Civil service inertia also needs to be overcome. Bureaucracies are often resistant to change, especially when organizations and jobs are threatened. Thus political will to implement reforms is important. The commitment of the Conservative government during the 1980s was crucial to bringing about alterations to the United Kingdom civil service.

Criticisms have been directed against the involvement of the private sector in administering public policy. It is alleged that the private sector's main concern is profitability. The organizations which administer privatised services are said to be primarily motivated by a desire to make profits rather than to deliver a service to the public. This resulted in an emphasis being placed on consumerism in the United Kingdom. The *Citizens' Charter* (1991) sought to make all providers of public services (including those administered by the private sector) aware of their duties to their clients and to establish standards of service which consumers had the right to expect.

Freedom of information and official secrecy

To what extent are the operations of central government subject to effective public scrutiny?

In a liberal democracy, members of the general public need to be in a position to evaluate the performance of a government in order to give or deny that government political support. To do so requires access to information by which public policy can be judged. In many liberal democracies this is provided by freedom of information legislation.

Freedom of information legislation requires public bodies or officials to make available to citizens a wide range of public documents. Public access was first granted in Sweden in 1766 but in other countries it has been a twentieth-century development. Freedom of information legislation exists in America and Germany where it is a considerable aid to investigative journalism. In America, the 1966 and 1974 Freedom of Information Acts provided citizens and interest groups with the right to inspect most federal records. Although access to some information may be denied, an appeal to the courts may secure the production of the desired information. New Zealand also has an Official Information Act which permits public access to a wide range of information and the United Kingdom will have a Freedom of Information Act in operation in 2005.

The 'right to know' is viewed as an important civil right in liberal democratic countries, enabling citizens to hold their governments to account for the actions they have taken. There are, however, limits placed on the public's ability to have access to official material. Typically, this is constrained by the desire to prevent unwarranted intrusion into an individual's privacy and also to safeguard national security. Legislation exists in a number of liberal democracies to restrict the release of official information which may be used to prevent the media from publishing material which is deemed to be contrary to state interests. This includes Ireland's 1939 Offences Against the State Act and the United Kingdom's Official Secrets legislation.

In the United Kingdom, the 1911 Official Secrets Act made any disclosure of official information a criminal offence. This posed dilemmas for some civil servants. They sometimes believed that politicians confused state interests with their own political considerations and sought to use the former grounds to suppress information which might have damaging political consequences. This gave rise to the phenomenon of whistle blowing, which involved a civil servant deliberately leaking information to bodies such as the media when he or she believed that the public's right to know superseded the concern of a government to keep such material secret.

Whistle blowing in the United Kingdom

One interesting example of whistle blowing occurred in the 1980s. Clive Ponting, a civil servant, leaked a document concerning the sinking during the Falklands War of the Argentinian cruiser, the *General Belgrano*, to a Labour member of parliament, Tam Dalyell. He justified his action by arguing that the government was misleading parliament and hence the country. He perceived that his duty to the nation as a public servant outweighed his loyalty to the government. Civil servants who engage in this activity run the risk of dismissal and imprisonment. Ponting was charged with breaking the Official Secrets Act but was acquitted in 1985 by a jury sympathetic to his arguments.

A danger posed by this activity is that it erodes the trust between ministers and civil servants. It might result in the politicization of the bureaucracy whereby politicians appoint persons to its upper ranks whose trust and loyalty can be relied upon.

In 1989, a new Official Secrets Act was enacted in the United Kingdom. The sanction of a criminal prosecution was limited to certain categories of official information, which were broadly associated with the interests of the state. Within these categories, an absolute ban was imposed on disclosure of some information (for example, by intelligence officers discussing the operations of the security services), while in other areas (such as defence) it would be necessary to demonstrate that the disclosure resulted in 'harm' or 'jeopardy' to state interests. The act contained no public interest defence which might be used by civil servants or investigative journalists who publicized government activities in these restricted areas.

The 'alternative' machinery of government

Through what machinery other than government departments can public policy be administered?

Our discussion so far in this chapter has primarily been concerned with the work performed by civil servants employed in government departments or executive agencies. However, in most countries there exists a vast range of alternative mechanisms whereby national public policy is discharged.

In America, regulatory agencies, government corporations and independent executive agencies perform federal government functions. In the United Kingdom, a range of bodies which include quangos (quasi-autonomous non-governmental organizations) deliver services at both national and sub-national levels. In Ireland, state-sponsored bodies or semi-state bodies discharge important areas of central government work. The staff employed in this 'alternative machinery' of government may be civil servants but often are not.

The main advantage arising from the use of such machinery is that it is implemented by organizations which are purpose built to perform a specific function. It does not have to accord to the organization and structure dictated by normal civil service requirements. Thus people can be recruited with expertise which would not normally be possessed by civil servants (for example, experience in conducting a large-scale business enterprise) and rewarded by a salary which does not have to conform to civil service pay scales. In both the United Kingdom and Ireland, these bodies have been used to link the public and private sectors.

There are two major problems affecting these bodies.

Accountability

The extent to which the 'alternative' machinery of government is adequately accountable for its actions has been questioned. It may be deliberately used to avoid the constant 'interference' of politicians. It is argued that organizations that pursue commercial activities require a certain amount of freedom so that enterprise can flourish. Others that pursue non-economic tasks may also justify a relative degree of insulation from political control on the grounds that the task with which they are concerned should not be subject to the constant to and fro of political debate: thus such bodies effectively depoliticize the function with which they are concerned. However, accountability remains an important issue as such bodies are concerned with the administration of public policy. Additionally, some rely on state funding to finance all or some of their activities.

Accountability may be secured in three ways – by the chairperson (a political appointee) reporting to the minister, by the chief executive (a paid official) reporting to the department associated with the body (perhaps in the form of an annual report or a corporate plan indicating targets and performance) or through scrutiny exercised by the legislature over the operations which such bodies perform.

The consideration of annual reports might aid legislative scrutiny of such bodies but parliamentary select committees (such as the Irish Joint Committee on State Sponsored Bodies, established in 1976) possibly possess greater potential for enabling legislatures effectively to examine the activities of these bodies.

Patronage

The second problem associated with the implementation of public policy by bodies other than government departments concerns the manner whereby those who manage these organizations are appointed. The main criterion for the appointment of managers to such organizations often seems to be their political sympathy to the government that appoints them. In the United Kingdom this led the Nolan Committee in 1995 to recommend that appointments to quangos should be scrutinized by an independent commissioner for public appointments. The role of this office was extended by the 1997

Labour government to ensure that future appointments were non-partisan and that a much wider group of people (including women and members of ethnic minorities) were encouraged to apply for these jobs.

Questions

1 Outline the main developments affecting the structure and organization of the civil service in any country with which you are familiar.

2 Using material from any country with which you are familiar, assess the manner in which government departments are organized.

3 Analyse the arguments for and against the view that policy making is dominated by civil servants rather than ministers.

4 To what extent have the principles underlying new public management influenced the reform of the civil service in any country with which you are familiar?

5 Discuss what limits, if any, a liberal democracy is entitled to impose on the access of citizens to public documents.

Taking it further

This chapter has considered the role played by the civil service, and in particular has examined the argument that civil servants exert a considerable role in the formulation of public policy in liberal democracies.

A more detailed examination of the role of the civil service in the United Kingdom and the process of adminstrative reform can be obtained from Peter Barberis (editor), *The Whitehall Reader* (Milton Keynes: Open University Press, 1996) and the same author's *The Elite of the Elite* (Aldershot: Dartsmouth, 1996).

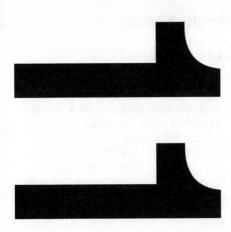

the legislative branch of government

In this chapter you will learn:
- the main functions carried out by legislatures
- the operations of unicameral and bicameral legislative bodies
- the contemporary problems affecting the conduct of legislatures

The functions of legislatures

What roles do legislatures perform?

Elected legislatures are viewed as the symbol of representative government: as it is not possible for all citizens to directly share in policy making, they elect persons who perform these duties on their behalf. These representatives convene in the country's legislature (which is referred to as Congress in America, parliament in the United Kingdom or the *Oireachtas* in Ireland). This is thus the institution that links the government and the governed. In addition to this symbolic function, legislatures undertake a number of specific tasks which we consider now.

Law making

Legislatures constitute the law-making body within a country's system of government. Thus making the law (or amending or repealing it) is a key function which they perform. A specific, although important, aspect of this role is approving the budget and granting authority for the collection of taxes.

A key issue concerns the extent to which legislatures themselves initiate law or respond to proposals put forward by the executive branch of government. Although there is a tendency for legislatures to respond to the initiatives of the executive branch in both presidential and parliamentary systems of government (thus transforming the legislature into a body which legitimizes decisions rather than one which initiates them), this is not invariably the case. The committee system of the German parliament is particularly influential in securing a policy-making role for this body. Much of the work of the *Bundestag* is carried out through specialized committees whose areas of activity correspond to the federal ministries. These committees provide a forum in which ministers, civil servants and members of parliament (including those of the opposition parties) jointly engage in the process of policy making.

We consider the process of law making in the United Kingdom parliament in the following sections.

Law making in the United Kingdom parliament

In the United Kingdom a difference exists between public and private legislation. The former constitutes the general law of the land, but the latter is limited in jurisdiction (often being promoted by public bodies such as local authorities to extend their powers). A number of stages are involved in translating a proposal into law. The following outline applies to public legislation. We are assuming that this legislation is first introduced into the House of Commons, which is generally (but not exclusively) the case.

First reading   This is merely the announcement of an intention to introduce legislation on a particular topic. No debate occurs at this stage.

Second reading   This is a debate on the general principles embodied in the legislative proposal (which is termed a 'bill'). If these principles are approved the bill progresses to the next stage in the legislative process.

Committee stage   This involves a detailed examination of the contents of the bill. Amendments can be made provided that they do not destroy the bill's fundamental principles which have been approved in the second reading.

    This stage usually takes place in a standing committee which involves a relatively small number of MPs, although a committee of the whole House or a select committee may be used instead.

Report stage   Here any changes to the bill proposed by the committee are considered by the full House of Commons and either approved or rejected.

Third reading   This is a consideration of the bill as amended in its progress through the House of Commons.

If the bill receives its third reading, it then goes through a similar process in the House of Lords.

If amendments are proposed by the House of Lords, these need to be separately considered by the House of Commons. By convention, the House of Lords will normally give way to the sentiments of the Commons if there is a dispute between the two chambers.

When such differences are reconciled, the bill is passed for royal assent. This is granted automatically, but is the process by which the 'bill' becomes an 'act'.

It is necessary for a bill to complete all of these stages in a single parliamentary session. If it fails to do this it may be reintroduced in the following session commencing at the first reading stage.

Scrutiny of the executive

Legislatures also scrutinize the actions of the executive branch of government. Governments are required to justify their actions to the legislature which may thus exert influence over the government's conduct. This scrutiny may be retrospective (that is, it occurs after a decision has been implemented and seeks to examine whether it was justified). In some cases, however, the legislature may be required to give its consent to an action which the executive branch wishes to undertake. In America, for example, Congress has to approve a declaration of war.

In parliamentary systems in which the legislature provides the personnel of government, scrutiny facilitates ministerial responsibility. Governments are collectively responsible to the legislature. Perceived deficiencies in the overall activities of the government may result in its dismissal by the legislature (usually through the mechanism of a vote of 'no confidence'). Individual ministers may also be individually responsible for the performance of specific aspects of the work of the executive branch. However, the ability of legislatures to force individual ministers to resign varies. In Germany, for example, the *Bundestag* lacks such a sanction although criticism by the legislature of a minister may result in that person's resignation.

Confirmation of governmental appointments

Scrutiny may also extend to approving the nomination of individual members of the government put forward by the chief executive. This form of legislative scrutiny operates in some parliamentary systems of government such as Ireland. The scrutiny of nominations for public office by the legislature is also a feature of some presidential systems of government such as America where the Senate is required to confirm a wide range of presidential appointments. The rationale for such a process is to ensure that those nominated for high government office have the relevant credentials to occupy such a post. In practice, however, this form of scrutiny might involve delving into a person's private life (to demonstrate personal failings which are allegedly incompatible with office holding) or might be determined on political grounds.

Investigatory functions

The investigation of issues of public importance is an important function of many legislative bodies. This may be separate from exercising scrutiny over the actions of the executive. In America, Congress has the right to *subpoena,* that is, to force persons to appear and answer questions on the topic which is the subject of investigation.

Supervisory functions

Legislatures may concern themselves with the manner in which an institution of government or an activity that is reliant on public funds is being performed. This function (which in America is termed *oversight*) is concerned with monitoring the bureaucracy and its administration of policy. This entails ensuring that an agency is meeting the goals specified for it, that the public money provided for it is being spent for the purposes for which it was intended or that an operation is conducted in accordance with any restrictions which were initially placed upon it by the legislature. The American Congress actively performs supervisory functions through committee hearings and the review of agency budgets but these procedures are less prominent in other legislatures such as Britain. An example of this were the hearings held by the Senate Finance Committee in 1997 into the operations of the Internal Revenue Service.

Raising issues of local and national importance

Legislatures debate policy and other issues of public importance. Such debates are published in official journals and through the media thus providing a source of information for the general public. This enables the electorate to be politically informed and educated. These bodies further provide a forum in which representatives can advance the interests of their constituencies and intercede on behalf of any of their constituents who have encountered problems in their dealings with the executive branch of government. Much work of this nature takes place in private, but it is usually possible to raise such issues publicly, within the legislative chamber.

Judicial functions

Legislatures may also perform judicial functions whereby members of all three branches of government may be tried and sentenced in connection with offences connected with the performance of their official duties.

In America, for example, Congress has a judicial power, that of *impeachment*. This is a formal charge that a member of the executive or judicial branch of government has committed an offence while in office. The accusation of inappropriate conduct is laid before the House of Representatives and if they believe that there is a case to answer a trial takes place in the Senate. If guilt is determined by this body the official would be dismissed from public office.

Legislatures may also exercise judicial-type functions in relation to the conduct of their members. The processes used vary. In America, for example, each House of Congress has an Ethics Committee to which accusations of wrongdoing contravening the rules of either body are referred. Members of Congress cannot be impeached, but wrongdoings by legislators may be punished by an alternative process of censureship. This rarely involves removal from office but embraces alternative sanctions which adversely affect the status of the condemned legislator.

Initiating constitutional change

Legislatures play a key role in the process of changing a country's constitution. In countries with a flexible constitution (that is, one which can be altered by the normal law-making process) the legislature is solely responsible for initiating and determining constitutional change. This is the situation in the United Kingdom. In countries with rigid constitutions (where amendment involves a separate process from the normal law-making procedure), the role of the legislature in providing for change is reduced, although important as the following examples show.

America

Two-thirds of both Houses of Congress (the House of Representatives and the Senate) must separately agree either to call a constitutional convention to determine change when asked to do so by two-thirds of the states (which last occurred in 1787), or themselves propose a specific amendment to the Constitution of which two-thirds of the states must then approve. Recent examples of this process were the Equal Rights Amendment proposed by Congress in 1972 which failed to secure the required level of support from state legislatures, since only 35 approved it.

Ireland

Proposed changes to the constitution are initially put before the *Oireachtas* and if approved are then placed before the country's citizens in a referendum. The number of amendments has been small. In 1972 the third amendment allowed Ireland to join the EEC and the tenth amendment authorized the state to ratify the 1987 Single European Act. In 1995 a proposal to legalize divorce was narrowly approved in a referendum.

The operations of legislatures

How do legislatures perform their functions?

Legislatures conduct their affairs through a number of mechanisms. We discuss the main ones in the sections that follow.

Debate

Legislatures are first and foremost debating institutions. This means that functions such as the consideration of legislation, the articulation of constituency issues or the discussion of matters of national importance are performed orally. Members of the legislature deliver speeches in which they put forward their views and listen to the judgements of their fellow legislators on the same issue. To facilitate debate, members of legislative bodies may enjoy certain immunities which ordinary members of the general public do not possess. In the United Kingdom, for example, members of the House of Commons enjoy freedom of speech. This is one of a number of 'parliamentary privileges'.

This means that in parliament members may effectively say what they want (subject to the speaker's rulings) to facilitate the maximum degree of openness in debate. Speeches made by a member of parliament, no matter how defamatory, cannot be subject to an action for slander.

Committees

Much of the work performed by contemporary legislative bodies is delegated to committees. In turn, these bodies may devolve responsibilities to sub-committees. These are useful devices as it enables a legislature to consider a number of matters at the same time and thus cope with increased volumes of work associated with the expanded role of the state in years following the Second World War and membership of supranational bodies. They further enable small groups of legislators to investigate the affairs of government in considerable detail, and through their reports the entire assembly becomes more knowledgeable of these matters and thus less dependent on government for the provision of information.

There are various types of committee existing in modern legislatures. In the United Kingdom's House of Commons a key division is between standing committees (which are used to consider legislation) and select committees (which are used for various purposes, including examination of the work performed by key government departments). A similar division exists in the American Congress. Both Houses of Congress have a wide array of standing committees which consider bills in different policy areas. Select committees may also be set up to investigate special problems. In countries whose legislatures consist of more than one chamber, joint committees may be established to enable the two chambers to co-operate for specific purposes.

Committees are an especially useful means for considering legislation. In countries such as America the examination of legislative proposals is aided by the system of hearings in which the committee or sub-committee considering the proposal invites interested parties to give evidence before it to ensure that their decisions are based on a wide range of informed opinion. The decision whether to report a measure out of committee with a favourable recommendation or to 'kill' it is influenced by this procedure.

The party system and party membership

The party system may have an important bearing on the effectiveness with which committees operate in modern legislatures. The appointment of members to committees usually involves the party leadership and the fact that committee members are affiliated to a political party may influence the manner in which issues before a committee are viewed by its members.

In countries with parliamentary forms of government, such as the United Kingdom, the party system may help the executive branch dominate committee proceedings since the governing party usually possesses a majority on committees considering legislation. In countries with presidential systems such as America, committees may exercise a far greater degree of autonomy since the executive branch is not directly involved in appointments. There, appointments are allocated by the party apparatus which exists in both Houses although a member's desire to serve on a particular committee may be taken into account. Membership is not confined to a particular session of Congress: once appointed to a committee a member will usually sit on it for the remainder of his or her career. The chairmanship of such bodies is largely – although now not exclusively – determined by seniority. This was a procedure whereby the longest serving committee member whose party controlled Congress headed the committee.

In some countries the work of committees extends beyond the consideration of legislative proposals. Legislation may be initiated by these bodies. The committee system of the German parliament is particularly influential in this respect. Much of the work of the *Bundestag* is carried out through specialized committees whose areas of activity correspond to the federal ministries. These committees provide a forum in which ministers, civil servants and members of parliament (including those of the opposition parties) jointly engage in the process of policy making.

Questions

Questions are a further means through which the work of the legislature is transacted in countries with parliamentary forms of government. These may be oral or written and are addressed to members of the executive branch of government. They can be of use in eliciting information, clarifying an issue or seeking to secure action by the executive branch of government, although they are rarely of importance to the process of policy making. They provide a mechanism whereby civil servants (who prepare the answers to these questions) respond to an agenda set by legislators as opposed to members of the executive branch of government. In the German *Bundestag*, questions aid the process of ministerial accountability. The oral questioning of a minister may be followed by a vote which enables members of the legislature to express whether they are satisfied with the answers with which they have been provided.

Bicameral and unicameral legislatures

Why do legislatures usually consist of more than one body?

In most liberal democratic political systems, the legislature is divided into two separate bodies. These bodies form separate debating chambers. For example, in the United Kingdom parliament consists of the House of Commons and the House of Lords. In America, the legislative branch is divided into the House of Representatives and the Senate. In Ireland, parliament (the *Oireachtas*) consists of the *Daíl éireann* and the *Seanad éireann*, while in France the legislative function of government is shared between the National Assembly and the Senate. All these countries have what is termed a bicameral legislature.

The opposite of this is a unicameral system in which the legislature consists of only one body. Examples of this are found in New Zealand, Finland, Denmark, Sweden and Israel.

The following sections consider the advantages of having a legislature composed of two bodies.

A revising chamber

An important benefit of a bicameral legislature is that one chamber can give the other an opportunity to think again, to reconsider its position. On occasions when the content of legislation is contentious and the period surrounding its passage through the first of the legislative bodies is charged with emotion for and against the measure, it is useful that a second chamber can coolly and calmly re-evaluate what has been done and if necessary invite the first chamber to reassess the situation by either rejecting the measure or proposing amendments to it. In this case, the second performs the function of a revising chamber.

Differences in composition

In bicameral systems, the two chambers of the legislature are often drawn from different constituencies (that is, composed in different ways). This may be an advantage in that it enables issues to be examined from different perspectives.

In some countries one chamber of the legislature is designed to represent public opinion while the other is concerned with territorial representation – advancing the more localized views of the areas, states or regions into which the country is divided. This was originally the justification for creating the American Senate. When the constitution was being drafted a conflict of interest emerged between the sparsely populated states and those in which large numbers of persons resided. Thus the constitution adopted a compromise position (which was termed the 'Connecticut Compromise'). This resulted in representation in one chamber (the House of Representatives) being based on population, which would give the populous states a greater voice in that body. However each state, regardless of size, was given equal representation in the second chamber, the Senate.

Bicameralism in Germany and France

In Germany, the *Bundestag* consists of representatives elected by the voters for a four-year term of office, whereas the *Bundesrat* provides a forum at national level in which the views of the states (or *Länder*) can be put forward. Members of the *Bundesrat* are not elected but are nominated by the individual state governments. Each state sends delegations to this body who are mandated to act in accordance with the instructions given to them by the state government. Each state is allotted three votes in the *Bundesrat*, with extra votes being given to the more populated states.

In France, members of the National Assembly are elected for a five-year term. Members of the second chamber, the Senate, are indirectly elected for a term of nine years by an electoral college which is composed of deputies of the National Assembly and local politicians, including mayors, members of departments and city councils.

Functional representation

Second chambers may also articulate concerns other than territorial ones. They may represent the interests of specific groups within a country. This is referred to as functional representation. The Irish *Seanad* is theoretically constituted in part on this basis. Members of this body are not directly elected but are supposed to reflect vocational interests. The majority of its members are thus chosen from lists of candidates representing key vocational groups in Irish society (education and culture, agriculture, industry and commerce, labour and public administration and social services). An electoral college composed of members of local authorities and parliament (the *Oireachtas*) then elects 43 senators from these lists. A further six are chosen from graduates of the National University of Ireland and Dublin University and the prime minister (*Taoiseach*) appoints a further 11 members. In reality, however, party affiliation is the key for election to this body.

The resolution of disagreements in bicameral legislatures

It is inevitable that disputes between the bodies that compose a bicameral legislature will sometimes arise. These situations are usually catered for in a country's constitution or by political practices that seek to avoid a situation in which one chamber effectively vetoes the work of the other which results in total inaction. Let us consider some examples.

In Ireland, the resolution of disagreement is catered for by the constitution. This established the *Seanad* as an inferior body to the *Dáil* in terms of the functions which it performs. The latter body nominates the *Taoiseach* and approves the government. The government is responsible only to the *Dáil* and most legislation is introduced into this house. The *Seanad*'s subsidiary role thus minimizes its ability to disrupt the process of government. In the United Kingdom, too, the two chambers of parliament are not co-equal in power and, in the case of disagreement between them, the views of the directly elected House of Commons will ultimately prevail. This situation is enshrined in the 1949 Parliament Act which gives the House of Lords the power to delay the progress of non-financial legislation which has been passed by the House of Commons for the maximum period of one year, after which (provided the measure is reintroduced in the House of Commons) it will become law.

The French constitution provides for the pre-eminence of the National Assembly over the Senate. Only the former body can dismiss a government and it also possesses the ultimate ability to determine legislation, although in the event of disagreements between the two chambers an attempt will usually be made to seek a compromise. The Senate does, however, possess important powers (including the need to consent to changes in the constitution) and has on occasions asserted itself, especially during periods of socialist government. This situation is referred to as 'conflictual bicameralism'.

'Pre-study' in Canada

One difficulty which may affect the operations of a bicameral legislature is the time available for a second chamber adequately to examine legislation sent to it by the first.

A solution to this is the process of 'pre-study' which has occasionally been utilized by the Canadian Senate since 1945. This is a process by which the subject matter of a bill under consideration in the House of Commons can be considered by a Senate committee at the same time. The report of this committee's deliberations is made available to the House of Commons which may consider the Senate's reactions to the proposal that is before it, and if necessary introduce amendments before transmitting the bill to that body.

This process enables the Senate to examine legislation placed before it relatively quickly, but also ensures that it is able to make a valid contribution to the law-making process by making its views on it known before it is formally sent to it for examination.

However, in America the two branches of the legislature are equal in status. The institution of direct election for senators in 1913 resulted in both Houses of Congress being popularly elected. Disagreements between the two chambers on legislation are resolved through the mechanism of a conference committee. If a bill is passed in different versions by the two Houses, a committee composed of members of each House is appointed to resolve the differences and draw up a single bill which is then returned to each House for a vote. Should either house reject this bill, it is returned to the conference committee for further deliberation. It is not necessary to resort to this mechanism frequently, but when it is used it may provide a forum in which 'trade-offs' between the House of Representatives and the Senate are made.

Changes affecting the power and authority of legislatures

For what reasons has the power and authority of legislatures declined in recent years?

The power of legislatures varies from one liberal democracy to another and is affected by constitutional and procedural rules which govern the powers and conduct of these bodies. In the United Kingdom, for example, scrutiny is aided by the opposition parties being granted a number of occasions during each parliamentary session when they may initiate debates which can be used to probe the actions of the executive. These are termed 'supply days', but such facilities are not found in all countries possessing a parliamentary form of government. However, changes affecting the power and authority of legislatures have occurred in a number of countries and in this section we seek to understand the nature of these developments.

The power of legislatures

Developments have taken place in a number of countries that have had an adverse effect on the ability of legislatures to perform the functions outlined earlier in this chapter. The decline in the power of such bodies has adversely affected their ability to carry out traditional functions. We consider some of the main factors affecting the power of legislatures in the sections that follow.

Membership of supranational bodies

The membership of supranational bodies has implications for both the law-making and scrutinizing role performed by national legislatures. In the United Kingdom, for example, membership of the European Union has resulted in the loss of some of parliament's traditional legislative functions but has also added to the volume of governmental activity which this body is expected to monitor.

Developments devaluing the law-making role of legislatures

The role of legislatures as law-making bodies has been undermined by a number of contemporary developments. These include referendum (whose usage has increased in countries such as the United Kingdom which traditionally made little use of them) and other aspects of 'people politics' in which citizens seek to secure changes in legislation by engaging in various forms of extra-parliamentary political action.

The role of legislatures as law-making bodies was especially affected by what is termed 'neo-corporatism'. This denotes a close working relationship between government, unions and business interests. One example of this was the National Economic Development Council (usually referred to as NEDDY) which was set up by the United Kingdom Conservative government headed by Harold Macmillan in 1962. It brought together ministers, civil servants, trade union leaders and representatives of employers, whose key role was to plan for industrial growth. Parliament thus became devalued as key economic and industrial policies were determined in this alternative body.

The role of the media

The ability of legislatures to scrutinize the actions of the executive, to air grievances or to educate the public concerning political affairs is often more effectively conducted by the media. Television interviews with leading politicians and investigative journalism perform important roles in enabling the public to be informed of political matters. Additionally, politicians may decide that the media offer them better opportunities to present arguments to the electorate than a debate which takes place in a legislative body.

Domination by the executive branch of government

A major explanation for the decline in the power of legislatures is the tendency for these bodies to be dominated by the executive branch of government. In many countries, the initiation of policy and the control over finance has passed to the executive branch. In the United Kingdom, for example, the bulk of public legislation is initiated by the government. Parliament thus responds to the agenda set for it by the government. It may subsequently be able to influence the detailed content of this legislation, but it is not the driving force behind it. Additionally, governments may be able to utilize procedural devices to expedite the progress of their legislation. In the United Kingdom, one such device is the guillotine. This is a mechanism that limits the time devoted to a debate which ensures that the progress of a government measure is not halted by unnecessary or excessive parliamentary debate.

Executive dominance of legislatures has occurred in both parliamentary and presidential forms of government. There are three reasons that might account for this development.

The first is the ability of the executive branch of government to act independently of legislatures in certain circumstances. This has enhanced the power of the former, eroding the latter's ability to initiate public policy or scrutinize the activites of government. In the United Kingdom, the government may make use of the *royal prerogative* and undertake certain actions without having to first obtain parliamentary approval. In other liberal democracies, chief executives are given emergency powers with which to act as they see fit to deal with an emergency or may govern by some form of decree. The American president, for example, may issue executive orders and thus act in certain matters without the approval of Congress.

The second explanation for executive domination of legislatures concerns the ability to cope with the volume of post-war state activity, much of which is of a complex and technical nature. This has made it difficult for members of legislatures to keep abreast of the affairs of modern government and has tended to result in ministers and civil servants within the executive branch exercising a dominant position in policy making because of the superior information they have at their disposal.

The final explanation for executive dominance of legislatures is the development of the party system. The party system possesses some obvious advantages for legislative bodies. It helps to prevent legislative anarchy (in the sense of members seeking to pursue individual interests to the exclusion of all else) and organizes the work of these bodies thus ensuring that specific goals and objectives are achieved. But there are also disadvantages for legislatures which arise from the party system.

The party system aligns members of the executive and legislative branches. Members of both branches, when belonging to the same party, have common ideological and policy interests. They have a vested interest in successfully translating these common concerns into law. These mutual interests are underlaid by party discipline which serves to induce members of the legislature to follow the lead given by their party leaders within the executive branch of government. In extreme cases, where party discipline is strong, disobedience to the wishes of the executive might result in expulsion from the party, a fate which befell the 'Eurorebels' in the United Kingdom Conservative Party in 1994.

The emergence of disciplined political parties has the effect of ensuring that legislatures do not act as corporate institutions exercising their functions on behalf of the nation as a whole. Instead, they operate under the direction of the executive branch of government.

The French party system

The emergence of disciplined political parties has been especially apparent in France. The situation of governments being placed at the mercy of constantly shifting coalitions in the National Assembly has been replaced by the development of parties organized in support of, or opposition to, the government. This situation is termed *le fait majoritaire*. It supplemented other developments contained in the 1958 Constitution that were designed to subordinate the legislature to the executive. These included limitations on the ability of the National Assembly to dismiss governments and facilities for governments to secure the passage of legislation lacking majority support in either the National Assembly or the Senate.

The authority of legislatures

In addition to developments affecting the power of legislatures, other changes have affected the aura and prestige enjoyed by these bodies and have had an adverse effect on their authority. In this section we consider some of the main factors which have had an adverse effect on the authority of legislatures.

Adversarial politics

The operations of the party system have one further consequence which may devalue the workings of the legislature. Party systems often give rise to adversarial politics. Britain and New Zealand are examples of countries whose political affairs are traditionally conducted in this manner. The political parties which compete for office put forward policies that are significantly different from those of their opponents, typically formulated on contrasting ideology.

Adversarial politics denotes a situation in which one party is automatically disposed to oppose the views and suggestions of another as a point of principle. If this style of politics influences the operations of the legislature, it means that this body lacks any sense of common purpose. The work of the legislature is less concerned with a genuine search for the best solutions to issues and problems regardless of party affiliation but is mainly activated by the furtherance of partisan acrimony and the pursuit of party advantage. Members of the legislature who are supporters of the same party from which the executive is drawn are likely to back that government and deride proposals made by the opposition party (or parties) regardless of the merits of the cases put forward. Similarly, those who are not supporters of the government are likely to make destructive rather than constructive assessments of initiatives put forward by the executive branch.

Thus, party systems may erode the ability of legislatures to take dispassionate consideration of a range of ideas and then support those which overall opinion within that body agrees is the best course of action in the national interest. This situation may affect the way in which members of the general public feel towards the legislature.

The economic climate

Public confidence in legislatures may be especially affected by the economic climate. Factors such as recession are likely to have an adverse impact on the way the public view all institutions of government, especially when it appears that they have no instant solutions to contemporary problems. Recession is further likely to reduce the capacity of institutions of government to act as innovators: rather than act as dynamic proponents of reform (which may enhance the standing of such bodies in the public eye) both executives and legislators are disposed towards inaction and to pruning public spending. This is a less adventurous exercise than initiating new programmes and may have an adverse effect on the way in which the public view the machinery of government.

Performance of a diverse range of functions

Legislatures perform a wide range of functions. However, not all of these are compatible. In particular, prominent attention to the role of promoting local considerations (which is termed parochialism) may detract from the legislature's ability to exercise superintendence over national affairs and provide the appearance of a fragmented body with no overall sense of purpose. This may also result in the decline of the aura and prestige of that body and thus its authority.

It has been argued that the parochialism of members of the American Congress detracts from that body's ability or willingness to view matters from an overall national perspective. Although American Congressional elections are fought by candidates who represent the nation's major parties, the main influence on the outcome of these elections is the personal vote a candidate can attract. This personal vote may be secured on the basis of that person's campaigning style and how they 'come across' to local voters. However, the key basis of a personal vote is the candidate's previous record when in office. This record can be based on factors which include accessibility to local constituents (especially the provision of help to those with problems), the voicing of support for local interests or causes and particularly the ability to attract government resources into the constituency the candidate represents.

Parochialism

The role which legislators perform in providing a service to their constituents is an important one in many countries. In Ireland, members of the *Dail* are often prominent participants in the local political affairs of the constituency they represent and view the promotion of local interests and articulation of individual grievances as roles which are of more importance than formulating national legislation. Even ministers are not immune to these parochial pressures.

In Britain, reference is often made to a member of parliament's 'personal vote'. This means that some candidates secure support from their local electors on the basis of who they are and what they have done (especially in connection with the service provided to their constituents). Such support is, however, far less important than a candidate's party label.

It follows, therefore, that incumbent candidates (that is, those who are striving for re-election) are in a far better position to win seats in the House of Representatives or Senate than is a candidate who has no record to advance and is seeking to win a seat for the first time. Only factors such as a dilatory record in advancing constituency interests or being involved in some form of scandal are likely to offset the incumbent's advantage. Although sitting candidates do sometimes lose, a key feature of elections to Congress is that incumbents are in a good position to win and usually do so.

It has been argued that this situation results in Congress having a dual character: it is at one and the same time a body composed of politicians with a keen interest (or even a preoccupation) with local affairs but is also a forum for making national policy. Concern with the former consideration may detract from the latter function and reduce Congress's effectiveness in responding to current or future problems.

Corruption

A further explanation affecting the decline in the authority enjoyed by legislative bodies concerns corruption or 'sleaze'. If the public perceive that the main purpose of seeking election to such bodies is to further a member's personal interests rather than to serve the nation, citizens are likely to hold both legislatures and legislators in low regard.

The decline of legislatures

To what extent are legislatures in a state of irreversible decline?

In the two previous sections we have referred to difficulties faced by contemporary legislatures. We have argued that they face two related sets of problems – changes affecting the power of these bodies that have hindered their ability to discharge traditional functions effectively and changes in public perceptions of the aura and prestige of such bodies that have had an adverse effect on their authority. These arguments can be amalgamated into the suggestion that there has been a decline in legislatures.

However, although we have charted major developments that have contributed to arguments alleging the decline of such bodies, it is important to appreciate that they continue to perform valuable and vital roles in political affairs. Some of the problems to which we have drawn attention are neither universal nor insuperable. For example, the dominant hold which governments exercise over the law-making process is greater in some countries than in others. In both Germany and Italy, for example, there remains a considerable degree of scope for legislation to be initiated by ordinary (or 'backbench') members of the legislature.

We have drawn attention to the impact of the party system on the role of legislatures. However, the strength of party varies from one liberal democracy to another and this has an obvious bearing on the subservience of legislature to the executive. For example, the nature of the American party relationship between Congress and the president is one factor that explains why Congress has retained an extremely significant role in law making.

Additionally, the dominance governments possess over the conduct of legislatures through the operations of the party system is not always a constant feature in the political affairs of a country. There are occasions on which legislatures may assert themselves to a greater degree. This is when (in a parliamentary system) no one party possesses overall majority support in the legislature or when (in a presidential system) the executive branch of government is controlled by a different party than that which controls the legislature.

Legislature assertiveness – some examples

In Ireland during the 1980s the absence of one party with an overall majority gave the *Dail* the opportunity to exercise its right to dismiss governments. Two were dismissed and a third was forced to resign and seek a dissolution.

When the presidency and National Assembly in France were controlled by different political parties during periods of what is termed *'cohabitation'* (1986–88,1993–95), the president was forced to appoint a prime minister who enjoyed the support of the National Assembly. This situation again occurred between 1997 and 2002 when President Chirac (of the conservative RPR party) was obliged to appoint his defeated opponent in the 1995 presidential election, the socialist Lionel Jospin, to the office of Prime Minister. In such situations, governments become accountable to the legislature rather than to the president thus enhancing the power of the former at the expense of the latter.

Thus, the party system is a double-edged sword. Although it sometimes aids executive dominance over the legislature, it may also enable legislatures to assert themselves at the expense of executive power. Their ability to do this may further be enhanced by reforms which we discuss in the following section.

The role of select committees

Legislatures may seek to provide themselves with mechanisms designed to elicit information on the affairs of government, thus enhancing that body's ability effectively to scrutinize the actions of the government. Individual legislators may be provided with financial aid to employ staff, one of whose roles could be to provide expert knowledge of specific policy areas. Members of the United Kingdom parliament and members of the Irish *Dail* are extremely poorly served in this respect while American legislators fare far better, with large personal staffs and the support of expert research services.

The use of select committees has been a key reform to facilitate legislative scrutiny of the affairs of government in a number of liberal democracies. Their deliberations provide a source of information which is separate from that provided by the executive branch. Further, the non-partisan climate within which select committee discussions are held may reduce the domination exerted by the executive branch of government thereby enhancing the status of the legislature. This has been the case in Ireland, France, the United Kingdom, New Zealand and Canada.

In the United Kingdom, the Public Accounts Committee was an early example of a select committee that monitored the work of government. Specifically, it examined the accounts of government departments and sought to ensure that money voted by parliament was spent effectively and for the purposes that parliament had agreed. Its work is aided by the comptroller and auditor-general and the National Audit Office.

In 1979, a new system of select committees was introduced into the House of Commons to monitor the work performed by all key government departments. Such bodies were designed to make all MPs more informed concerning the work of government. To aid them in their deliberations, such committees were empowered to hire staff with expertise in the area of government with which they were concerned and to secure evidence from persons who were not MPs but who possessed knowledge of the subject area under discussion. This reform was not universally welcomed, however. Some politicians feared that the power of these committees would further devalue parliament as an institution and that key legislative functions would be transferred to committees. It was also argued that these bodies would promote consensus politics since committee members would feel pressurized to compromise their views in order to produce a unanimous report.

In Ireland, the *Fine Gael*–Labour coalition (1982–87) established a number of select committees in 1983 but most of them were abandoned by the *Fianna Fail* government in 1987.

Major reforms to the system of select committees were introduced into the New Zealand parliament by the incoming Labour government in 1985. These reforms were designed to subject the process of government to enhanced parliamentary and public scrutiny. One significant innovation was the power of such committees to inquire on their own initiative into any area of government administration, policy or spending.

Questions

1 Using examples of your own drawn from a country with which you are familiar, assess the main functions performed by legislatures.

2 Examine the role performed by committees in the legislature of any country with which you are familiar.

3 Using some examples of your own, assess the strengths and weaknesses of bicameral legislatures.

4 Using examples of your own, assess the main reasons to account for the decline in the power and authority of contemporary legislatures.

5 Using examples of your own, assess the extent to which contemporary legislatures are able to overcome domination by the executive branch of government.

Taking it further

This chapter has examined the role performed by law-making bodies in liberal democracies. A comparative study of these bodies is provided in Gerhard Loewenberg, *Legislatures: Comparative Perspectives on Representative Assemblies* (Michigan: University of Michigan Press, 2002). A more detailed consideration of the relationship between legislatures and executives can be found in Philip Norton, *Legislatures* (Oxford: Oxford University Press, 1990) and (in connection with America) Michael Foley and John Owen, *Congress and the Presidency* (Manchester: Manchester University Press, 1996).

The legislatures of many countries now televise their proceedings and these provide us with an interesting insight into how these bodies operate. In the United Kingdom, debates in both the House of Commons and the House of Lords are to be found on the BBC's *Parliamentary Channel*. Additionally, the House of Commons's website (www.parliament.uk) provides the full text of bills and debates which take place in the House of Commons.

12

the judiciary
and law
enforcement

In this chapter you will learn:
- how police forces are controlled
- the way courts and judges operate
- how politics may influence the work of judges

The politics of law enforcement

Why is law enforcement of interest to students of politics?

A system of law enforcement in any country must be seen as impartial if it is to be accepted as legitimate by its citizens. This is most easily guaranteed when the agencies engaged in the system of law enforcement (especially the courts and the police) are free from political pressures and biases and thus able to apply the law in the same manner to all persons within a country. However, total freedom from political pressures or involvement is impossible in any system of government. The courts and the police do not operate in a vacuum. These bodies are subject to political pressures and the role they perform and the decisions which they make may project them forcibly into the arena of politics.

Law enforcement and political control in the United Kingdom

The police service and judges traditionally exercised a considerable degree of autonomy in the exercise of their functions in the United Kingdom. However, the perception that this freedom was not necessarily compatible with the government's political objectives resulted in reforms designed to curb the discretion of professionals working in these two agencies.

The 1994 Police and Magistrates' Courts Act required police forces to attain objectives set for them by the home secretary thus limiting the ability of chief constables to set out the priorities for their forces as had previously been the case and central control was developed by subsequent home secretaries after 1997. The 1997 Crime (Sentences) Act aimed to limit the freedom which judges exercised over sentencing by introducing a range of mandatory sentences covering crimes which included murder and domestic burglary.

Thus, as students of politics, we need to be aware of the nature of the work performed by the police and the courts. We also need to consider the extent to which their activities are influenced by political considerations and the way in which the work they perform has significance for the manner in which political issues are resolved.

The control and accountability of the police

Who should exercise control over the police and to whom should the police account for their actions?

We are familiar with the sight of police officers patrolling our neighbourhoods on foot or in cars. Their main role is to ensure that all citizens obey the law. If they fail to do so the police can invoke a range of sanctions. These may include cautioning or arresting a person who is breaking the law, but we need to ensure that the police carry out their duties fairly and impartially. These objectives highlight the importance of the mechanisms that exist for the exercise of control over police work and through which the police can be made to account for their actions. These are important issues in liberal democratic systems of government.

National government control of policing

If a police force is controlled by, and accountable to, national government there is a danger that the main role of that organization will be to promote the political interests of the party or parties from which the government is formed. Typically, the government will identify its interests with those of the state. Thus, police operations might be directed by the national government or legislation might be interpreted for the police by that government. The police are then answerable to this body for the manner in which they have discharged their duties. The police therefore personify the state. They are the 'state in uniform'. Such a situation existed, for example, when South Africa was subject to white minority rule.

National control of policing

In France, central government performs a major role in police affairs. There are two main police forces. The *police nationale* is controlled by the Ministry of the Interior, while the *gendarmerie nationale* is technically part of the armed forces under the control of the Ministry of Defence. Officers from these bodies are also used as investigating officers to conduct inquiries under the supervision of an investigating judge or a public prosecutor. In this capacity they are termed the *police judiciaire* and are responsible to the judiciary.

In Ireland, the *garda siochana* operates on a national scale, controlled by a commissioner appointed by the minister of justice to whom the commissioner is theoretically responsible.

The main danger which might arise from such a close identification between the police and national government concerns the style of policing. If the main role of the police is to uphold the interests of the government, policing may be coercive in nature, directed against all those who disagree with the policies pursued by that government. Coercive policing is frequently pursued by paramilitary police bodies which take their orders from a minister in the national government. Their attitude may be that of 'shoot first and ask questions later' since there is no body other than the government to hold the police accountable for their actions.

Local government control of policing

A second possibility is that the police should be subject to local control. This may be performed by state governments, local authorities or by the direct election of police chiefs. The police would then be accountable to these local bodies for their activities. This would ensure that a number of police forces rather than a unified police service operated within the country. It may thus guard against police work being concerned with the advancement of the interests of one particular political party (or group of parties acting in alliance). It is likely that a range of political parties will exercise control over the large number of state or local governments found in any one country. This will prevent police work being primarily directed towards attaining one overriding political aim.

In this situation police work can be orientated towards issues felt to be of concern to ordinary members of the general public. Police activity is directed towards matters such as responding to crime and lawlessness rather than towards achieving the politicial priorities of national government. This role is appreciated by the public who support the police in their work. Policing is thus carried out with the consent of most members of the population.

Control of American policing

In America, policing is primarily a local affair, controlled by units of local government operating at county or municipal levels. The national guard which exists at state level may also perform police-related functions. Additionally the Federal Bureau of Investigation (FBI) is an agency of the justice department with the responsibility of enforcing federal laws and whose remit is thus nationwide. Local control, however, does not necessarily take the politics out of policing. State or local governments also have political objectives which they wish to fulfil and the police may be used to further these.

The development of urban policing in America, for example, was considerably influenced by local machine politics in which jobs and promotion in police forces and the tasks which the police fulfilled were greatly influenced by local politicians. Lack of efficiency and even corruption stemmed from this situation which persisted for a number of decades in the late nineteenth and early twentieth centuries.

Professional control of policing

A final option is that police work should be controlled by, and accountable to, those professionals who actually perform the work. Under this model, senior police officers in charge of police forces exercise control over such bodies and individual police officers are accountable for their actions to these commanders. This system of control and accountability might seem the best guarantee of political impartiality in the exercise of police work. It leaves the police free to determine what are the most important functions to discharge and thereby enhance the trust and co-operation of the general public.

There are, however, problems with such a system. The police and the public may have different views concerning issues such as what matters should receive priority attention. There is the danger that the police and public may become so distanced that their role is seen as illegitimate by citizens. It is also possible that members of the general public will distrust a system in which police officers are subject only to internal mechanisms of accountability. Remedies against abuse of power are difficult in a situation in which the police are a 'law unto themselves'. The United Kingdom concept of constabulary independence perhaps comes closest to the model of police work being subjected to the control of senior police officers. Their ability to direct policing was, however, considerably undermined when the 1994 Police and Magistrates' Courts Act enabled the home secretary to set national objectives which each force was required to meet.

The judicial system

What do the courts do?

The main role of the courts is to adjudicate a dispute between two parties. These two parties may be private citizens who are in dispute with each other. Alternatively, the state may be party to a case that comes before the courts.

No two liberal democratic countries have an identical judicial system. Differences especially exist concerning the conduct of trials. The United Kingdom and America utilize the adversarial system in which two parties seek to prove their case by discrediting that put forward by their opponents. The trial is presided over by a judge whose main function is to ensure fair play. Many European countries utilize an inquisitorial system. Here the gathering of evidence is the responsibility of the judge and the main function of the trial is to resolve issues uncovered in the earlier investigation. The judge will actively intervene in the trial in order to arrive at the truth.

In the remainder of this section we consider some of the main work performed by judicial systems.

Civil and criminal law

Civil law is concerned with the resolution of disagreements in which, typically, one party seeks some form of redress (such as damages) from a second party. Criminal law embraces activities that have broader social implications and which thus require the state to initiate a prosecution with a view to punishing the offender. Slander is an example of a civil action, murder is a criminal charge.

In many countries, civil and criminal matters are heard in different courts. This is not invariably the case, however. In France civil and criminal matters are heard in the one court, the *ordre judiciaire*, utilizing the same judicial personnel. In England and Wales a circuit judge may hear both civil and criminal cases and magistrates' courts perform some civil functions.

The organization of the courts in England and Wales

The civil and criminal courts in England and Wales are organized in a hierarchical fashion.

Most criminal cases are tried in magistrates' courts. The more serious, carrying heavier sentences, are heard in crown courts presided over by a judge and making use of a jury. Appeals against the verdicts reached in crown courts are heard by the Court of Appeal (Criminal Division).

Minor civil matters may be handled by the small claims procedure which seeks to resolve a dispute without the need to take it to open court. Most civil cases which go to court are heard by county courts, although the high court of justice may hear cases in which large sums of money are claimed. Appeals against a verdict reached in a county court or the high court will be heard by the Court of Appeal (Civil Division).

The House of Lords is the final court of appeal for both criminal and civil cases.

Scotland has a legal system which is different from that in England and Wales and the courts in Northern Ireland also function differently from their English and Welsh counterparts.

Administrative law

Administrative law is concerned with the relationship between a government and its citizens. In the United Kingdom challenges mounted by the general public to the actions or operations of the executive branch of government may be heard in the courts. The legality of delegated legislation or accusations of abuse of power may be challenged in this manner. Minor issues (such as a challenge to a decision taken by a civil servant) may, however, be resolved by a tribunal. Complaints of maladministration (that is an accusation that incorrect procedures were followed to arrive at a decision) may be submitted to the ombudsman.

In other countries, however, a separate court system exists to adjudicate upon such matters. Germany and France have a distinct system of courts concerned with administrative law.

The French system of administrative courts

A belief that the executive branch of government would become subordinate to the judiciary if the ordinary courts were able to review actions undertaken by the executive resulted in the establishment of a separate system of administrative courts in France. These have exclusive jurisdiction in a wide range of cases covered by public law, which involve disagreements between individuals and the workings of the state, including allegations of illegal actions undertaken by ministers, civil servants and public bodies.

The French system of administrative courts is headed by the *Conseil d'État*, which acts as both an advisory and a judicial body. The 1958 constitution specified a range of issues on which the government must consult this court before taking action. Below this is the *cour administrative d'appel*. This court possesses judicial powers alone and hears appeals from the *tribunal administratif*. The latter operates on a regional level and like the *Conseil d'État* is an advisory and judicial body.

Constitutional law

In some countries the courts may be also called upon to adjudicate disputes arising from the constitution. This is termed 'judicial review'. Typically, it involves assessing whether acts passed by the legislature accord with the statement of fundamental law contained in a country's constitution. But it may also scrutinize actions undertaken by the executive branch (such as the executive orders issued by the American president). If the courts decide that such actions are in breach of the constitution they may be declared 'unconstitutional'. This has the effect of overturning them: they are rendered 'null and void'.

Additionally, the courts may be required to determine the constitutionality of actions undertaken by sub-national bodies such as state governments. This form of adjudication is frequently required in federal states. The courts may also have to ensure that the allocation of responsibilities within and between the institutions of government remains as was provided for in the constitution.

In America, the process of judicial review is performed by the supreme court. This consists of nine judges appointed by the president subject to the consent of the Senate. Their intervention occurs when cases are referred to them on appeal either from the highest courts of appeal in the states or from the federal court of appeal. Judicial review provides the supreme court with considerable political power. In the 1950s and 1960s its decisions were influential in establishing the civil rights of black Americans.

The French Constitutional Court

In France, the *Conseil Constitutionnel* is responsible for ensuring that the constitution is adhered to. This body was instituted in the 1958 Constitution. It consists of nine members who are not required to be legally trained judges. Three of these are apppointed by the president of France, three by the president of the National Assembly and three by the president of the Senate. They serve for nine years and may not be renominated. Former presidents of the republic may also serve on this body.

Unlike the American supreme court, there are some limitations placed on the jurisdiction of this body and it further exercises a range of advisory power (including the requirement that it has to be consulted if the president intends to exercise emergency powers).

In Germany, the Federal Constitutional Court ensures that the constitution is obeyed. This body was established in 1951 and it is staffed by 16 judges who are formally appointed by the *Bundesrat* and *Bundestag* following nomination by all-party committees. In addition to its ability to declare law unconstitutional, it has further involved itself in the process of law making by suggesting how a law which it has declared to be unconstitutional can be amended in order to comply with the constitution. In Italy, the task of upholding the constitution is shared between a constitutional court and the president of the republic. The former's role includes acting as a court of impeachment for the president, prime minister and other ministers. The latter's tasks include ensuring that the actions of the executive and legislature conform to the relationship specified in the constitution.

A country that lacks a codified constitution (such as the United Kingdom) does not have any process whereby the actions of bodies such as parliament can be overturned. This procedure would be contrary to the concept of the sovereignty of parliament. This doctrine insists that parliament is the sole source of law-making power whose actions cannot be overruled by any other body. In countries with uncodified constitutions, judicial review has a more limited scope, that of scrutinizing the actions undertaken by the legislature, executive or other tiers of government to ensure that they accord with the requirements imposed upon them by legislation.

Judicial interpretation

In what sense can it be argued that judges are law makers?

In theory, the role of judges is to apply the law or the constitution to the matter that comes before them. However, it is often argued that judges go beyond this role and effectively determine its contents which are subsequently binding on courts dealing with similar cases. This situation arises as a result of judicial interpretation of such documents which may effectively give judges the ability to act in a law-making capacity. Judges differ, however, in the principles which they apply when interpreting the law or constitution. These are now discussed.

The strict letter of the law

Some judges rigidly apply the wording of the statute or constitution to the case that is before them. The judge's interpretation, therefore, is little more than the citation of existing sources as the basis for the decision which they reach. A case is determined according to the strict letter of the law. This strict interpretation view of the role of the judiciary tends to promote a conservative approach to judicial interpretation. It suggests that issues that are not contained in a country's law or constitution cannot be inserted into it by judges. Those who endorse such a view regard this as either the work of legislators or as a matter which should be responded to by the process of constitutional amendment.

Judicial activism

Other judges, however, exercise a wider degree of discretion when interpreting the law or constitution. Some who are faced with a situation that is not strictly covered by existing law or constitutional provision may believe it to be their responsibility to bring the existing law or the constitution up to date.

Alternatively, a statute or constitutional provision at issue in a case may lack precision or be ambiguous and thus capable of having more than one meaning. The judge will thus be required to give an opinion as to the correct course of action that should be pursued in the case with which they are dealing. In these situations judicial interpretation departs from the precise wording of the law or constitution. It may be guided by one or other of two principles.

Judges may decide a case according to the spirit of the law or constitution. That is, they reach a verdict based on what they view to be compatible with existing law or constitutional enactments rather than what is actually contained in them. In reaching their decision, judges may seek to determine what was in the minds of those who initially drafted the law or constitution and apply this to the case before them. Other judges may go beyond this. They may consider it their duty to adjudicate a case according to what they believe should be contained in the law or constitution rather than what actually is there.

Both of these principles enable a judge to advance beyond the mere administration of the law and, instead, to act in the capacity of a legislator. That is, they advance existing law or create new law through the ability they give themselves to interpret laws and constitutions. The term 'judicial activism' is applied to the situation in which judges exercise a positive role in policy making.

Judicial interpretation may help to ensure that the law or constitution is kept up to date or accords with changing public sentiments as to what constitutes reasonable conduct. However, critics of this role argue that judges ought to distinguish between interpreting the law and actually writing it. They assert that judicial interpretation leads judges to perform a role which ought to be carried out by the legislative branch of government or through the process of constitutional amendment.

The politics of the judiciary

To what extent is the operation of the judiciary subject to political considerations?

We know from our own experiences that it is difficult to act in a totally detached and neutral manner. Our actions are likely to be based upon our personal values. Judges are no exception to this. The following evaluates some of the factors that might influence the way in which judges discharge their responsibilities and the extent to which they are sufficiently accountable for their actions.

Personal values

The personal values of judges may exert considerable influence on the way in which they perform their duties. These values may be influenced by factors including the judges' social background or legal training. This suggests that it is desirable that judges should be representative of the society in which they operate in terms such as class, gender or race. If judges are socially unrepresentative they may be open to the accusation of discriminatory conduct towards those from a different background.

Political opinions

The political opinions held by a judge may also influence how that official operates. These may derive from the position which the judiciary operates in the machinery of the state. In a liberal democracy judges may regard the preservation of this system of government to be of paramount importance. This may influence the attitude which judges display in cases when state interests are involved. Alternatively, these opinions may consist of the judge's own political preferences. In many countries the executive branch of government has the ability to appoint judges. In America, for example, presidents often seek to promote their political values through the appointments they make to the federal judicial system, especially to the supreme court. They thus appoint judges to these positions whose political views mirror their own.

The politics of judicial appointment in America

In America, all federal judges and justices of the Supreme Court are appointed by the president. Inquiries into a candidate's background are initiated on behalf of the chief executive. Following this, however, they are required to be confirmed by the Senate whose judiciary committee conducts hearings into a nominee's suitability. Judges of the Supreme Court serve for life subject to 'good behaviour'. The ability of this body to overrule state and federal legislators and the chief executive influences presidents to appoint judges whose political views closely correspond to their own. For similar reasons, the Senate may pay regard to issues other than the professional competence of a nominee who comes before them for confirmation.

Some presidents have the opportunity to appoint a large number of federal judges and others very few. However, when one party has filled the office of president for a number of years, it is likely that the composition of the federal courts will reflect this control. Thus, when President Clinton entered office in 1992, he was faced with a conservative Supreme Court whose personnel had been mainly chosen by previous Republican presidents. During his presidency he was able to nominate only two members of this nine-member court.

Judicial accountability

We have suggested that the personal views of judges and political considerations might influence the way in which the courts operate. If we accept that judges are able to inject personal or political biases into their work, especially when interpreting the law or constitution, we need to examine the sufficiency of mechanisms through which judges can be made to explain and justify their actions and, if necessary, be punished for them. In a liberal democracy members of the legislative and executive branches of government (who in theory are charged with initiating and carrying out legislation) are accountable for their actions. Ultimately, they rely on public support to enter or remain in public office. Judges, however, are usually insulated from any direct form of political accountability for their actions, even when these have a fundamental bearing on political affairs. They are usually unelected (although this method of appointment does apply in some American states) and once appointed enjoy security of tenure.

There are, however, some formal controls over the activities of judges. These include the ability of politicians to intervene in the operations of the criminal justice system (which in the United Kingdom includes legislation setting out a wide range of mandatory sentences which judges are required to implement). The use of juries may help to offset judicial biases. The decisions of judges can also be set aside by a revision to the law or an amendment to the constitution.

Judges and politics in America

The ability of the executive branch of government to appoint members to the judicial branch may be of considerable political importance. In 2000, the US Supreme Court was able to determine the outcome of that year's presidential election.

Concern about voting practices in the state of Florida (especially in connection with discounted votes) resulted in manual recounts being commenced. The Supreme Court intervened in this process, first by halting this process and then by ruling that there was no time to stage proper recounts of disputed ballots. This decision meant that Florida's 25 electoral college votes were given to the Republican candidate, George W. Bush, who obtained a majority of 537 votes out of the almost six million votes which were cast in that state. These 25 electoral college votes gave Bush a narrow majority in the electoral college and he thus became President.

This decision contravened the traditional reluctance of the Supreme Court to intervene in elections (which were regarded as functions administered by the states) and eroded the defence of state rights which this court had upheld in recent years. Some commentators believed that party politics were a factor in the decision of the court (seven of whose nine members had been nominated by previous Republican presidents).

The tenure of judges

Liberal democratic political systems usually give judges considerable security of tenure. This is designed to ensure that these public officials cannot be placed under pressure to determine cases according to the wishes of the government of the day. In the United Kingdom, for example, senior judges can only be removed by an address of both Houses of Parliament to the Queen. In Ireland, judges can only be dismissed for misbehaviour and incapacity, and to do this requires resolutions from the *Dail* and the *Seanad*. Additionally, an Irish judge's remuneration may not be reduced during that official's continuance in office.

Security of tenure tends to make judges insufficiently accountable for their actions. They are able to say and do more or less what they like in the sure knowledge that they do not have to answer directly to politicians or to the public at large.

This is particularly a problem when judicial interpretation effectively gives judges a key role in the determination of public policy.

Additionally, judges may be subject to informal pressures. In particular they may be influenced by a consideration of what is acceptable to the public at large and seek to ensure that their judgements accord with what they discern as the prevailing political consensus. It has been argued that the American Supreme Court watches the election returns. This suggests that public and political opinion may play a role in determining judicial decisions.

Questions

1 'Policing is a local function which should be controlled by local government.' Examine the strengths and weaknesses of this form of control over policing.
2 In what ways can judges act as law makers? Is this a good or a bad development?
3 Do you believe it is desirable to make judges more politically accountable for their actions?

Taking it further

This chapter has discussed the process of law enforcement and the role performed by judges and the courts in liberal democracies. Particular attention has been devoted to the politics of the judiciary. Greater consideration of this issue can be found in Richard Hodder-Williams, *Judges and Politics in the Contemporary Age* (London: Bowerdean, 1996) (which contains comparative discussion based on the United Kingdom and America), John Griffith, *The Politics of the Judiciary* (London: Fontana Press, 1997) and Robert Stevens, The Independence of the Judiciary (Oxford: Clarendon, 1997).

Further information concerning the process of reform affecting the judiciary in the United Kingdom can be found at the web site of the Department for Constitutional Affairs which was set up in June 2003 (www.lcd.gov.uk).

sub-national government

In this chapter you will learn:
- the operations of unitary and federal states
- the role performed by local government
- the process of local government reform in Britain

Definition

What is meant by the term 'sub-national government'?

A major role performed by government is to provide services for the benefit of the general public. Many of these are provided by national government. However, others are controlled and administered by bodies covering only part of a particular country. There are a wide variety of these, but in this chapter we will confine our attention to state, regional and local authorities. These constitute important examples of what is meant by 'sub-national government'.

Sub-national governments are subject to considerable variation. A key distinction concerns the autonomy which such units enjoy. In federal states, such as Germany, Australia or America, power is divided between the national (or federal) government and the constituent units of government. The division of responsibilities is provided for in a single source, usually a written constitution, which allocates specific functions to each sphere of government. Each enjoys autonomy in its own area of jurisdiction which means that one may not intrude into the operations of the other. There may also be functions which are exercised jointly by both tiers of government.

The alternative to a federal state is a unitary one. In unitary states, political power is centralized in the hands of the national government. Countries including the United Kingdom, Sweden and France possess such forms of government. However, unitary states often possess a unit of government which is intermediate between national and local government. These are usually regional bodies which provide services for a relatively wide geographic area where the inhabitants share some form of common identity such as language, culture or race. Regional authorities vary according to the autonomy they possess: some exercise power which is devolved from national government thus giving them a wide degree of control over such delegated responsibilities, while others merely function as administrative bodies whose role is to provide regional services according to guidelines laid down by national government.

In both federal and unitary states a range of services are provided by subordinate authorities, termed 'local government'. The scope of their activities and extent of their autonomy is subject to wide variation. In many western European and

Scandinavian countries and in America, local government is created by constitutional enactment and has the ability to perform any function unless expressly forbidden to do so by law. This is termed 'general competence'. In the United Kingdom and Ireland, however, local government has no constitutional status. Its existence is derived from legislation and it may only perform those functions which are expressly allocated to it by legislation. This situation tends to vastly curtail the autonomy which is exercised by local authorities in these two countries, although in the United Kingdom discretionary powers provide such bodies with a significant degree of operational and innovatory freedom.

Federalism

What are the strengths and weaknesses of a federal political structure?

Federal political structures possess strengths and weaknesses. We consider these in the sections that follow.

Advantages

We have identified the division of power between a national government and constituent units such as states or provinces as the essence of a federal form of government. This situation possesses a number of advantages.

An aid to the relationship between the government and its citizens

Federalism was historically viewed as a safeguard against the overbearing power of a strong, central government. In large countries it breaks down the remoteness which would otherwise occur if government were provided by a distant national authority. Government is thus brought closer to the people who additionally are provided with the means to participate in its activities through the process of voting or through their involvement with locally orientated pressure groups.

Facilitating diversity in one country

New right ideology emphasizes the virtues that derive from the diversity with which a federal system of government may be associated. Variations within one country in matters such as taxation or the level of services may prove attractive to citizens or to commercial organizations which are encouraged to move from part of the country to another to benefit themselves. Diversity may thus encourage competition between states to attract people and industry.

Maintenance of national unity

The autonomy possessed by state governments in a federal system may be of benefit to nations whose existence is threatened by significant internal division. Provided that a nation provides recognizable political or economic benefits to all of its citizens, groups with divergent interests may be encouraged to remain within the one state when the power possessed by the national government is limited with most functions being provided by governments controlled by local people. Federalism thus empowers localities to run most aspects of their affairs in accordance with the wishes of the people who reside there with restricted 'interference' by a national government. It may thus contribute towards retaining the existence of states threatened by separatist tendencies. Belgium granted considerable powers of self-government to its Flemish and Walloon communities within the confines of a federation in order to prevent the break-up of the state along linguistic lines. For similar reasons a wide degree of autonomy has been granted to the Canadian province of Quebec.

Federalism in Canada

Canada consists of a federation of provinces. There exist strong separatist forces in one of these, Quebec. This is underlaid by its French language and culture.

In an attempt to retain national unity, Canada's federal system of government has provided Quebec with considerable powers of self-government especially in connection with the official use of French. However, this situation has not been to the satisfaction of many Quebeckers who desire separation. This would enable Quebec to negotiate future relations with the remainder of Canada on its own terms. In 1995, a referendum was held on the issue of separation. Quebeckers rejected it by the narrowest of margins.

The existing level of self-government contributed to the rejection of separation: the continued unity of the nation may depend on the ability of the national government to redefine its relations with Quebec through the provision of a special status designed to provide an enhanced degree of autonomy within a federal structure of government.

Disadvantages

There are, however, problems associated with federal systems of government. We discuss the main ones now.

Fragmention of government

Federalism results in government in one country being fragmented. Diverse standards of service provision operating in a single country are not necessarily desirable. Further, the autonomy granted to sub-national units of government may provide a minority with the means to frustrate the will of the majority. The progress of civil rights in America has been impeded by the ability of southern state governments to resist or to slow down the implementation of such legislation. Some of these problems may, however, be mitigated. In America, for example, the existence of intergovernmental bureaucracies, composed of paid officials operating at all levels of government, has served to promote common approaches to problems pursued by all tiers of government.

Enhancement of the power of national governments

One particular difficulty with federalism concerns the distribution of power between the national and constituent governments. This division is provided for in the constitution and disputes between the two tiers of government are arbitrated by a constitutional court. However, a tendency for the power of national governments to be enhanced at the expense of states has been observed in many federal countries. In America, this alteration to the fundamental nature of federalism has partly arisen from the willingness of the Supreme Court to interpret the constitution in a manner which is favourable towards national governments playing an increased role in economic and social policies. A particular consequence has been increased reliance by the states on revenue provided by national government. This has made for a style of government in which collaboration between the two tiers (and especially by their public officials) has become essential.

Financial aid to state governments may erode the independence of the latter. This became a particular issue in Germany following reunification in 1990 since the states which comprised the former country of East Germany were heavily dependent on federal financial support. Such money may be given to states largely to use as they please (as occurs in Germany and was the case with President Nixon's General Revenue Sharing policy in America) or it may be attached to stringent conditions which states have to meet (as occurred under President Reagan in America). The states' freedom of action may also be circumscribed by action imposed by the national government which is designed to enforce conformity and set minimum standards of service provision. In America, pre-emption is an example of the latter. This imposes a legal requirement on states to meet certain minimum standards or to provide stipulated services.

Nonetheless, states continue to play an important role in the economic and social life of a federal country. In America, for example, the ability of the states to raise some of their own revenue and their role as implementators of public policy may enhance their image as dynamic institutions even if they are subject to the strong central control exerted by the federal government over many aspects of their operations.

Confederation

A confederation is a political structure in which a group of nations agree to co-operate to achieve common aims which are frequently of a defensive or economic nature. It bears some relationship to federalism, the key difference concerning the powers of the national government. In a federal structure the central government has a wide degree of power which may (as has been the case in America) be expanded at the expense of the state governments. By contrast, the national government of a confederation has extremely limited powers with most tasks of government being performed by those states or countries which are part of it. These retain their sovereignty and their right to secede. A particular feature of a confederation is that the national government has no direct powers over citizens: functions such as taxation and law enforcement are exercised by the constituent governments.

The main difficulties associated with confederations include the absence of a strong central government able effectively to co-ordinate the actions of its members, which may especially be required in times of crisis. These structures are also often dominated by the larger of its members.

A confederal system of government was established by the American colonies engaged in the War of Independence against Britain. The Articles of Confederation which were drawn up by the Continental Congress in 1777 provided for a confederacy to be known as the United States of America. The 11 southern states of America which seceded in the Civil War were also subject to this form of government between 1861 and 1865. The Commonwealth of Independent States (established in 1991 following the collapse of the Soviet Union) is a more recent creation.

Further examples of federations are also found in organizations which seek to promote social, political or economic matters that are in the mutual interests of those who are members. Membership of such organizations is typically voluntary and includes the North Atlantic Treaty Organisation. The European Union has some elements of a confederal political structure. Confederations may develop into federal structures of government (as happened in Switzerland, which became a federation in the fourteenth century despite retaining the title *Confédération Helvétique*).

Governing a divided nation – consociationalism

Consociationalism (which is often referred to as power sharing) seeks to provide a stable system of government in a plural society which is characterized by the existence of fundamental divisions (which may be based upon religion, race, language, ideology or culture) and in which other key aspects of civic affairs (such as political parties, pressure groups and the educational system) are organized on the same basis. The groups into which society is divided compete for control of the same territory.

This model for governing divided societies was developed by a Dutch political scientist, Arend Lijphart, who wrote *Democracy in Plural Societies* (published in 1977). He put forward four key features of consociational democracy. The first feature was government by a grand coalition of the political leaders of all the significant sections into which society was divided. This entails co-operation by political elites in the formation of an executive branch of government. The second feature was the introduction of a veto which the various sections could use to defend their interests against majority decisions and a third was that political representation should be based on proportional principles. The final aspect of consociationalism was that each section of society should be granted a high degree of autonomy to regulate its own affairs.

Consociationalism, entailing the establishment of a coalition government composed of representatives of various ethnic groups to provide unified government for the territory which they share, is practised in Northern Ireland. The 1998 Northern Ireland

Act provided for an assembly elected under proportional representation and an executive committee composed of ministers drawn from the major parties represented in the assembly. This arrangement brought together the leaders of Northern Ireland's nationalist and unionist communities.

Regionalism

What functions are served by regional machinery of government?

States with unitary political structures are often accused of being centralized: power resides in the capital and citizens living in areas that are geographically distant from this area may feel neglected by a government which they regard as remote. Some unitary states, therefore, have utilized regional apparatus to offset the disadvantages which are sometimes perceived in a centralized state. This involves a state being divided into a number of smaller areas within which certain tasks of government can be discharged. The role and composition of regional machinery is variable and many different forms may be used even in one state. We consider the main varieties of regional machinery in the following sections.

Advisory

Regional machinery may be purely advisory. It can be utilized as a consultative mechanism to facilitate overall government planning of particular activities (such as the nation's economic development) or it might be established by individual government departments to aid the flow of information between that department and citizens living in each region. This may enable central government to adjust the operations of a policy to suit the particular requirements of a region and its inhabitants, or it may be used to provide advice on government policies to people or public authorities residing there. This machinery is typically staffed by civil servants and possesses no power other than the ability to act as a vehicle which facilitates a two-way process of communication between government and the governed.

Administrative and governmental

A region may alternatively provide the geographic unit around which services are administered. This embraces the decentralized regional apparatus used by national governmental organizations but also includes regional machinery that has been established to provide services. Regional machinery may be established to discharge individual services: in Ireland, for example, health services have been provided by area health boards since 1971. Alternatively several governmental functions can be co-ordinated at a regional level. This was the case in the United Kingdom until the devolution legislation affecting Scotland, Wales and Northern Ireland was passed in 1998. Previously, the Scottish and Welsh Offices had been responsible for a range of services in these two countries which were performed by individual government departments in England. Those who administer services in this fashion may possess some discretion to tailor them to address specific regional needs or requirements.

Regional machinery may be given some degree of power. This will often be exercised by representatives who are elected at regional level and who then discharge a range of services over which they possess partial or total control. Italy, for example, is divided into 20 regions, each of which has a directly elected council that exercises control over a wide range of functions. A considerable proportion of the national budget is under the control of Italy's regional councils. In the United Kingdom the Scottish parliament and the Welsh and Northern Ireland assemblies have exercised responsibilities allocated to them by the 1998 devolution legislation. This process may be expanded by the establishment of regional authorities in England in control of substantial budgets to spend on services such as transport, planning and training.

Devolution, federalism and home rule

Devolution involves the transfer of power from a superior to an inferior political authority. The dominance of the former is generally exhibited through its ability to reform or take away the power which it has given.

Federalism necessitates a division of power between central and sub-national governments. The existence of the latter and the general range of powers they possess is usually embodied in the provisions of a codified constitution.

Home rule requires the break-up of a nation into a number of sovereign states, each exercising total control over its internal and external affairs. This demand is usually based on the existence of a national identity.

Regional administration in Spain

Regional government may possess sufficient power to alter the nature of a unitary political structure into one that approximates a federal one. This degree of power may be important in enabling national government and strong regional affiliations to be reconciled. This is the case in Spain and may be illustrated by the example of the attempts made by the regional government of Cataluxa (Catalonia) to promote the use of their language (Catalan) in that area.

In 1979, 17 regions (or 'autonomous communities') were set up, each with an assembly (elected by the party list form of proportional representation) and a president (elected by the assembly). The 1978 Constitution made Castilian the pre-eminent language in Spain but at the same time also recognized others, leaving regional parliaments with the ability to determine the balance. In 1983, the regional parliament in Catalonia decreed the mandatory use of Catalan in regional government. In 1998, a law was proposed to require that 50 per cent of new films shown in Catalonia should use this language and that private radio stations operating there should broadcast half their output in that language.

Local government

What advantages does local government bring to the operations of liberal democratic political systems?

Local government has responsibility for providing a range of services to people living in part of a country. Many of the functions traditionally associated with local government constitute services that are utilized by large numbers of citizens on a daily basis. These include the provision of housing, social services, environmental services, refuse disposal and planning. Education is frequently provided by local government, although in France this service has traditionally been subject to a considerable degree of central control. Changes proposed in the late 1990s, however, sought to devolve increased control over this service to local level.

The scope of the activities of local government and the extent of its autonomy is widely varied. In many western European and Scandinavian countries local government is created by constitutional enactment, and in America it is provided for in state constitutions. In countries which include France, Italy, Sweden and Denmark, local government has 'general competence', that is, the ability to perform any function unless expressly forbidden to do so by law. In the United Kingdom and Ireland, however, local government has no constitutional status. Its existence is derived from legislation and it may only perform those functions that are expressly allocated to it by law passed by parliament. This situation tends vastly to curtail the autonomy which is exercised by local authorities in these two countries, although in the United Kingdom discretionary powers provide some degree of operational and innovatory freedom.

We now go on to consider the functions that local government may perform in a liberal democratic political system.

Public involvement in policy making

The existence of local government enhances the ability of citizens to take part in the administration of their own affairs. They may do this by voting in local government elections or by serving as elected members of local authorities. Local government thus increases the number of people in a state able to take decisions related to the administration of its affairs.

Local accountability

A major advantage of local government stems from the fact that it is composed of elected officials. In English-speaking liberal democracies these are usually termed 'councillors'. They can be held accountable to the local electorate for the way in which services are provided. In this way the functions discharged by government can be made compatible with what local people desire. There are alternative ways to provide services (such as through development corporations which have been used selectively in the United Kingdom since 1979) but the elected dimension of local government is the key to its responsiveness to local issues and problems.

Efficiency in service provision

It has been further suggested that local government is the most efficient way to provide public services. Its size enables local problems (which may be untypical of the nation as a whole) to

Consultation and participation

In addition to voting or standing for office, local people may also be enabled to play a role in the day-to-day affairs of local government. This is achieved through the processes of consultation and participation.

Consultation involves mechanisms whereby the general public are able to make their views known to those who take decisions. This may be achieved through surveys, exhibitions or advisory bodies. The key feature of consultation is that policy makers are not bound to follow the opinions expressed to them: they agree to listen but are not required to act in accordance with them.

Participation entails a change in the power relationship between citizens and policy makers. It is thus more radical than consultation since power is shared with the general public and policy making becomes a joint exercise involving governors and the governed. In the United Kingdom, mechanisms to achieve this include a local authority ceding to tenants' associations the ability to exercise control over the running of a council housing estate.

Consultation and participation might be regarded as beneficial to liberal democracies as they permit the views of the public to be considered or acted upon by public officials. However, the lack of information in the hands of the general public might make meaningful discussion impossible and may even result in the public being manipulated into giving their backing to contentious proposals put forward by the policy makers.

be addressed, which might be overlooked were all government services administered by larger geographic units such as state or local governments. Local government is also flexible in its approach to problems and has the ability to innovate in an attempt to find solutions to them. In the United Kingdom reforms to the management of local government introduced by the 1997 Labour government (which are referred to on pages 258–9) were influenced by experiments in local authoritites such as Hammersmith and Fulham, which had installed a mayor and small cabinet to speed up decision making.

Pursuit of social objectives

Local government may serve as a vehicle to advance social objectives such as gender or racial equality which may have a low priority on the national political agenda. It may do so through its role as an employer, purchaser or provider of services. Since the passage of the 1976 Race Relations Act, local government in the United Kingdom has had a statutory duty to eliminate racial discrimination and has been at the forefront of developing equal opportunities policies.

The receptiveness of local government to social concerns may help to overcome the problem of marginalization, whereby particular minority groups perceive that the operations of the conventional political system do not cater for their needs. These may be encouraged to become involved in conventional political activity at local level as it presents a realistic possibility that some of their concerns might be addressed. In both the United Kingdom and America, a significant number of councillors derive from ethnic minority backgrounds. This involvement may reduce the likelihood of such minority groups having to resort to more extreme forms of political activity that have a damaging effect on social harmony.

Linking citizens with national government

In many countries local government is viewed as a training ground for politicians who later occupy high national office. It may also serve as an institutional mechanism linking local people with national government. This is especially apparent in France where leading politicians sometimes hold elected office in municipal government. This situation provides national politicians with powerful localized bases of support.

Acting as a pressure group

An important role performed by local government is acting as a pressure group, putting forward local needs or concerns to other tiers of government and seeking remedies, perhaps through the provision of increased funds to the locality or by changes in central government policy. The early 1980s witnessed some Labour-controlled local authorities in the United Kingdom providing confrontational opposition to Conservative government policies which they believed were harmful to local people. The ability of local government to act in this manner is enhanced by its elected base, which implies it is acting at the behest of local majority opinion.

Barometers of public opinion

Although local government elections should be concerned with local issues, their outcome is frequently determined by national considerations. This arises because, in many liberal democracies, local government elections are contested by the same parties that compete for power nationally. This may mean that the outcome of such contests is heavily influenced by voters' opinions on the performance of the parties (including the record of the government) at national level. Local government elections may thus provide evidence of the political mood of the nation and serve as a means whereby the general public can exert influence over the conduct or composition of the national government.

The performance of local government

The benefits which are meant to derive from the operations of local government are not always fully realized. Local government may be unable to respond effectively to contemporary issues. Its organizational base may be inappropriate and its revenue-generating capacity inadequate to offer workable solutions to problems such as urban poverty which are manifested at local level, especially in inner city areas. In such places the demand for services is high but the ability of people to pay for them is low. This tends to drive up the level of local taxes and encourage wealthier people to move away. This situation may result in increased reliance on finance supplied by state or national governments or lead to the delivery of services by purpose-built bodies detached from the organizational structure of local government.

Local government may not always be adequately responsive to local needs and problems. Its ability to act in this way may be diminished by factors such as the working practices adopted by local government officers or the lack of social representativeness of those elected to local office. Party politics may require elected councillors to put the interests of their party above the concerns of those they represent. Services are administered by full-time officers who may put their professional interests above the requirements of those they view as their 'clients'. In some countries, the political power is centralized within a local authority so that power is wielded by a handful of people. This has the effect of making local government seem remote and unapproachable to ordinary people. The decentralization of locally administered services is one solution to this problem, but it has not been pursued in the UK with the vigour found in other countries such as France and Spain.

Perhaps as a result of these two deficiencies, public interest in local government is low in some countries. In the UK, for example, the turnout in local elections rarely rises above 40 per cent. This suggests that here local government is not particularly effective as a vehicle through which people can take part in government.

Further, in most liberal democracies, local elections are contested by the national political parties. This means that the outcome of local election contests is greatly influenced by national political issues: factors such as the degree of popular support for the national government may be more influential in determining the outcome of a local election than the performance of the authority.

Central control and local autonomy

In what ways are the operations of local government subject to control by national government?

In most liberal democracies, local government is subject to a considerable degree of control by national or state governments. This may be exercised in a number of ways.

Control by the executive branch

The executive branch may impose a range of controls on the operations of local government. These include specific controls over individual services, limits on local government spending or detailed controls over local government borrowing. In Ireland, central supervision is also exerted over the personnel employed by local authorities.

The prefectoral system

The prefectoral system offers a way in which local government can be controlled by higher political authorities. This involves the imposition of an official appointed by central government to act as its eyes and ears in the localities and provide a link between central and local government, effectively fusing the two levels of administration.

The system whereby a representative of central government (usually termed a 'prefect' or 'governor') is appointed alongside an elected regional or provincial assembly is relatively common in Europe. The main purpose of such an official is to provide a link between local and national government, which is sometimes aided by regional assemblies appointing a board of representatives who meet under the prefect's chairmanship. Arrangements of this nature exist in Denmark, Sweden, Spain, Greece and Italy. In Italy, the prefect is the state's representative in the localities (termed 'provinces'). This official is usually an official of the Ministry of the Interior, but is sometimes a career politician. In theory, the prefect's main role is to co-ordinate the work of central government ministries at local level, although in practice much attention is directed at the maintenance of public order and security.

The prefectoral system in France

In France, the prefect (who was termed 'commissioner of the republic' between 1982 and 1987) is a civil servant appointed by the Ministry of the Interior and placed in each department and, after 1972, in each region. The prefect formerly exerted considerable day-to-day powers over the departments and their constituent local government units (termed 'communes'). The extent of such power over local authority actions was subject to variation, but was universally reduced by reforms enacted by the Socialist government in the 1980s. These served to reduce the previously highly centralized nature of French local government. However, prefects continue to wield supervisory powers over local government.

Judicial control

In countries in which the powers of local government are rigidly controlled by legislation, judicial control may constitute an important control. In the United Kingdom, for example, the courts are able to intervene and prevent local authorities from performing functions which they are not legally empowered to perform and may also force a council to discharge its mandatory duties if it was ignoring these.

Local government reform in Britain

What innovations to local government have been introduced since 1979?

Conservative governments between 1979 and 1997 displayed a critical attitude towards local government. They accused it of waste and inefficiency aggravated by poor management and of putting political interests before service to the community. This resulted in increased central control being exerted over local government and a loss of functions with which it has traditionally been associated.

Reform to the structure of local government

The structure of local government was altered. The two-tier system of county and district councils that had been implemented under the provisions of the 1972 Local Government Act was abandoned in the major urban areas in 1986 when the Greater London Council and the metropolitan county councils were abolished. There was subsequently a move towards creating single-tier, or unitary authorities, throughout much of the United Kingdom in the belief that it was more efficient and cost effective for services to be administered by one set of hands. Additionally, the Labour government provided a new directly elected assembly for London in the 1999 London Government Act.

Loss of functions

Services were also being taken out of the hands of local government and transferred to a range of alternative authorities including joint boards, quangos and central government. The involvement of central government greatly increased in policy areas such as education, which was traditionally viewed as a local responsibility. Government policy has also served to weaken the role performed by local government in functions which include the provision of public housing. Government policy initiated in the 1980 Housing Act resulted in the sale of vast numbers of council houses and much of the work previously carried out by local authorities in the area of what became known as 'social housing' became assumed by housing associations.

Controls over local government spending

Additional controls were introduced to curtail the level of expenditure by local government. This was justified by the argument that the national government was required to exercise overall control over the level of public spending. Key legislation to achieve this objective included the 1980 Local Government, Planning and Land Act, the 1982 Local Government Finance Act and the 1984 Rates Act.

Estimates of what each local authority needed to spend were drawn up by central government initially in the form of grant-related expenditure. This determined the level of local government grant paid to local authorities by central government, but it was possible to exceed the government's overall estimate by raising additional funds locally through the rates. Accordingly, 'capping' was introduced in 1984, which allowed the government to enforce a ceiling on the overall expenditure of those authorities which were viewed as particularly spendthrift. In 1990, Standard Spending Assessments were introduced to influence the level of locally raised revenue. Like the previous grant-related expenditure, these limits were also underlaid by the sanction of capping.

The key reform introduced by the Conservative Party which sought to curb local government spending was the introduction of a new source of finance through which local government would fund its operations. The rates (which was a tax levied on property) was replaced by a tax on individuals. This was the community charge, more infamously known as 'poll tax'. It was designed to enhance the accountability of local government to its residents by forcing all citizens to contribute towards the costs of local government. In this way it was envisaged that high spending councils would be more readily sanctioned by local electors since exemptions and rebates associated with the rating system resulted in a significant number of local residents having to make no financial contribution to the costs of local services. This new tax became law in 1988 and was first introduced in England and Wales in 1990.

However, the introduction of poll tax was surrounded with controversy. It was an extremely difficult and expensive tax to collect, and its problems were compounded by a campaign seeking to encourage people not to pay. It was argued that the tax was essentially unfair by making all contribute regardless of their means. Eventually, the government was forced to back down. Poll tax was abandoned and replaced by the council tax as local government's independent source of finance. This was essentially a tax on property, the level of which was determined by the value of property (which was viewed as suggestive of the financial means of its occupants). In 1990, a uniform business rate was introduced to govern the financial contribution made by business concerns towards the costs of local authorities in which they are situated.

Conservative reforms to local government finance served to enhance the power of central government over the level of local spending and also established central government as the main contributor towards it.

Privatization

The concept of market forces was introduced into the operations of local government in order to make local government provide enhanced value for money. A large number of services were transferred from direct local government control and made subject to competitive tendering. Legislation which included the 1980 Local Government, Planning and Land Act and the 1988 and 1990 Local Government Acts has moved local government in the direction of an enabling authority rather than one which directly provided services. The implication that people may be attracted to move to the most efficient and cost-effective local authorities has been enhanced by the Audit Commission's publication of local authority performance indicators, commencing in 1995. Conservative governments also sought to involve the private sector in projects which included the rejuvenation of declining urban areas. Although this sometimes involved local government working in partnership with financial and business interests, this approach has, on occasions, resulted in the establishment of bodies such as urban development corporations and task forces which have bypassed local government.

Internal control of local government

The internal arrangements affecting the operations of local government are subject to wide variation between and within liberal democractic political systems.

The executive arm of local government is composed in different ways. A key distinction exists between a directly elected executive (such as the American mayor) or an executive selected from the leading members of the largest political party represented on the local authority.

Internal management is also subject to variation. Ireland utilizes the council manager system in which all services are co-ordinated by one person. The manager's position and powers are based on legislation. In other countries, individual local government committees may exercise a considerable degree of autonomy.

The 1997 Labour government abandoned compulsory competitive tendering in favour of what is termed 'best value', which replaced the Conservative emphasis on value for money. Best value sought to promote economy and efficiency in service provision by requiring service providers to demonstrate to a process of independent audit that they were providing best value. However, this approach went beyond the measurement of quantifiable data by suggesting that the cheapest service provider was not always the best choice.

In the United Kingdom, changes to local government introduced by the 1997 Labour government have included reforms to its management. The 1999 London Government Act created a directly elected mayor for London. Elsewhere a white paper issued in 1998, *Modern Local Government: In Touch with the People,* initiated changes in the management structure of local government by requiring local authorities to prepare plans for new structures based on a directly elected mayor and a cabinet, a cabinet with a leader of the council or a directly elected mayor and a council manager.

Questions

1 Drawing examples from countries with federal political structures, evaluate the strengths and weaknesses of this form of government.
2 Using examples of your own, distinguish between federalism and regionalism.
3 To what extent can it be argued that local government performs a key role in liberal democractic political systems?

Taking it further

This chapter has examined the concept of federalism and has discussed the role performed by local goverment in liberal democratic systems of government.

An interesting account of federalism in European countries is found in Jurg Steiner, *European Democracies* (Harlow: Longman, 1998). American federalism is discussed in a number of general accounts of American government which include Philip Davies and Fredric Waldstein (editors), *Political Issues in America Today: The 1990s Revisited* (Manchester: Manchester University Press, 1996), David McKay and D.D. Raphael, *American Politics and Society* (Oxford: Blackwell, 2001) and Duncan Watts, *Understanding American Government and Politics* (Manchester: Manchester University Press, 2002).

Contemporary developments affecting sub-national government in the United Kingdom include consideration of the establishment of regional assemblies in England which would operate alongside devolved government in Northern Ireland, Scotland and Wales. Details of the campaign to promote this reform can be found at the Campaign for English Regions website address, www. cfer.org.uk.

A useful account on the development of local government in Britain is provided by Andrew Stevens, *Politico's Guide to Local Government* (London: Politicos Publishing, 2003). Information on current policies affecting local government can be obtained from the Local Government Association whose address is 1st Floor, Local Government House, Smith Square, London, SW1P 3HZ (www.lga.gov.uk).

14

the nation state in the modern world

In this chapter you will learn:
- what is meant by the term 'sovereignty'
- why states cannot control all aspects of their domestic affairs
- the key changes affecting the development of the European Union

Definition

What does the term 'sovereignty' mean?

Sovereignty entails a body possessing unrestricted power. In contemporary politics it has two dimensions. Internal sovereignty refers to the existence of a supreme legal or political authority which has the power to make decisions that are binding on all of its citizens.

Internal sovereignty is divided within federal states. In countries which include America, Australia, Canada and Germany, the national government may enact legislation in certain areas of activity while other matters are regulated by the states or provinces into which these countries are divided. In unitary countries such as the United Kingdom and France, sovereignty is not divided but resides in the institutions of national government that have the sole right to regulate these nations' affairs.

External sovereignty refers to self-determination and suggests that a state has the ability to control its own affairs without interference from outside bodies and countries. External sovereignty has been eroded by the increasing interdependence of nations which has arisen as the result of a number of factors that we discuss in more detail in the following sections.

Nationalism

Nationalism is a sentiment underpinning a people's desire to exercise control over their own political affairs. Those who live in a particular locality are united by a desire to be independent of other nations and live under a political system which they control. This unity may be based on a common ethnic identity or cultural heritage (including language and literature) or be grounded upon a sense of shared citizenship which may transcend ethnic or cultural differences. 'Nation state' is the term used to describe the political community that arises when the boundaries of nation and state are the same.

Nationalism may justify attempts by conquered or colonized countries, or those dominated either economically or politically by another country, to shake off the burden of foreign domination and attain self-government. Post-war history contains numerous examples of national identity being the motivating force for movements seeking the establishment of self-governing states. It inspired independence movements in African countries directed against European colonial powers. In Latin America, it was the main force behind anti-American movements in many countries, including Cuba and Nicaragua. The desire to establish a self-governing state has considerable influence on the contemporary politics of Canada and Spain, where national minorities (the Quebeckers, Catalans and Basques) desire self-government. In the United Kingdom, the demand for Scottish and Welsh home rule resulted in devolution legislation being enacted in 1998.

The United Kingdom concept of the sovereignty of parliament

The term 'sovereignty of parliament' implies that parliament may pass any legislation it wishes whose implementation cannot then be challenged by any other body within the state (such as a court or a local authority). This concept is at the heart of the United Kingdom's system of government. Initially, this doctrine was designed to provide for the pre-eminence of parliament over the monarchy.

A further aspect of the sovereignty of parliament is that one parliament cannot bind a successor to a course of action. Any law passed by one parliament can be subsequently amended or repealed by a successor. Thus, while the United Kingdom's membership of the European Union asserts that European law has precedence over that enacted by the United Kingdom parliament, this apparent undermining of the sovereignty of parliament is addressed by the theoretical ability of a future parliament to withdraw the United Kingdom from this supranational arrangement.

Nationalism may be a progressive force when it seeks the liberation of subjugated peoples from oppressive, foreign rule. However, it may also be a reactionary movement. The love of one's country (or patriotism) may lead to the hatred of other foreign peoples or races, which is termed *xenophobia*. For example, nationalism was the justification for 'ethnic cleansing' (or genocide) carried out in Bosnia-Hercegovina by the Bosnian Serbs against the Bosnian Muslims in 1992 and subsequently by the Serbs against ethnic Albanians in Kosovo in 1999.

Threats to external sovereignty

Does external sovereignty remain a viable concept in the late twentieth century?

It is doubtful whether any state has ever enjoyed total control over the conduct of its affairs. The nineteenth-century nation state perhaps went some way to approximating this ideal, but such countries were often required to pay regard to outside factors when administering their internal or external activities. In the twentieth century sovereignty is even less of a reality: the ability of any state to function autonomously has been jeopardized by a wide range of factors. The term 'globalization' is used to refer to the increased interconnectedness of nation states in political, economic or cultural affairs which has undermined the traditional distinction between 'national' and 'international' politics.

Supranational governmental institutions

Many countries affiliate to governmental organizations that operate across national boundaries. The European Union is an example of such a body. Membership of supranational institutions places limitations on the activities of the member countries whose sovereignty is thus restricted by the expectation that they will adhere to the policies determined by the central decision-making machinery of the organization. The refusal of any member country to do so may result in the deployment of sanctions against it.

Globalization

Globalization refers to the increasing integration of nations which affects a wide range of issues including cultural and political affairs (especially the spread of liberal democratic political values). It has arisen as the result of a number of developments. One of these is communications technology, such as the internet, and satellite television, which has made it difficult for governments to censure the spread of ideas and has also facilitated the organization of protest on an international scale (such as the worldwide anti-capitalist movement). A particularly important aspect of globalization is the increasing integration of world economies arising from the ease with which goods and capital can be transferred across national boundaries. This has resulted in the emergence of world money markets and aided the development of transnational corporations.

The global economy emphasizes the interrelationships of the economies of nation states, and the success or failure of the economy of one nation, or bloc of nations, has a major impact throughout the world. This may result in a 'governance gap' whereby nation states are powerless to control processes that occur at global level.

It has often been assumed that the economic aspects of globalization have a detrimental effect on the poorer nations, for example by enabling industrialized nations to advance rules of trade that are advantageous to themselves. However, global institutions such as the World Trade Organization have the ability to create economic growth for developing countries by insisting on more open trade. This situation may help to reduce the inequalities between rich and poor nations provided that the benefits of increased economic growth are fairly distributed.

The cultural aspects of globalization have been enhanced by developments affecting communications. Developments such as satellite and cable television, and particularly the internet have transformed the media into a global mechanism which transmits across national frontiers. These new forms of communication have made it difficult for governments to exercise control over the spread of information to their citizens since it may be transmitted from installations which operate outside their frontiers and which are thus beyond their supervision or control.

Organizations to secure intergovernmental co-operation

In addition to supranational organizations which exercise governmental powers across national boundaries, other international bodies primarily serve as forums for co-operation, often in limited areas of state activity. These bodies may operate on a worldwide basis (such as the United Nations or the Commonwealth) or be confined to countries in specific regions of the world (such as the North Atlantic Treaty Organization). These organizations may seek to influence the direction of member (and sometimes non-member) countries through the application of moral pressure, sanctions or force. Trade embargoes are a potent sanction which international bodies may use to force a government to change the direction of its politics. They may also utilize military intervention to accomplish their aims. The use of grounds troops in Bosnia under the auspices of NATO in 1995 sought to ensure the successful implementation of the peace agreement following its endorsement by the presidents of Croatia, Bosnia and Serbia.

The emergence of a global economy

In addition to the existence of various formal institutions that have undermined national sovereignty by encouraging nations to co-operate, economic factors have also served to erode the significance of national boundaries. These factors have given rise to the emergence of a global economy which has been brought about by international trade and the international character of contemporary commerce and finance. The concept of a global economy rejects the view that the economies of nation states can be seen as independent entities and instead places emphasis on their interrelationships. This concept emphasizes that the success or failure of the economy of one nation, or bloc of nations, has a major impact on countries throughout the world.

We consider some of the main ways in which economic factors have undermined the relevance of the boundaries of nations in the sections that follow.

International trade

International trade has placed restraints on the actions of national governments. Membership of regional trading blocs, such as the European Union or wider arrangements such as the General Agreement on Tariffs and Trade, limit the ability of member countries to pursue policies such as tariff protection against other participating nations. Broader agreements have also been made to regulate the world's trading system through international actions, which included the Bretton Woods Agreement (1944) and the Group of Seven (G-7) summit meetings consisting of America, the United Kingdom, France, Italy, Canada, Germany and Japan. These initiatives restrict the control that individual nations can exert over economic policies. This discretion is further reduced by the need to consider the reaction of financial markets to political decisions taken by individual governments.

Multinational companies

The concentration of large-scale economic activity has resulted in the formation of multinational (or transnational) companies. These have their headquarters in one country but their commercial activities are conducted throughout the world. Incentives for them to do this include access to raw materials and (in the case of firms locating in the Third World) the availability of cheap labour. Such multinational companies (many of which are American or Japanese owned) possess considerable influence over the operations of the government of the countries in which they invest, thereby undermining the economic and political independence of such countries. In return for providing jobs and revenue derived from taxing their operations, multinational companies may demand concessions from governments as the price for their investment in that country. They may seek direct or indirect control over a country's political system to ensure that government policy is compatible with the needs of the company. If these conflict the government may suffer: in Guatemala, for example, President Jacobo Arbenz's quarrels with the American United Fruit Company resulted in his replacement by an American-backed military government in 1954.

Foreign aid

Some countries, especially in the developing world, are in receipt of aid. This includes grants, loans or gifts, which may stimulate agricultural and industrial development or be concerned with military purposes. Aid of this nature is provided either by individual governments (termed 'bilateral aid') or by international bodies such as the World Bank or the International Monetary Fund (termed 'multilateral aid'). Foreign aid may be awarded subject to conditions which the receiving government is forced to adopt. These may include fundamental alterations in domestic policy. Aid provided by Western liberal democracies, for example, may require improvements in the receiving country's human rights record.

American involvement in Latin America

The post-war political affairs of countries in Latin America have been heavily influenced by the United States. There are two reasons for this – military and economic.

Latin America lies in close proximity to the United States. The spectre of Soviet missiles being sited in Cuba (which had been removed from the American sphere of influence by a revolution headed by Fidel Castro in 1959) almost triggered a nuclear war in 1962. Central America (particularly the Panama Canal zone) is viewed as the jugular vein of the United States which needs to be controlled by governments that are friendly to that country.

Economic considerations (especially the availability of cheap labour, raw materials and a market for American goods) have made Latin America attractive to American multinational companies. They require political stability, which has often been delivered by governments reliant on American support that can be trusted to safeguard their interests. National revolutions (such as that which occurred in Nicaragua in 1979) are often opposed by America on economic as well as strategic grounds.

Dependency

Dependency seeks to explain the unequal relationship that exists between first world countries over those in the third (or developing) world. It suggests that the overt political control formerly exercised by developed nations over their colonies (which were sometimes referred to as 'dependencies') has given way to a new form of dominance exerted over third world countries based on the economic power of the first world. Factors such as the superior market position of first world countries, and the reliance of the third world on foreign aid and development loans from the first world, form the basis for the economic imbalance between countries of the first and third world and from which the latter find escape hard.

Dependency suggests the existence of an economic form of colonialism which seeks to ensure that third world countries serve the economic interests of the industrially advanced nations by supplying raw materials required by the industries of the first world, and latterly by serving as a market for the goods they produce. This tends to distort the pattern of economic development in such countries, which is typically concentrated on agriculture and the mining of minerals to the detriment of the development of domestic manufacturing industry. Dependency is buttressed by loans made available to third world countries by bodies such as the International Monetary Fund. The interest rates charged and the conditions stipulated by the lending body erode the sovereignty of the receiving country and may result in the pursuance of policies which are to the detriment of many of its inhabitants. The need to export agricultural produce to pay the interest on foreign loans may, for example, result in the local population suffering from hunger and starvation and place the country in a very weak position from which to pursue economic development.

The economically subordinate position of third world countries is not, however, totally irreversible. Oil-exporting countries, for example, have been able to turn the tables on the first world when, acting in concert through the Organization of the

Petroleum Exporting Countries (OPEC), they quadrupled the cost of oil in 1973. Its members have subsequently been able to initiate major changes in its price by their ability to raise or cut production.

The end of sovereignty?

Is external sovereignty a meaningful concept in the early twenty-first century?

The sections thus far in this chapter have documented some of the restrictions imposed on the freedom of action possessed by national governments. But it would be wrong to assert that nations now have no meaningful control over their internal or external affairs. National economies are subject to broad global considerations and restraints. However, individual governments retain the ability to manage their economies, at least in the short term. In many liberal democracies incumbent governments will initiate policies such as taxation cuts or reductions in the rates of interests in order to court popularity with the electorate.

Individual governments may further pursue actions regardless of the opinions of other countries. The decision by the French government in 1995 to resume its programme of nuclear weapon testing in the Pacific Ocean provoked widespread opposition from individual countries such as Australia and New Zealand, from international pressure groups such as Greenpeace and from international organizations such as the Commonwealth. Economic pressure in the form of boycotts against French produce, especially wine, was applied. But the French government ignored such pressures and proceeded with this policy.

Sovereignty remains a term which enters into the rhetoric of political debate and influences political behaviour. In the United Kingdom, allegations that sovereignty is threatened by the policies of the European Union mean that it remains a potent argument that crosses traditional political divisions.

The European Union

What is the European Union and how does it operate?

The European Union (EU) is an important example of a supra-national governmental body. Countries that join this organization forego control over their own affairs in areas which are encompassed by its treaties. Decision making in these areas becomes a collective exercise involving representatives of all the member countries. The United Kingdom's voice in the European Union, for example, is put forward by its 87 members of the European Parliament, two commissioners (who are nominated by the UK government) and the one vote it possesses in common with every other member in the Council of Ministers.

In the following section we briefly discuss the evolution of the European Union and describe how its work is performed

The evolution of the European Union

The Second World War provided a key motivating force for the movement towards closer co-operation between the countries of Europe. There was a desire by leading politicians from the victorious and defeated nations to establish institutions to avoid a further war in Europe. The first step towards co-operation was the establishment in 1951 of the European Coal and Steel Community. It was envisaged that the sharing of basic raw materials that were essential to the machinery of war would avoid outbreaks of hostilities. This initiative was followed in 1955 by the formation of the European Investment Fund. The body now known as the 'European Union' developed from an organization initially popularly known as the 'Common Market'. The main developments in the progress of the EU are as follows.

The Treaty of Rome (1957)
This treaty established the European Economic Community (EEC) and Euratom (the European Atomic Energy Community). The EEC initially consisted of six countries (France, West Germany, Italy, the Netherlands, Belgium and Luxembourg). Britain, the Irish Republic and Denmark joined in 1973, Greece in 1981, Spain and Portugal in 1986 and Austria, Finland and Sweden in 1995.

The Single European Act (1986)
This Act sought to remove obstacles to a frontier-free community by providing the legal framework to achieve a single market by 31 December 1992. This would entail the free movement of goods, services, capital and people between member states.

The Maastricht Treaty (1991)
This treaty was drawn up by the heads of member governments at a meeting of the European Council and sought to provide a

legal basis for developments concerned with European political union and economic and monetary union. The treaty laid down the conditions for member countries joining a single currency. These required a high degree of sustainable economic convergence measured by indicators which covered inflation, budget deficits, exchange rate stability (which would be guaranteed by membership of the Exchange Rate Mechanism) and long-term interest rates. Moves towards common foreign and security policies and an extension of responsibilities in areas which included justice, home affairs and social policy were also proposed.

The then Conservative government in the United Kingdom objected to the 'Social Chapter' designed to protect workers' rights and had reservations concerning the terms and timing of monetary union. It thus signed the treaty only when it was agreed to exempt Britain from the former and leave parliament to determine the latter issue. It was further satisfied that the inclusion of the subsidiarity principle in the treaty would limit the scope of the future policy making by the EEC (although the precise meaning of the term 'subsidiarity' was subject to diverse interpretation across Europe). Other countries also experienced problems with this treaty. It was rejected in 1992 by a referendum in Denmark, a result that was reversed after this country succeeded in securing four opt-out provisions.

Following ratification of this treaty in 1993, the term 'European Union' was employed, implying the creation of an organization that went beyond the original aims of the EEC.

The Treaty of Amsterdam (1997)

This was agreed at an intergovernmental conference in 1997 and amended and updated the Treaties of Rome and Maastricht. It sought to strengthen the commitment to fundamental human rights and freedoms, expressed opposition to discrimination, racism and xenophobia and aimed for greater foreign policy co-ordination between member states and the development of a common defence policy. It also proposed enhanced policy and judicial co-operation. It promised a move towards common decision making on immigration, asylum and visa policies, although Britain and Ireland were given opt-outs in these areas.

The Brussels Summit (1998)

At a summit of the European heads of government in May 1998, the finance ministers of 11 countries agreed to implement the objectives of the Maastricht Treaty and create a single European currency, the Euro. On 1 January 1999, the currency of these 11 countries was fixed in relation to the Euro and a new European central bank established to manage monetary policy. The Euro was used for paper and electronic transactions after January 1999 and went into general circulation in 2002 when national currencies were withdrawn by the participating nations. The United Kingdom, Denmark and Sweden remained outside the single currency. However, the United Kingdom had joined the Exchange Rate Mechanism in 1990 which required her to maintain the value of the pound against other EU currencies, using interest rates to achieve this, regardless of domestic considerations. The United Kingdom left in 1992 in the belief that high interest rates were prolonging recession.

A single European currency places restrictions on the sovereignty of those nations that join. The ability of individual governments to use interest rates to control the growth of their economies was ended and it seemed likely that, as the economies of participating converged, there would be intense pressures for equalization to take place between wage rates, taxes and social security systems.

Political union, possibly leading to the creation of a European state, was a logical development stemming from the creation of single currency. However, the subsequent adoption at the 1998 Cardiff summit meeting of a proposal to establish a council of deputy prime ministers to co-ordinate the work of EU institutions and national governments was designed to enhance the degree of political control exerted by individual governments over Brussels.

The Nice Summit (2000)

This intergovernmental conference took a number of major decisions relating to the future development of the EU when enlargement (that is, the admission of ten new member states) occurs in 2004. It was agreed to alter the weighting of national votes in the Council of Ministers. This change was designed to prevent the larger countries from being outvoted by a combination of smaller ones, although it would also entrench the power of the six founder members (whose voting strength was increased from 48 to 51 per cent) provided that they voted as a unified bloc. In 2005 the total number of commissioners was to be capped at 27, requiring the United Kingdom, France, Germany, Italy and Spain each to lose one commissioner. Qualified majority voting was extended to a number of new areas (which included international trade agreements, external EU border controls and state aid to EU industry), but was retained for matters affecting tax, social security, regional aid and state subsidies and core immigration policy.

The Salonika Summit (2003)

In 2002 *The Convention on the Future of Europe* was held in Brussels to consider proposals for a new EU constitutional treaty which would define the powers of the EU when its membership was expanded in 2004. A draft of this document was subsequently drawn up by the former President of France, Valery Giscard d'Estaing.

Giscard D'Estaing's proposals entailed creating a new office of president to replace the present system whereby this office rotates among member states every six months. The draft proposed that the president would be elected by EU leaders, serve a maximum of two-and-a-half year terms of office and would head the Council of Ministers. The European Commission would be reduced in number, and the European Parliament would acquire added status by obtaining 34 more areas where it had the power of 'co-decision' to approve laws. A new post of EU foreign minister would be set up, and the draft constitution also suggested a common defence policy and an EU mutual defence guarantee as currently exists within NATO. The constitution proposed to establish a European public prosecutor to tackle serious cross-border crimes and a common EU asylum policy would be instituted, entailing common definitions of who should qualify for refugee status and agreements to provide similar standards of accommodation and welfare. Enhanced tax harmonization by the abolition of the veto of national governments in taxation areas such as excise duties and corporation tax was also suggested.

The main institutions of the European Union

The Commission

The Commision is based in Brussels and consists of 20 members appointed by the governments of each member state. Each state appoints one commissioner and the larger select two. Each commissioner serves a four-year term which may be renewable. On appointment, commissioners take an oath not to promote national interests and in sense this provides the EU with its most obvious supranational dimension. The commissioners appoint a president who has a five-year term of office. The commissioners are allocated specific responsibilities (termed 'portfolios') by the EU president. They are served by a civil service organized into what are termed directorates general. The Commission performs a number of key tasks connected with its operations. These include:

- **Initiation of policy:** This task is performed through the preparation of proposals for the consideration of the Council of Ministers.
- **Implementation of policy:** Laws passed by the Council of Ministers are passed to the Commission for implementation which thus serves as the EU's executive arm. This role often includes enacting delegated or secondary legislation. Much policy is not directly administered through the Commission's civil service but is discharged by the member states.
- **Supervisory functions:** This body also serves as a watchdog and may draw the attention of the Court of Justice when measures are not being implemented.
- **Financial:** The Commission is responsible for preparing draft budget proposals. In 1998 it published the Agenda 2000 proposals which were designed to set the framework of the EU budget for the millennium and beyond.

The Council of Ministers
The Council is also based in Brussels and is composed of ministers of the member states. It is the EU's supreme law-making (legislative) body.

European law making
European law is delivered in two main forms: regulations (which are immediately embodied into the law of each member country) and directives (which require a member country to take action to adopt the principles contained in a directive into national law by a process termed 'transposition'; this procedure gives member countries some flexibility in implementation).

The European Court of Justice rules in the event of disputes arising concerning the adoption of law by or within member countries. A number of national courts (including those of France and Britain) have upheld the view that European law has precedence over national law.

Parliaments in member nations have sought to monitor the activities of the EU by setting up specialist committees. These include Ireland's Joint Committee of the *Oireachtas* on Secondary Legislation, the British House of Commons Select Committee on European Legislation and the short-lived (1983–87) German *Europa-Kommission* composed of members drawn from the *Bundestag* and the European Parliament.

Voting in the Council of Ministers is weighted in favour of the larger member states, although this process is rarely used. When approved by the Council, legislation becomes part of the national law of member states and it is in this sense that membership of the EU results in a loss of sovereignty. Initially, this was safeguarded by the practice of unanimity, whereby all members of the Council were required to approve a proposal in order for it to be adopted. This effectively gave individual governments the power to veto proposals and thereby preserve national interests. Since the mid-1980s, however, there has been a movement towards taking decisions on the basis of qualified majority voting which erodes the single-nation veto. The Single European Act, the Maastricht Treaty and the Nice Summit extended the areas which could be determined in this manner.

The presidency of the Council changes hands at six-monthly intervals, with each member state taking its turn.

The European Council

This body has no permanent venue although it is effectively the most senior level of political authority in the EU. It is composed of the heads of government and foreign ministers of the member countries and the president and one vice-president of the Commission. Its existence was formally recognized in the Single European Act. Its main purpose is to discuss political issues of overall importance to the EU and in this capacity has performed a prominent role in the area of foreign affairs. It is not, however, a law-making body, and its decisions would have to be ratified by the Council of Ministers to acquire legal status.

The European Parliament

The European Parliament meets in Brussels and Strasbourg and consists of representatives who (since 1979) have been directly elected by the citizens of each member country, the number of representatives being determined by population. MEPs serve for a term of five years. For much of its existence the European Parliament was regarded as an advisory body, a 'talking shop' which considered proposals put forward by the Commission but which exercised little power over decisions. However, the Single

European Act and particularly the Maastricht Treaty sought to provide it with a more vigorous role. Its new responsibilities included the right to reject the EU budget, to be consulted on the appointment of commissioners and the ability to play a more significant role in the law-making process. In 1998, it rejected the EU budget in protest against accusations of fraud and mismanagement by the Commission and in 1999 proposed that individual commissioners alleged to be responsible for this situation should resign. The dispute between the EU Parliament and Commission resulted in the collective resignation of the latter in March 1999.

The EU Parliament makes wide use of committees whose role includes considering the content of proposed EU laws. A key deficiency in the Parliament's powers concerns its lack of control over the Council of Ministers.

The European Court of Justice

The Court of Justice (not to be confused with the European Court of Human Rights), which sits in Luxembourg, is staffed by judges and advocates drawn from member countries. They serve for six years. The main purpose of the Court is to ensure that EU law is adhered to within member countries. Disputes between member states, between the European Union and member states, between individuals and the European Union or between the institutions of the EU are referred to this court. It has the power to declare unlawful any national law which contravenes European law and also has the power to fine companies found to be in breach of such legislation. A number of national courts (including those of France and the United Kingdom) have upheld the view that European law has precedence over national law.

In the United Kingdom, for example, a European secretariat within the Cabinet Office co-ordinates national policy towards the EU and government departments (especially those concerned with trade, agriculture and industry) have divisions concerned with the European dimension to their activities. One key function is to ensure that British and European law are harmonized. Local authorities in the United Kingdom have established formal links with Brussels in connection with proposed bids for aid from sources such as the European Regional Development Fund.

The transfer of much decision making to the institutions of the EU has had significant implications for those who seek to influence the policy-making process. As was observed in Chapter 6, pressure groups are widely engaged in liaison with the Commission and its officials. Lobbying by groups in Brussels is especially apparent in the areas of agriculture, environmental policy, regional and economic policy.

International terrorism

Terrorism is a difficult term to define precisely, but it entails the use of violence to further a political objective. Those who carry out acts of violence do not seek to confront the state directly (indeed they are typically too weak to do so) but, alternatively, aim to eliminate its key personnel (such as politicians or judges) or intimidate ordinary members of the general public in order to attain their ends. The violence which terrorists use may be of a spectacular nature, designed to secure publicity for their cause.

Developments associated with globalization and technological developments affecting means of communication have helped to promote terrorism on the international stage. Thus the grievances of citizens in one country may result in acts of violence in another (perhaps carried out by a third party), especially when the policies pursued by a government or interests with which it is associated are deemed responsible for these problems. This was graphically demonstrated in America on 11 September 2001, when terrorist attacks directed at New York's World Trade Centre and the Pentagon Building in Washington resulted in the deaths of many thousands of people who just happened to be in the wrong place at the wrong time. These attacks were blamed on Muslim extremists who were seeking to force the problems of poor countries onto the agenda of western nations and in particular to highlight the plight of Palestinian Arabs arising from American policy, especially its support for Israel's policy towards these people. The aim of this violence was thus to promote a changed power relationship between western nations and poorer countries, especially those in Arab world.

Terrorist activities have prompted governments to amend their laws. The main legislation in the United Kingdom is the 2000 Terrorism Act and the 2001 Anti-terrorism, Crime and Security Act. However, legislation which is designed to restrict terrorism tends to reduce civil and political liberties. A particular problem is that legislation which is designed to outlaw political violence fails to draw an adequate distinction between direct action and terrorism and effectively enables the state to prohibit the activities of almost any group which uses some form of physical activity to further its cause.

Questions

1 Distinguish between the terms 'sovereignty' and 'sovereignty of parliament'.
2 Illustrate, with examples of your own, what you understand by the term 'globalization'.
3 Select one of the following:
   - the European Commission
   - the Council of Ministers
   - the European Parliament
   - the European Court of Justice

Compile your own information on this EU institution. This should include its membership, the role it performs, the power it wields and contemporary developments affecting its evolution.

Taking it further

This chapter has focused on the extent to which national sovereignty is a meaningful concept in the twenty-first century and has considered a number of factors which have eroded the ability of individual nations to exercise total control over the conduct of their own affairs.

Globalization is an important consideration when discussing national sovereignty. More detailed information on this topic can be found in Barrie Axford, *The Global System – Economics, Politics and Culture* (Cambridge: Polity Press, 1995).

There are many books which consider the development and operations of the European Union. Good accounts include those by Stephen George, *Politics and Policy in the European Union* (Oxford: Oxford Univesity Press, 1996), John McCormick, *The EU: Politics and Policies* (Colorado: Westview Press, 1996) Paul Taylor, *The EU in the 1990s* (Oxford: Oxford University Press, 1996), Helen Wallace and William Wallace, *Policy-Making in the European Union* (Oxford: Oxford University Press, 2000) and Clive Archer, *The European Union Structure and Process* (London: Continuum, 2000).

The EU is constantly undergoing change and development and summaries of contemporary developments can be found at the EU's website www.europa.eu.int.

taking it further

This book has attempted to provide you with some basic information concerning the operations of liberal democractic political systems in the first world. You are now in a position to build on your knowledge. The following books will help you to do this.

Barrie Axford, Gary Browning, Richard Huggins, Ben Rosamund and John Turner, *Politics – An Introduction* (Routledge, London, 1977). Useful to students with some prior knowledge of politics.

Alan Ball and B. Guy Peters, *Modern Politics and Government* (Macmillan, Basingstoke, 2000, 6th edn). Well-established text concerned with the study of politics in a wide range of countries.

Andrew Heywood, *Political Ideas and Concepts* (Macmillan, Basingstoke, 1994). Covers a wide range of issues in a lucid manner and is therefore readily understandable to those with little grounding in this subject area. See also the same author's *Politics* (Macmillan, Basingstoke, 1997) which deals with the study of politics in a comparative context.

Peter Joyce, *An Introduction to Politics* (Hodder & Stoughton, London, 1999). Covers key concepts and issues, political systems and policy making, the institutions of government and a number of contemporary political issues, including racial and gender discrimination and terrorism.

Bill Jones, Dennis Kavanagh, Michael Moran and Philip Norton, *Politics UK* (Pearson Education Limited, Harlow, 2001)

Dennis Kavanagh, *British Politics, Continuities and Change* (Oxford University Press, Oxford, 2000)

David McKay, *American Politics and Society* (Blackwell, Oxford, 1993, 3rd edn)

Peter Morris, *French Politics Today* (Manchester University Press, Manchester, 1994)

Clive S. Thomas (ed.), *First World Interest Groups, A Comparative Perspective* (Greenwood Press, Westport, Connecticut, 1993)

index